Decision-Making for Sustainable Transport and Mobility

TRANSPORT, MOBILITIES AND SPATIAL CHANGE

Series Editors: Richard Knowles, *School of Environment & Life Sciences, University of Salford, UK* and Markus Hesse, *Maison des Sciences Humaines, Université du Luxembourg, Luxembourg*

Published in association with the Transport Geography Research Group (TGRG) of the Royal Geographical Society with the Institute of British Geographers.

This series provides an important new forum for cutting-edge research into transport, mobilities and spatial change, for all modes, and at local to global scales. Analysis of transport policies, processes and behaviours that influence the movement of people, goods and information is essential in an increasingly globalized and urbanized world – not only since such mobilities are posing serious environmental concerns, but also as they have important repercussions for urban and regional developments.

Titles in the series include:

Automated and Autonomous Spatial Mobilities
Aharon Kellerman

Decision-Making for Sustainable Transport and Mobility
Multi Actor Multi Criteria Analysis
Edited by Cathy Macharis and Gino Baudry

Decision-Making for Sustainable Transport and Mobility

Multi Actor Multi Criteria Analysis

Edited by

Cathy Macharis

Professor, Vrije Universiteit Brussel-Research group MOBI (Mobility, Logistics and Automotive Technology), dep. BUTO, Belgium

Gino Baudry

Research Associate, CEP – Centre for Environmental Policy, Imperial College London, UK

TRANSPORT, MOBILITIES AND SPATIAL CHANGE

Edward Elgar
PUBLISHING

Cheltenham, UK • Northampton, MA, USA

Published by
Edward Elgar Publishing Limited
The Lypiatts
15 Lansdown Road
Cheltenham
Glos GL50 2JA
UK

Edward Elgar Publishing, Inc.
William Pratt House
9 Dewey Court
Northampton
Massachusetts 01060
USA

A catalogue record for this book
is available from the British Library

Library of Congress Control Number: 2018944041

This book is available electronically in the **Elgar**online
Social and Political Science subject collection
DOI 10.4337/9781788111805

ISBN 978 1 78811 179 9 (cased)
ISBN 978 1 78811 180 5 (eBook)

Typeset by Servis Filmsetting Ltd, Stockport, Cheshire
Printed and bound in Great Britain by TJ International Ltd, Padstow

Contents

v

Contributors

Susanne Balm works at the Amsterdam University of Applied Sciences (AUAS), the Netherlands as project leader in the research programme Urban Technology. She is responsible for multi-disciplinary projects in the field of city logistics and electric mobility. The project participants include logistics service providers, vehicle suppliers, shippers, logistics clients and public organizations. Together they are developing and applying knowledge on new logistics concepts and business models. Before her career at AUAS, Susanne worked as consultant at TNO where she gained experience in national and European projects in the field of sustainable logistics and urban freight transport. One of the research projects she worked on was the European Union STRAIGHTOL (2011–14, funded in the 7th Framework Programme). Within STRAIGHTSOL the Multi Actor Multi Criteria Analysis (MAMCA) methodology was further developed and tested. Susanne worked closely with VUB in this period and continued the cooperation when she moved to AUAS.

Socrates Basbas is Professor at the School of Rural & Surveying Engineering, Aristotle University of Thessaloniki, Greece. His research interests include Transportation Engineering and Transportation Planning. As author and co-author, he has published more than 350 scientific papers in the field of transportation.

Gino Baudry is a full-time researcher in energy modelling and decision-making support at Imperial College London, UK and an associate researcher at the University of Nantes, France, working on the interplay between lifestyles, economic development, energy systems, land use, greenhouse gas emissions, food security and the sustainable use of natural resources. He teaches courses on Energy Policy and Economics, and Decision-Making in the context of Climate Change through role-playing games to simulate the climate change negotiation environment.

Geert te Boveldt is a research associate at the MOBI (Mobility, Logistics and Automotive Technology) research group led by Professor Cathy Macharis at the Vrije Universiteit Brussel, Belgium. His research focuses on political decision-making in sustainable mobility and logistics. After having obtained a degree in Geography and Urban Planning at the universities of Utrecht and Amsterdam, Geert has worked for several semi-public and non-profit employers in urban planning and mobility both in Belgium and the Netherlands.

Heleen Buldeo Rai acquired the degree of Master of Science in Communication Sciences at Vrije Universiteit Brussel, after completing a Bachelor's degree in Business Management at UC Leuven-Limburg, Belgium. Currently, she is a research associate at the MOBI research group led by Professor Cathy Macharis. Her PhD work focuses on the changing retail landscape due to e-commerce and omnichannel and its impacts on passenger and goods transport. Her research has a strong focus on urban areas in general and the Brussels-Capital Region in particular.

Ewa Chojnacka is Associate Professor at the Department of Accounting, Faculty of Economic Sciences and Management (FESM), Nicolaus Copernicus University (NCU) in Torun, Poland. Her PhD thesis concerned capital structure determinants in selected public limited companies in Poland, focusing on determinants indicated by the pecking order theory. Apart from capital structure, her research interests concern financial statements (financial statements analysis, financial statements as a source of information) and non-financial information reporting.

Klaas De Brucker is Associate Professor at KU Leuven-University of Leuven, Belgium, Faculty of Economics and Business, where he teaches Micro-economics and Decision Making. At the Research Centre for Economics and Corporate Sustainability he conducts research on the strategic evaluation of complex projects and policy measures, in both the public and private sectors, in particular related to transport policy. Klaas's approach consists of combining multiple (and eclectic) evaluation methodologies into a multi-criteria framework with multiple stakeholders. His area of expertise also lies in the field of institutional economics, especially regarding the contribution of the multi-stakeholder approach to the field of institutional economics and sustainable development. Klaas has been involved in several national and European research projects related to transport (and road safety) policy and has published numerous articles in several top journals such as the *European Journal of Operational Research*.

Marco Dean is a PhD candidate at the Bartlett School of Planning, University College London, UK. His research investigates the applicability of participatory Multi-Criteria Analysis methodologies to the appraisal of large-scale transport infrastructure. Marco's principal areas of research lie in the fields of transport, logistics, complexity in strategic decision-making on major transport projects, quantitative and qualitative appraisal methodologies, and participatory tools and techniques. He has published several articles on these topics.

Dorota Górecka is Associate Professor at the Department of Applied Informatics and Mathematics in Economics, Faculty of Economic Sciences and Management (FESM), Nicolaus Copernicus University (NCU) in Torun, Poland. She obtained her PhD in 2009 having defended the thesis entitled "Multi-criteria selection aiding of the projects in the process of applying for co-financing by the European Union funds". Her research interests include decision support, especially multi-criteria decision aiding (MCDA), sensitivity and robustness issues, verbal decision analysis (VDA), decision-making under conditions of risk and uncertainty as well as applications of MCDA, for instance, in international expansion, non-profit performance evaluation, negotiations and environmental management. Dorota teaches mainly courses in Operational Research, Project Management and Quantitative Methods in Project Management. She is also a head of the FESM AACSB Accreditation Team, which is responsible for the realization of all tasks related to the AACSB accreditation process.

Robin Hickman is a Reader at the Bartlett School of Planning and Director of the MSc in Transport and City Planning at University College London, UK. His research interests are in transport and climate change, urban structure and travel, integrated transport and urban planning strategies, the affective dimensions of travel, discourses in travel, multi-criteria appraisal, and sustainable transport strategies in the UK, Europe and Asia. His most recent books are *Handbook on Transport and Development* (Edward Elgar, 2015) and *Transport, Climate Change and the City* (Routledge, 2014).

Cathy Macharis is Professor at the Vrije Universiteit Brussel, Belgium. She teaches courses in Supply Chain Management and Sustainable Mobility and Logistics. Cathy specializes in the assessment of policy measures and innovative concepts in the field of sustainable logistics and urban mobility. She is head of the research group MOBI (Mobility, Logistics and Automotive Technology) and the department BUTO (Business Technology and Operations). She is also the chairwoman of the Brussels Mobility Commission.

Dries Meers acquired the degree of Master of Science in Urban Geography in a joint programme of the universities of Leuven and Brussels in Belgium. Currently, he is a research associate at the MOBI (Mobility, Logistics and Automotive Technology) research group of Professor Cathy Macharis at the Vrije Universiteit Brussel, where he completed his PhD on intermodal transport and the further development of a Location Analysis Model for Belgian Intermodal Terminals.

Anastasia Roukouni is a Transportation Engineer (MSc, Imperial College London; PhD, Aristotle University of Thessaloniki, Greece). She is currently working as a postdoctoral researcher at the Policy Analysis Group, Department of Multi-Actor Systems, Faculty of Technology, Policy and Management, TU Delft, the Netherlands. Anastasia's research focuses on how simulation games can be used to foster the implementation of innovation in the transport and logistics sector.

Thomas Vallée is Professor of Economics at the University of Nantes, France. His current research focuses on bioeconomy modelling, decision theory and game theory. Thomas is the coordinator of two Erasmus plus capacity building projects dealing with environmental issues. He was the former director of the research laboratory LEMNA at the University of Nantes.

Tom van Lier is a postdoctoral research associate in the research group MOBI (Mobility, Logistics and Automotive Technology) led by Professor Cathy Macharis at the Vrije Universiteit Brussel, Belgium. His work focuses on evaluating the sustainability of transport solutions by means of external transport cost calculations. Tom has been involved in several research projects dealing with topics such as social cost-benefit analysis of transport options, external cost savings of freight bundling, carbon footprint calculations and life-cycle assessment of transport services. His PhD in Applied Economics Business Engineering concerned the development of an external cost calculator framework for evaluating the sustainability of transport solutions. Within MOBI, he is also involved in the carbon emission reducing Lean & Green project of the Flemish Institute for Logistics as neutral assessor.

Koen Van Raemdonck is a postdoctoral research associate in the research group MOBI (Mobility, Logistics and Automotive Technology) led by Professor Cathy Macharis at the Vrije Universiteit Brussel, Belgium. He obtained his PhD in Business Economics in September 2013 entitled "The development of a GIS-based tool to identify dangerous road segments on the road network". Koen's research focuses on evaluation methodologies and Multi Actor Multi Criteria Analysis (MAMCA) methodology in particular. He has been involved in different research projects dealing with traffic safety, sustainable mobility, external costs and the socioeconomic evaluation of transport and traffic projects.

Foreword

More than 30 years of European Union (EU) funded transport research is behind us. A treasure of knowledge and empirical tests and demonstration activities has been built up. Giant steps forward have been taken to make the European transport system seamless with more capacity; vehicles are greener, smarter, faster, safer; infrastructures more lasting and safer. However, each step forward has been followed by two backwards, or so it seems. The very same technologies brought in their wake and triggered further new demand and supply for transport, the effect of which is bigger than the gains from the research projects. And so the transport sector, one of the very few, has seen its eco-footprint increasing.

The big beneficiaries of the research results have been the private sector car manufacturers, rail industry, shipbuilders, logistic companies, to mention just a few. The public sector saw only that transport had become more and more of a liability, a societal cost. Yet, it remained passive. It had long considered that technological progress would benefit the industry with a knock-on effect on society as a whole – the results of many years of research would one day be brought together by an invisible hand. The public sector, therefore, did not involve itself. The degree of its participation of about 15 per cent in EU-RTD projects related to urban transport. In contrast, 60 per cent of the partners of a typical consortium were from the same stakeholder group: academics. The project SUGAR provides an extensive analysis of projects on urban transport and confirms this situation. Further, lack of an integrated vision, fragmentism, lack of leadership, citizens' awareness are primary consequences of the technology-driven projects with a passive public sector.

The EU Commission came, finally, with a response, launching the Horizon2020 EU-RTD programme, a paradigm shift in transport research. It recognised that technology solutions are a double-edged cutting sword and that acceptance and implementation of innovative solutions are not a matter for a few but require the cooperation of all of us. A real societal challenge. This changes the focus of research, to address primarily the actors and factors determining the outcome of a project, to find the balance between individual gains towards collective societal consensus on how a combination of innovations, incentives, legislation can support the livable society.

As a consequence, a new analysis model is required, raising different questions and providing different answers. In other words, a new way of thinking, different from the way we have been thinking over the last 30 years or so, when we created today's problems. This book suggests that more than ever the public sector needs to be proactive and show entrepreneurship. It must kick-start the bargaining process with the relevant actors within a long-term vision. Knowing the limitations and opportunities, being able to identify the opponents and protagonists will strengthen the ability to plan and implement a working strategy. It may call for contingency planning to cover risks and uncertainty.

The book, following the above-mentioned paradigm shift, demonstrates that we need new decision support systems to support this shift.

In the final years of the Seventh European Framework Programme (FP7), the Straightsol project applied the analytical tool "MAMCA", which was developed some years before by Cathy Macharis. MAMCA stands for Multi Actor Multi Criteria Analysis and it focuses on actors and factors that determine the outcome and implementation of a research project. In other words, the focus is on identifying constraints and barriers, interests and stimuli to determine ways and means to make a project relevant and acceptable for society, adapting the project on the basis of the analysis where necessary. This kind of analysis should not be made once a project comes to an end, but from the beginning. Knowing the limitations and opportunities, being able to identify the opponents and protagonists will strengthen the ability to plan and implement a working strategy. It may call for contingency planning to cover risks and uncertainty. This is rarely found in projects and is the cause of lack of follow-up or implementation. MAMCA, in contrast, anchors projects in a wider societal context with respect for all people's values. Given that currently research projects have no or very limited "after-life", the MAMCA tool is of great interest to many other European co-funded research projects in urban transport.

Only by combining paradigm and mind-set shifts will we be able to successfully solve societal challenges. Society is not an administrative matter for a few but entails the cooperation of all of us.

Joost De Bock, 28 December 2017

Introduction

Cathy Macharis and Gino Baudry

Project assessment in the field of mobility and logistics are by their nature, on the one hand, multi-dimensional and, on the other hand, impacting and involve many stakeholders. Awareness about the multi-dimensionality of projects has been growing over the last decades through including different sustainability dimensions in the appraisal of mobility projects, for example, by increasingly using Multi Criteria Analysis as an assessment method or by including external costs in the Cost-Benefit Analysis (CBA) framework. The awareness that involving stakeholders is important in achieving successful implementations is being voiced more and more. Also, in large and exceptional events like the Olympic Games, Metropolitan areas need a broader means of appraisal, beyond just functional and economic assessment criteria.

However, bringing this explicitly into the evaluation process was missing. Consequently, we developed the Multi Actor Multi Criteria Analysis (MAMCA) framework some 20 years ago. With the MAMCA, the involvement of the stakeholders and their multi-dimensional preferences is made possible from the very beginning of the decision-making process in a structured and sound way. In this book we bring the state of the art on the MAMCA methodology and its software together. We invited the chapter authors to write about their experiences of MAMCA in the field of mobility and logistics in order to show the multitude of applications that are possible.

MAMCA is mostly used as an *ex ante* evaluation tool, so before the actual implementation, to obtain insight on the support for different options. MAMCA gives as an output a good overview of the advantages and disadvantages of the different options. By using it as an *ex ante* tool, it enables policy makers and project developers to get an insight of what is at stake. MAMCA can also be used as an *ex post* evaluation tool. In this case, more data on the real impact of the different options can be gathered to get a structured overview of the impacts of the options for each stakeholder. In addition, MAMCA can be used for participation in real-life workshops in which case, a fruitful discussion can take place and a complete set of preferences and evaluations can be gathered and discussed in a few hours.

Fighting against climate change, designing and implementing sustainability policy, raising people's awareness about sustainable development and so on – one cannot enumerate the wide range of problem settings that require people empowerment and multi-dimensional analysis to move towards a more sustainable society. Beyond the case studies that are presented in this book, MAMCA mainly aims at strengthening the interaction between sciences and society by fostering the empowerment of stakeholders and enabling consideration of a wide range of sustainability issues, including those which cannot be expressed in monetary value. Through this book, the authors want to bring forward the MAMCA methodology and methodological advances that have been realized to reach these objectives. The first part aims at providing the reader with the theoretical basis concerning the MAMCA methodology to enable its replicability. The second part illustrates the deployment of the methodology through different but complementary real-life case studies.

Part I comprises five chapters. In Chapter 1 Cathy Macharis and Gino Baudry present the MAMCA methodology, step by step, through an educative case study. The chapter positions the MAMCA methodology within the multi-criteria group decision-making literature and presents some applications. In Chapter 2 Cathy Macharis, Klaas De Brucker and Koen Van Raemdonck develop a decision tree for the *ex ante* evaluation of transport projects to guide decision-makers in choosing the most appropriate evaluation method(s).

Over the years, an associated software has been developed[1] which enables the support of MAMCA applications in a very user-friendly way. In Chapter 3 Gino Baudry, Koen Van Raemdonck and Cathy Macharis present this software and describe how to use it alongside MAMCA. The authors also explain the mathematical methods behind MAMCA that can be used within the software.

In recent years, the methodology has been extended to include institutional levels (Competence-based Multi Criteria Analysis or COMCA, developed by Geert te Boveldt, Cathy Macharis and Koen Van Raemdonck) and uncertainty (the range-based MAMCA, developed by Gino Baudry, Thomas Vallée and Cathy Macharis). These frameworks are presented in Chapters 4 and 5, respectively. The COMCA was developed to cope with complex decision problems where different institutional actors are involved and who also might have different competences to get the solution

---

[1] http://www.mamca.be/en/ (accessed 4 June 2018).

implemented. The range-based MAMCA was developed to cope with high uncertainty contexts. It combines the traditional MAMCA and a Monte-Carlo Simulation within a unique framework to model how uncertainty may affect the decision-making process.

Part II comprises six chapters that present different applications in various countries in the field of sustainable transport and mobility. In Chapter 6 Marco Dean and Robin Hickman compare CBA and MAMCA methodologies by evaluating three potential alternative improvements of a rail line between Blackpool and Preston (United Kingdom). Based on this analysis, the authors contend that, particularly in areas characterized by severe social deprivation problems, a MAMCA approach to appraisal may be preferable to analyst-led, economic-centric tools such as CBA.

The effectiveness of applied transport financing policies depends significantly on the level of agreement among stakeholders, making collaboration a prerequisite for success. In Chapter 7 Anastasia Roukouni, Cathy Macharis and Socrates Basbas propose an assessment of financing options for urban public transportation using the MAMCA in the context of the under-construction of the metro system of Thessaloniki (Greece). The approach provides valuable insight into the extremely critical and sensitive issue of transportation financing and it is expected to stimulate and enhance interaction between actors on the policy level in Greece. It demonstrates that an in-depth dialogue with all involved stakeholders is needed before the introduction of new financial mechanisms for transportation infrastructure to achieve the challenging task of planning sustainable cities.

Logistics is a key sustainable issue for cities. In Chapter 8 Tom van Lier, Dries Meers, Heleen Buldeo Rai and Cathy Macharis propose a MAMCA application that evaluates the interest of stakeholders for innovative solutions impacting city logistics in Mechelen (Belgium). The local authorities decided to implement the two alternatives that were supported by most stakeholder groups and tried to mitigate the drawbacks for the stakeholders who were negatively affected.

Chapter 9 describes how the MAMCA has been used by Susanne Balm for educational purposes at the Amsterdam University of Applied Sciences. As part of the Minor Urban Logistics, the use of the MAMCA framework proved to be in line with the goals of practical-oriented research as it helps to make education more responsive, improves the quality of graduates and enhances innovation in professional practice.

In Chapter 10 Gino Baudry and Thomas Vallée present an application of the range-based MAMCA extension in the field of energy policy design. The authors assess stakeholder support for different biofuel options in France by 2030. The results show that the biomass to liquid biodiesel is the most suited option with a probability of 80 per cent support. More importantly, the application demonstrates that uncertainty unequally affects different stakeholders. For some groups, such as non-governmental organizations, the biofuel ranking is unchanged whatever the uncertainty. In contrast, for other groups such as distributors or producers, the evolution of our complex socio-economic system may imply rank reversal and lead to support for unsuited options. The framework may thus help in coping with such uncertainty.

The last chapter presents a MAMCA application beyond the scope of transport and mobility to demonstrate that it can fit a wide range of decision-making problem settings. In Chapter 11, a MAMCA application developed by Ewa Chojnacka and Dorota Górecka is presented that focuses on the evaluation of non-profitable organizations in Poland to help donors make reliable decisions regarding financial support.

Over the years, the MAMCA has been deployed in various ways and contexts, for example, to support real-life decision-making in the transport sector and beyond, and to raise students' awareness through role play, and so on. This book is based on such a wide range of contributions and hopefully will lead to even more applications and cooperation in the years to come.

PART I

The Multi Actor Multi Criteria Analysis
framework

1. The Multi Actor Multi Criteria Analysis framework

Cathy Macharis and Gino Baudry

1.1 INTRODUCTION

Decision-making in the context of sustainable mobility and the transport sector requires addressing complex problems featuring multiple interests and perspectives, conflicting objectives and different types of data and information. Typically, several levels of public policy are involved (local, province, regional, state and European levels) and several stakeholders (such as freight forwarders, investors, citizens, industry and so on) which have a vested interest in the ultimate decision, whether they encompass environmental, social, economic, technical or legal issues. If the decision-making process fails to take these interests into account, projects may fail the implementation step, lead to unacceptable delays, be ignored by policymakers, or may be attacked by the stakeholders (Macharis et al., 2012).

The question is, however, how to organize and structure the decision-making process to enable the social actors to participate? The Multi Actor Multi Criteria Analysis (MAMCA) has been developed to address such issues. It explicitly considers and involves the stakeholders from the very beginning to the very end of the decision-making process. The following section positions the MAMCA methodology within the multi-criteria group decision-making literature. In Section 1.3 we present some MAMCA application cases in the field of sustainable mobility, transport and logistics. In Section 1.4 we present the methodology step by step through an educative case study. In Section 1.5 examples of MAMCA applications in the field of sustainable mobility, transport and logistics are provided. Section 1.6 concludes.

1.2 A CHANGING CONTEXT: SUSTAINABILITY AT THE CORE OF MOBILITY AND LOGISTICS PROBLEMS

This section presents the key concepts in addressing decision-making problems in the field of sustainable mobility and logistics.

1.2.1 Sustainability Concept

The concept of sustainability was formally defined by the well-known Brundtland Commission as:

> a development that meets the needs of the present without compromising the ability of future generations to meet their own needs. (Brundtland et al., 1987)

According to Pope et al. (2004), the scope of the concept may change depending on the dimensions incorporated into the sustainability assessment. The single pillar concept is the oldest approach. It focuses on environmental impacts, assuming that socio-economic aspects can never take priority over ecological preservation (Gallego Carrera and Mack, 2010). The two-pillar concept assumes a possible substitution between economic growth and the ecological integrity. The three-pillar concept adds a consideration for social aspects (Pope et al., 2004). The four- and five-pillar approaches include considerations for cultural and institutional dimensions (Parris and Kates, 2003).

Fundamentally, the sustainability concept implies defining: What is to be sustained? How is it possible to cope with the multi-dimensional needs? How it is possible to balance the present and future needs? The answers to those questions may vary depending on the temporal and spatial scale (Mayer, 2008), but also on the preferences of individuals or geographical region too (Buchholz et al., 2009).

Focusing on these latter aspects, Sala et al. (2015) speak about cross-pillar dimensions. From their point of view, addressing sustainability issues requires appropriate ways to strengthen the legitimacy and relevance of the decision-making process by engaging stakeholders at an early stage. Stakeholder-based approaches help in structuring the scope of the problem by identifying the multiple and sometimes conflicting perspectives of stakeholders concerning their own sustainability criteria (Buchholz et al., 2009; Cuppen et al., 2010; Gallego Carrera and Mack, 2010; van Dam and Junginger, 2011). The question is, thus, how to identify and make the relevant stakeholders participate?

1.2.2   Stakeholder Concept

Given the rising concerns for corporate social responsibility, the concept of stakeholder was introduced in the research field of strategic management (Buysse and Verbeke, 2003; Donaldson and Preston, 1995; Williamson, 1991). According to Freeman (1984), the stakeholder concept refers to an individual or a group of individuals who can influence or be influenced by the objectives of an organization. Banville et al. (1998) pointed out the importance of including stakeholders within Multi Criteria Decision Aid frameworks on the basis of their role in the decision-making process, implicitly suggesting that those whose potential for cooperation is low will be less likely retained for participation (Macharis et al., 2012). Such a definition is thus also influenced by organizational problem settings. Nevertheless, all relevant points of view should be incorporated when addressing socio-environmental problems.

Facing this ethical issue, Munda (2004) proposed broadening the scope of participation in the decision-making context by involving all the relevant social actors. By social actors, Munda refers to organized groups but also to unorganized actors, such as, for example, future generations. Grimble and Wellard (1997) proposed to broaden the scope of stakeholders by involving groups of people, organized or not organized, who share a common interest or stake in a particular issue or system. From our perspective, the scope of the concept should be limited based on the stakeholders' values at stake in the issue. Otherwise, this leaves the door open for any person or group who, with just intellectual curiosity, would like to be involved, which may lead to an unmanageable procedure.

In the MAMCA framework, we refer to stakeholders as people who have an interest, financial or otherwise, in the consequences of any decision taken. Focusing on sustainable mobility and logistics and depending on the problem, stakeholders may, for example, include terminal infrastructures managers, network infrastructures managers, vehicle manufacturers, passenger service operators, travelers' representatives, disabled and/or elderly transport users' representatives and/or associations, freight service operators, transport authorities, policy makers, socio-environmental non-governmental organizations (NGOs), future generation representatives, citizens, residents and so on.

1.2.3   Multi Criteria Analysis: A Methodological Framework to Support Decision-makers in Making More Sustainable Decisions

Decision-makers require a wide range of information to demonstrate whether our complex human-based system is becoming more or less sustainable. Without an adequate methodology, the decision-makers tend to focus on a small set of decision criteria, leading to decisions taken based on insufficient information. Rising concerns for environmental and social impacts have made Multi Criteria Decision Aid (MCDA) processes increasingly popular (Løken, 2007; Wang et al., 2009) as it allows the integration of different dimensions in the decision-making process. The MCDA offers structured and comprehensive frameworks in addressing complex problem settings.

The core of the MCDA procedure is the formal specification of how the different inputs are combined together to come to multi-criteria outputs (Damart and Roy, 2009). MCDA frameworks usually adopt a rather similar pathway: (1) the scope of the problem has to be defined; (2) a relevant set of options – or alternatives – and a criteria set have to be defined; (3) criteria can eventually be prioritized through the weight elicitation step; (4) the different options are evaluated based on the different criteria; (5) the multi-criteria evaluation is performed; (6) results have to be presented and discussed; (7) decision-makers make the final decision. Depending on the method and problem setting, steps may be executed in a different order, executed in parallel and the learning process during the procedure may also lead to the repeat of some steps (Lahdelma et al., 2014; Salo and Hämäläinen, 2010).

When addressing sustainable mobility and logistics problems, a wide range of stakeholders may be affected. Depending on the problem characteristics, stakeholder participation may take many forms and different degrees of involvement ranging from informing the public to co-producing knowledge (Cuppen et al., 2010). The questions are thus: Who should participate? In which steps? To what extent? Table 1.1 presents how the participants should be involved in these typical MCDA framework steps.

Typically, MCDA processes require involving the decision-maker(s), various stakeholders, experts in the appropriate fields, planner(s) and analyst(s) who manage the process (Lahdelma et al., 2014). Most of the decision-making methods have been adapted to enable group decision-making (for an overview, see Álvarez-Carillo et al., 2010). The difference between the methods mainly lies on the extent to which the information is brought together. Traditional methods aim at reaching a consensus among the stakeholders about the election of a common set of criteria. However, such an approach often fails to capture the whole variety of viewpoints, and thus the full scope of the problem (Cuppen et al., 2010).

The prerequisite consensus between social actors is not necessarily an achievable target at the very beginning of the procedure because of the high divergence between their respective interests. Such a lack of consensus may hamper the decision-process and the eventual implementation of

Table 1.1 Typical MCDA steps and actors' involvement

Actors	Define problem scope	Define alternatives & criteria	Elicit stakeholders' preferences	Measure of alternative performance	MCDA method choice	Perform MCA analysis	Make the final decision
Decision-makers	x	x	x		(x)		x
Stakeholders	x	x	x	(x)	(x)		
Experts	x	x		x	x		
Planners	x	x		x	x	x	

Note: x: participant is involved; (x): depends on the decision-context characteristics and on the methodological choices.

Source: Designed by the authors. Adapted from Lahdelma et al. (2014).

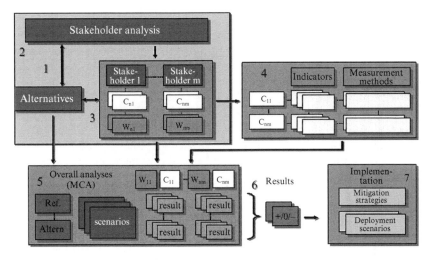

Source: Macharis et al. (2012).

Figure 1.1   Overview of the MAMCA methodology

solutions (Breukers and Wolsink, 2007; Di Lucia and Nilsson, 2007; Elghali et al., 2007). The MAMCA approach takes into account a specific criteria tree for each stakeholder to overcome this inherent consensus requirement (Macharis et al., 2009).

1.3   MAMCA METHODOLOGY

The MAMCA is an iterative methodology that consists of seven steps (Figure 1.1). The first three steps are very important and will influence each other (Macharis et al., 2012). This is why the methodology should be done in an iterative way.

1.3.1   Step 1: Defining the Problem and the Alternatives

The first stage of the methodology aims at defining the scope of the decision-making problem, including identification of the relevant alternatives. Depending on the problem setting, alternatives can take various forms such as policy options, technological solutions, site locations and so on. A reference alternative may be added to provide a benchmark against which the other alternatives can be compared, typically a "business as usual" reference.

For some problem settings, alternatives can be pre-determined. In such cases, the alternative identification step is straightforward. Otherwise, the set of alternatives can be tracked from a literature overview, possibly complemented by stakeholders' interviews. Alternatives may also be screened in terms of feasibility regarding legal, economic, social, environmental and technical issues.

This screening can be performed through risk analysis, early involvement of the stakeholders combined with an insight into their concerns (Lahdelma et al., 2014). In this case, stakeholders have to be involved at the very beginning of the process, which means performing Steps 2 and 3 before defining the alternatives.

1.3.2   Step 2: Stakeholder Analysis

An in-depth understanding of the stakeholder's objectives is critical in order to appropriately assess the different alternatives. Stakeholder analysis can be considered an aid to properly identify the range of stakeholders – the people or group of people who may affect or may be affected by the consequences, financial or otherwise, of any decision taken – who need to be consulted and whose views should be considered in the decision-making process.

Although there are no strict rules or consensus about stakeholders' involvement, the literature provides several appropriate methods to identify the relevant stakeholders (Banville et al., 1998). Savage et al. (1991) suggest identifying the stakeholders based on their potential for cooperation within the decision-process. Weiner and Brown (1986) suggest identifying the potential reasons for people to mobilize around any aspects of the decision-problem. Munda (2004) propose performing an in-depth analysis of historical legislative and administrative documents complemented with stakeholders' interviews to identify the relevant social actors.

The approach proposed by Munda (2004) and Weiner and Brown (1986) may be considered a good start to identify the stakeholders in the MAMCA framework. Next, one should define the border of the problem regarding its impacts, for example, through the scope of the policy level (community, region, country and so on) or through the scope of the demand and supply side, the supply chain and so on. Stakeholders can themselves be involved in the identification of the relevant actors to integrate into the process.

Given the sustainability issues within the mobility and transport context, special care has to be given when the consequences of decisions may affect unorganized groups (Munda, 2004). As an illustration, there is the risk of child labour in the production of palm oil, which is one of the main feedstocks for biofuels in Europe. In such cases, specialized NGOs and associations may be included to represent those values at stake within the decision-context. In other words, all the relevant points of view have to be captured in the process. This is called the completeness requirement (Macharis et al., 2012).

Stakeholder groups may consist of one or several actors characterized by quite homogeneous objectives and priorities. In other words, stakeholders with divergent viewpoints must be considered in separate groups. The priorities and weights might differ a little, but the same criteria tree is used within the stakeholder group. Stakeholder groups' weights are aggregated by the geometric mean, in which case analytic hierarchy process (AHP) is used, or the average. A sensitivity analysis should be executed when the stakeholders' weights differ markedly within a group (see Chapter 3).

1.3.3   Step 3: Defining Criteria and Weights

In the MAMCA, the definition of criteria is primarily based on the identification of the stakeholders' objectives and the purposes of the considered alternatives, not the impacts of the actions per se as is usually done in a MCA. Nevertheless, if all the relevant stakeholder groups are considered, these impacts should naturally be reflected in the objectives of the stakeholders.

From a theoretical perspective, the identification of the stakeholders' criteria can be determined through a bottom-up (Roy, 1985) and/or a top-down (Keeney and Raiffa, 1993) approach(es). The first approach consists of revealing criteria starting from how the alternatives affect the stakeholders. The second one consists in constructing the criteria through the decomposition of the stakeholders' objectives. The aggregation of the multiple social actors within stakeholder groups depends on their concerns and priorities. Each stakeholder group has to be homogeneous in term of concerns and preferences in order to draw a common criteria tree ().

On the one hand, the definition of criteria must comply with methodological requirements (Keeney and Raiffa, 1993; Macharis et al., 2012), which can be addressed by the researcher as mentioned by Munda (2014):

- Non-redundancy: the criteria should not measure the same thing within each stakeholder group. Nevertheless, two groups can have common criteria as long as they represent their own preferences.
- Minimality: the number of criteria should be kept to a minimum to remain manageable.
- Homogeneity: an agreement about the set of criteria within each group is required. Otherwise, two separate groups need to be considered.

- Operationality: anticipating the requirements of Step 4, criteria can be used meaningfully in the process. In other words, the alternative capacity to fulfil criteria must be properly measurable through indicator(s).

On the other hand, elicitation of the criteria is usually pursued through an interactive discussion with the stakeholder groups. From an operational perspective, criteria lists can first be provided to the different stakeholder groups based on a literature overview. Next, each stakeholder group gets the opportunity to evaluate and validate the pre-defined criteria, for example, in workshops or by telephone. It is important to come to an agreement concerning the meaning, the definition, of each criterion. Sub-criteria elicitation may be considered in detailing the stakeholders' objectives. On this basis, a hierarchical tree can be set up.

Within each group, weights can be allocated to capture the expression of the stakeholders' priorities between their criteria. Literature provides various methods to express these weights, such as pairwise comparisons, direct ratings, points allocation and so on (Eckenrode, 1965; Nijkamp et al., 2013). The choice of method depends on the MCA framework that is used in Step 5 concerning the type of required inputs. Moreover, the choice of the MCA framework may also depend on operational constraints. For example, the time availability of stakeholders may rule out the most time-consuming methods.

Wang and Yang (1998) studied the theoretical validity, predictive and perceived performance of three weight measurement methods: Saaty's AHP (Saaty, 2008), Edward's simple multi-attribute rating technique (SMART) and the functional measurement (FM) method as a theoretical validity standard (Zhu and Anderson, 1991). All three methods were perceived as equally valid but in terms of perceived performance, AHP is significantly preferred and perceived as easier to use. The AHP friendliness and understandability for users is widely highlighted in the literature, particularly in decision-contexts that address sustainability and energy issues (Kaya and Kahraman, 2011; Løken, 2007; Pohekar and Ramachandran, 2004; Wang and Yang, 1998). In these contexts, PROMETHEE is one of the most popular methods but no specific guidelines yet exist to determine the weights. Indeed, PROMETHEE assumes that decision-makers are able to weight their criteria appropriately, at least when the number of criteria is not too large. A combination of different methods can also be used (Marttunen et al., 2017). Macharis et al. (2004), for example, suggest combining the strengths of the weight elicitation of AHP (Step 3) and the PROMETHEE tool as the decision-method (Step 5) in the MAMCA. Consequently, most of the MAMCA case studies use Saaty's AHP process

Table 1.2   An illustration of Step 3's inputs

Stakeholder	Criterion	Criterion definition	Weight (%)
Retailer	High level of service	Customer satisfaction, deliveries on time and of the right quantity	30.0
	Socio-environmental concerns	Positive attitude towards environmental impact	25.0
	Profitable operations	Making a profit	16.5
	Viability of investment	A positive return on investment	16.5
	Employee satisfaction	Employees are satisfied with their work and working environment	8.0
	Security	Security of the goods and the drivers; no thieves and no attacks	4.0
Local authorities	Quality of life	Attractive environment for citizens	58.7
	Network optimization	Optimal use of existing infrastructure	21.6
	Social and political acceptance	Citizens' support for measures	9.4
	Cost measures	Low costs to implement measures	6.5
	Positive business climate	Attractive environment for companies	3.9
Citizens	Safety	Positive impact on road safety	31.0
	Emissions	Reduce emissions of CO2, NOX, PM2.5, PM10	26.4
	Urban accessibility	Reduce freight transport; less congestion	20.8
	Noise nuisance	Reduce noise nuisance	15.7
	Visual nuisance	Less space occupancy by trucks	6.1

Source: Verlinde and Macharis (2016).

for the elicitation of stakeholders' weights (AHP and PROMETHEE procedures are explained step by step in Chapter 3).

Table 1.2 presents the set of criteria and their associated weights extracted from the MAMCA application performed by Verlinde and

Macharis (2016) that compared different scenarios on off-hours deliveries to supermarkets in Brussels. Three stakeholder groups were identified who were asked to define their objectives (criteria) and priorities (weights).

One may also consider weights to express the prioritization between the different stakeholder groups. All stakeholder groups are considered of equal importance in all the MAMCA applications so far. In other words, stakeholder groups are given an equal weight to consider each point of view on an equal basis. Nevertheless, sensitivity analysis can be performed to consider different weight setting, which may lead to new insights.

The first three steps of the methodology should be considered circularly interlinked until all the relevant stakeholders, alternatives and criteria are identified. Indeed, each step may provide new ideas, visions or inputs, leading to consider new stakeholders, alternatives or criteria. This circle may be seen as a refinement process for the problem structuration.

1.3.4   Step 4: Indicators and Measurement Methods

Step 4 aims at "operationalizing" the criteria by constructing quantitative or qualitative indicators that will measure the extent or the capacity of each alternative to contribute in meeting each stakeholder's criterion. These indicators must remain explicit for understanding purposes.

Based on the literature and/or expert consultations, alternative performance regarding each criterion can be evaluated. Expert consultation can provide a scientific and solid foundation for the evaluation process, which may help social acceptance of the results. Indeed, depending on the complexity of the decision-making context, the analyst can try to acquire the necessary knowledge and expertise to properly complete the evaluation. This evaluation can be performed by the analyst and/or the experts, based on the literature, empirical data collection and expert consultations. When the decision-context features multi-dimensional issues, it may be preferable to cooperate with a multidisciplinary team of experts to ensure a solid basis for the evaluation. The evaluation has then to feed the decision-method, which requires data to be suited to the selected method.

1.3.5   Step 5: Overall Analysis

Using the measurement methods (Step 4), Step 5 consists of the evaluation of the alternatives through a MCA framework. It is possible to translate alternatives into scenarios to get a clearer evaluation. Different actors may provide the inputs for the evaluation of alternatives depending on the decision-making process objective: (1) the analysts, (2) the experts or (3) the stakeholders. Analysts may acquire the necessary expertise for the problem to make the evaluation properly. Nevertheless, cooperating with interdisciplinary experts may be more suited when addressing multi-dimensional problems, as previously mentioned. Stakeholders may also evaluate the alternatives themselves (for example: when the problem requires assessing stakeholder support for an alternative). Such an approach could, however, induce strategic bias because stakeholder groups could influence the decision towards their own strategic ultimate outcome. Stakeholders may also be consulted to validate the input given by the analyst or the experts.

The literature provides a wide range of MCA methods which can be used in the MAMCA framework. Among the most popular methods: the MACBETH approach (Bana and Costa, 1986); the Multi Attribute Utility Theory (MAUT) (Keeney and Raiffa, 1993); the AHP method (Saaty, 2008); ELECTRE (Roy, 1991); PROMETHEE (Brans and Vincke, 1985). The choice of a particular method depends on the decision-context and group members' characteristics (Salo and Hämäläinen, 2010). For example, the researcher/project manager may be more familiar with a particular method; the degree of participation in the process may imply operational constraints; the availability/price/friendliness of the software may drive the choice a specific method and so on (Kurka and Blackwood, 2013).

1.3.6   Step 6: Results and Sensitivity Analysis

Based on the decision-method output, the MAMCA eventually leads to a classification of the different options but more importantly reveals the critical stakeholders and their criteria. In other words, the strengths and weaknesses of each option with regard to each of the stakeholder groups' concerns can be identified. The MAMCA provides a comparison of the support of the stakeholder for the different options while pointing out the elements that have positive or negative impacts. In other words, it clearly shows which points of view are in disagreement and which ones could possibly come to a consensus.

As an illustration, Figure 1.2 shows the government's point of view extracted from the case study proposed by Turcksin et al. (2011) that evaluates the support of stakeholders for different biofuel options in Belgium.

The X-axis presents the extent to which biofuel options contribute to the government regarding each criterion presented in the Y-axis. The higher the score, the better the option contributes to comply with the objective. The importance of the criteria for the stakeholders – the weights – is represented through bars for each criterion (Y-axis). The higher the bar, the higher the criterion importance for the stakeholder group.

Biogas constitutes the most suited option regarding the government's

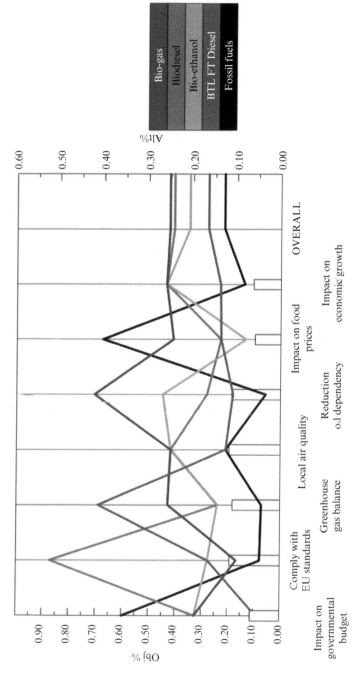

Figure 1.2   An example of MAMCA output (using AHP, governement output)

criteria (Figure 1.2). Even if the overall line might suggest that the final ranking will also lead to the best solution, we think that this is not the aim of the MAMCA output. Its objective is to provide insights into what is important, what is affecting positively or negatively each stakeholder group but certainly not to just sum up these perspectives to come to a final decision. Consequently, the overall line should always be commented on with care.

1.3.7   Step 7: Implementation and Recommendations

Based on the MAMCA outputs, policy recommendations can be formulated by the decision-maker, which is often a public authority. These recommendations are defined to help the decision-maker in the search for a deployment scenario, suited to the concerns of each stakeholder group, and ensuring overall coherence and sustainability. To this end, two approaches may be considered.

The first approach consists in considering the public authority to follow as it is the most relevant in representing the viewpoint of society. Based on its perspective, the public authority may choose its most suited option while considering the extent of the other stakeholders' support for it. The decision-maker can then develop additional and well-suited measures to compensate the negative consequences for some stakeholder groups (if any). In other words, the decision-maker can identify and tackle the barriers that may occur to facilitate the implementation of an option. For example, in Figure 1.2, biogas constitutes the most suited option for the government but it is also an unsuited alternative for end-users, especially given its user-unfriendliness. The government may, for example, implement additional measures to lower the cost for end-users and to demonstrate user-friendliness through advertising campaigns to overcome rejection by end-users.

In a second approach, the decision-maker may choose the option that offers the best consensus, that may face less barriers or simply prevent stakeholders' opposition. For example, in the case of the Oosterweel connection (Macharis et al., 2012), several "bridge and tunnel" possibilities were evaluated and the public authority finally chose an option that faced less barriers and was more socially acceptable, regardless of its own preferences.

In any case, the "consensus process" might take place through a negotiation round with all the stakeholders and possibly with a facilitator. During the process, new options can potentially be identified which will lead to a feedback loop towards the beginning of the procedure.

1.4   A MAMCA EDUCATIVE CASE STUDY

The following sub-sections present the methodology step by step through an educative case study.

1.4.1   Step 1: Defining the Problem and the Alternatives

Our daily lives are full of multi-criteria decisions which may range from simple to complex problems: buying a new phone, a new car, hiring an employee and so on. In real life, decisions are rarely based on a single criterion and they rarely affect the decider only. In this chapter, we illustrate the MAMCA methodology by means of an intuitive case study. Let us consider a group of people who want to choose among four skiing holiday destinations: Morzine, Châtel, St Martin and Les Menuires.

1.4.2   Step 2: Stakeholder Analysis

Step 2 consists in identifying the relevant participants to involve in the decision-process. Let us consider three families – the Corijn, Demeester and Macharis families – as our stakeholder groups. The families have different objectives, for example, the Corijn family is gourmand while the Demeester family is sportive.

1.4.3   Step 3: Defining the Criteria and Weights

To properly structure the decision-problem, each family has to define its own criteria tree and, potentially, they may elicit weights, expressing their preferences in between their criteria. Depending on the decision-method (Step 5), weights may be elicited to express the relative preferences between the criteria for each family.

Table 1.3 presents the criteria trees and the weights of our three families. Some decision criteria are common between the families such as the proximity to ski runs. The weights express the trade-offs between the families' preferences. For example, the Corijn family considers the conviviality 2.3 times more important than being near the ski runs.

1.4.4   Step 4: Indicators and Measurement Methods

Indicators enable the capacity of each alternative to be measured that fulfil the different criteria, that is, the alternatives' performances. Quantitative and continuous scales may, for example, be used to measure the proximity to ski runs. Discrete scales may be used to measure the presence (1) or the

Table 1.3   Families' criteria and weights

Stakeholder group	Criterion	Weight (%)
Family Corijn	Kitchen	67
	Conviviality of the chalet	23
	Near ski runs and bus	10
Family Demeester	Large ski resort	47
	Near ski runs	34
	Sauna	13
	Conviviality of the chalet	6
Family Macharis	Room setting	54
	Conviviality of the chalet	22
	Near ski runs	15
	Large ski resort	9

Source: Designed by the authors.

Table 1.4   Macharis family's score evaluation

Criterion	Morzine	Châtel	Menuires	St Martin	Unit
Room setting	Neutral	Very negative	Positive	Neutral	Qualitative
Near ski runs	6.8	7.1	1.2	1	km
Conviviality of the chalet	Neutral	Very negative	Positive	Neutral	Qualitative
Large ski resort	2.4	2	4.8	5.2	km

Source: Designed by the authors.

absence (0) of a sauna. Qualitative scales can be used for criteria such as the room setting, allowing preferences to be ranked for different chalets. For some criteria, composite indicators may be required to measure the option performance. As an illustration, the "conviviality of the chalet" criterion may refer to different sub-criteria such as the availability of a chimney and the surface of the living room. Table 1.4 illustrates the score evaluation of the different chalets.

1.4.5   Step 5: Overall Analysis

In this step, the final scores can be compared and ranked (Step 5). In the MAMCA software, two decision-methods are available (see Chapter 3 for further details) which are both very popular in the context of sustainability problem settings: the AHP – the analytic hierarchy process – developed by Saaty (2008) and the PROMETHEE – the preference ranking organization method for enrichment evaluations – developed by Brans and Vincke (1985).

1.4.6   Step 6: Results and Sensitivity Analysis

Figure 1.3 presents the alternatives ranking of the Demeester family. The right Y-axis represents the evaluation scores, the left one the weights (vertical bar) regarding the different criteria (X-axis). Les Menuires and St Martin are equally suited at the overall level and regarding the "large ski resort" and "near the ski runs" criteria.

When focusing on the "sauna" criterion, St Martin outperforms Les Menuires whereas it is the opposite regarding the "conviviality of the "chalet". The strengths and weaknesses of each chalet for each family's concerns can be identified.

Figure 1.4 presents the alternatives ranking of all the families. The X-axis presents the families, the Y-axis the alternatives scores. The figure clearly shows that the chalet in Châtel is the worst option for all the families. Nevertheless, the most suited option of each family differs. For the Corijn family, Morzine constitute the most suited option, followed by Les Menuires, St Martin and Châtel. As mentioned previously, Les Menuires and St Martin contribute equally to the Demeester family's criteria. For the Macharis family, Les Menuires is the best option, followed by St Martin, Morzine and Châtel.

1.4.7   Step 7: Implementation and Recommendations

Based on the MAMCA outputs, a structured discussion among the stakeholders can be set up and suitable recommendations can be formulated. These recommendations are defined to help in the search for a deployment scenario, ensuring overall coherence and sustainability of the solution. Thanks to the structured way of sharing the pros and cons for each option, the stakeholders can come to a shared solution. In our present illustration, Les Menuires may be the best compromise as it is the most suited option for two families and the second best for the third family. Nevertheless, another alternative can be chosen and implemented.

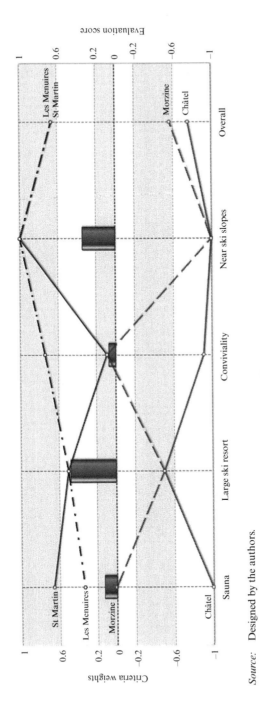

Source: Designed by the authors.

Figure 1.3   Chalet alternatives ranking of the Demeester family

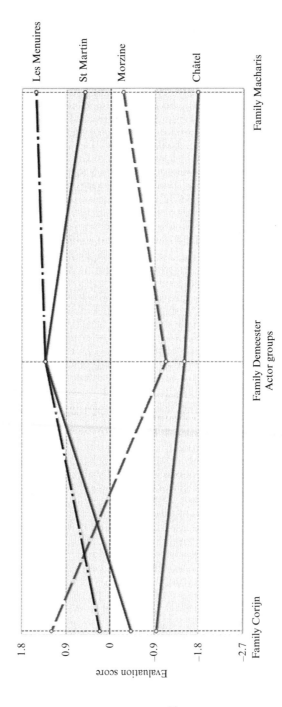

Source: Designed by the authors.

Figure 1.4 Chalet alternatives ranking of the three families

Figure 1.5 presents the alternatives ranking of the Corijn family which shows that the weakness of Les Menuires is related to the "kitchen" criterion. For example, the two other families may compensate this weakness by inviting the Corijn family to the restaurant.

1.5 SOME MAMCA APPLICATIONS IN THE FIELD OF SUSTAINABLE MOBILITY, TRANSPORT AND LOGISTICS

The MAMCA was developed by Cathy Macharis in the 2000s and it has been applied in multiple case studies in the field of sustainable mobility and transport since then. The methodology can cope with a variety of problem settings such as the evaluation of technology options, location sites, policy alternatives and so on. This section provides examples of the most recent MAMCA applications starting from 2010 – the previous ones can be found in Macharis et al. (2012).

Macharis et al. (2010) deployed the MAMCA in the context of the "Flanders in Action" project to provide insight into the support by different stakeholder groups for different policy measures to fulfil the sustainability ambitions of the Flemish Government for 2020. What was specific about this application was that criteria were pre-defined and common for the 11 stakeholder groups. Each group was, however, invited to express their criteria preferences through the elicitation of the weights. They were also allowed to assess the impact of the different measures of these criteria. Out of these measures, spatial planning, multimodality and bundling were identified as the most effective options for attracting logistic activities and that technology, multimodality and tax reformation would be best suited for reducing the detrimental impact of mobility and logistics on the environment.

Turcksin et al. (2011) deployed the MAMCA to assess stakeholder support for different biofuel options in Belgium in the context of the 2020 objectives for climate change. Results showed that biodiesel, ethanol and biomass-to-liquid are the most suited options to comply with the different stakeholders' objectives while reaching the Belgium renewable energy objectives in the transport sector. The research also pointed out the lack of adequate biofuel support measures for end-users and vehicle manufacturers whose preferences were still higher for the fossil fuel reference.

Vermote et al. (2013) assessed four alternatives of freight transport infrastructure at Anzegem (Flanders). The research led to the most interesting transportation infrastructure option, namely, the external western ring,

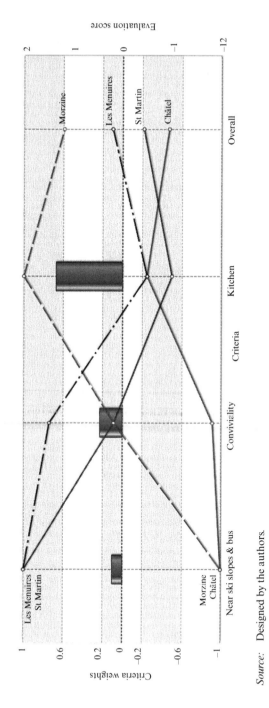

Source: Designed by the authors.

Figure 1.5   Chalet alternatives ranking of the Corijn family

to reconcile accessibility and livability, based on the transport companies, public authorities and citizens' criteria.

Brucker et al. (2014) used the MAMCA to obtain a selection and preliminary ranking for several ways to design innovative tools that have the potential to improve road safety. Results showed that alternatives based on speeding receive the highest priority except for users and manufacturers. Manufacturers generally prefer autonomous infrastructure-based alternatives because of liability issues. Users give low priority to vehicle-related alternatives because of the high user cost and the relatively small effect on driver safety.

Kourtit et al. (2014) analysed, by means of the MAMCA, the performances of 40 world cities regarding managers', researchers', visitors', residents' and artists' viewpoints. Based on 70 indicators, results showed that there is no single efficient city but there are dominant cities that score higher on all indicators than others, namely, Paris, London, New York and Tokyo.

Macharis and Crompvoets (2014) deployed the MAMCA to evaluate different alternatives for spatial data infrastructure (SDI) for Flanders. The results showed that each of the considered alternatives has their own drawbacks. The results also showed that the development of SDI in Flanders is more than just implementing the European INSPIRE directive, but also requires the integration of the market in the SDI. Decision-makers may thus consider a combination of different alternatives/measures to deal with the different stakeholders' objectives.

Verlinde et al. (2014) applied the MAMCA to research when a mobile depot for last-mile deliveries and first-mile pick-ups could become profitable and how stakeholders would be impacted. A mobile depot is a trailer fitted with a loading dock, warehousing facilities and an office. Results showed that the objectives of the economic stakeholders (TNT Express, shippers and receivers) are well addressed while the objectives of the societal stakeholders (citizens and local authorities) are better addressed. Nevertheless, the research also showed that the viability of the investment and profitable operations criteria of TNT Express must be met better to become interesting, for example, by using the mobile depot at full capacity and by increasing the drop density.

Verlinde and Macharis (2016) compared different scenarios on off-hours deliveries to supermarkets in Brussels. Their analysis showed that a shift towards such deliveries should receive overall support because the scenarios that envision a high proportion of night deliveries receive a high score.

Lebeau et al. (2015) used the MAMCA methodology to assess the support of stakeholder groups for the electrification of city logistics. Other applications are currently being performed.

1.6 CONCLUSION

Effective decision-making requires an explicit structure that jointly considers the objectives of the different stakeholders in evaluating alternatives. Contrary to traditional MCDA methods, the MAMCA methodology enables the objectives of each stakeholder group to be considered. In other words, the methodology enables visualization of the different points of view and facilitates the structuring of the discussion between stakeholders. Moreover, by enabling stakeholders to be involved throughout the whole process, it fosters social acceptance and facilitates implementation of the solutions. The MAMCA methodology has been further developed into different tools, namely, the COMCA (Competence-based Multi Criteria Analysis) and the range-based MAMCA, to cope with a wider range of decision-making settings.

REFERENCES

Álvarez-Carillo, P.A., Durate, A., Leyva-Lopez, J.C., 2010. A group multicriteria decision support system for ranking a finite set of alternatives. Paper presented at the EURO XXIV, Lisbon, Portugal.

Banville, C., Landry, M., Martel, J.-M., Boulaire, C., 1998. A stakeholder approach to MCDA. *Systems Research and Behavioral Sciences* 15, 15–32. https://doi.org/10.1002/(SICI)1099-1743(199801/02)15:1<15::AID-SRES179>3.0.CO;2-B (accessed 4 June 2018).

Brans, J.P., Vincke, P., 1985. Note – a preference ranking organisation method. *Management Science* 31, 647–56. https://doi.org/10.1287/mnsc.31.6.647 (accessed 4 June 2018).

Breukers, S., Wolsink, M., 2007. Wind power implementation in changing institutional landscapes: an international comparison. *Energy Policy* 35, 2737–50. https://doi.org/10.1016/j.enpol.2006.12.004 (accessed 4 June 2018).

Brucker, K.D., Macharis, C., Wiethoff, M., Marchau, V., 2014. Strategic analysis of stakeholder preferences regarding the design of ITS-based road safety measures. *IET Intelligent Transport Systems* 8, 190–9. https://doi.org/10.1049/iet-its.2012.0171 (accessed 4 June 2018).

Brundtland, G., Khalid, M., Agnelli, S., Al-Athel, S., Chidzero, B., Fadika, L., Hauff, V., Lang, I., Shijun, M., Morino de Botero, M., Singh, M., Okita, S., Others, A., 1987. *Our Common Future* ("Brundtland report"). New York: Oxford University Press.

Buchholz, T., Luzadis, V.A., Volk, T.A., 2009. Sustainability criteria for bioenergy systems: results from an expert survey. *Journal of Cleaner Production, International Trade in Biofuels* 17, Suppl. 1, S86–S98. https://doi.org/10.1016/j.jclepro.2009.04.015 (accessed 4 June 2018).

Buysse, K., Verbeke, A., 2003. Proactive environmental strategies: a stakeholder management perspective. *Strategic Management Journal* 24, 453–70. https://doi.org/10.1002/smj.299 (accessed 4 June 2018).

Cuppen, E., Breukers, S., Hisschemöller, M., Bergsma, E., 2010. Q methodology to select participants for a stakeholder dialogue on energy options from biomass in the Netherlands. *Ecological Economics* **69**, 579–91.

Damart, S., Roy, B., 2009. The uses of cost–benefit analysis in public transportation decision-making in France. *Transport Policy* **16**, 200–12. https://doi.org/10.1016/j. tranpol.2009.06.002 (accessed 4 June 2018).

Di Lucia, L., Nilsson, L.J., 2007. Transport biofuels in the European Union: the state of play. *Transport Policy* **14**, 533–43.

Donaldson, T., Preston, L.E., 1995. The stakeholder theory of the corporation: concepts, evidence, and implications. *Academy of Management Review* **20**, 65–91. https://doi.org/10.5465/AMR.1995.9503271992 (accessed 4 June 2018).

Eckenrode, R.T., 1965. Weighting multiple criteria. *Management Science* **12**, 180–92. https://doi.org/10.1287/mnsc.12.3.180 (accessed 4 June 2018).

Elghali, L., Clift, R., Sinclair, P., Panoutsou, C., Bauen, A., 2007. Developing a sustainability framework for the assessment of bioenergy systems. *Energy Policy* **35**, 6075–83. https://doi.org/10.1016/j.enpol.2007.08.036 (accessed 4 June 2018).

Freeman, R.E., 1984. Strategic Management: *A Stakeholder Approach*. Boston, MA: Pitman.

Gallego Carrera, D., Mack, A., 2010. Sustainability assessment of energy technologies via social indicators: results of a survey among European energy experts. *Energy Policy* **38**, 1030–9.

Grimble, R., Wellard, K., 1997. Stakeholder methodologies in natural resource management: a review of principles, contexts, experiences and opportunities. *Agricultural Systems* **55**, 173–93.

Kaya, T., Kahraman, C., 2011. Multicriteria decision making in energy planning using a modified fuzzy TOPSIS methodology. *Expert Systems with Applications* **38**, 6577–85. https://doi.org/10.1016/j.eswa.2010.11.081 (accessed 4 June 2018).

Keeney, R.L., Raiffa, H., 1993. *Decisions with Multiple Objectives: Preferences and Value Trade-offs*. New York: Cambridge University Press.

Kourtit, K., Macharis, C., Nijkamp, P., 2014. A Multi Actor Multi Criteria analysis of the performance of global cities. *Applied Geography, The New Urban World* **49**, 24–36. https://doi.org/10.1016/j.apgeog.2013.09.006 (accessed 4 June 2018).

Kurka, T., Blackwood, D., 2013. Selection of MCA methods to support decision making for renewable energy developments. *Renewable & Sustainable Energy Reviews* **27**, 225–33. https://doi.org/10.1016/j.rser.2013.07.001 (accessed 4 June 2018).

Lahdelma, R., Salminen, P., Hokkanen, J., 2014. Using multicriteria methods in environmental planning and management. *Environmental Management* **26**, 595–605. https://doi.org/10.1007/s002670010118 (accessed 4 June 2018).

Lebeau, P., Macharis, C., Van Mierlo, J., Janjevic, M., 2015. Implementing an urban consolidation centre: involving stakeholders in a bottom-up approach. Paper presented at the URBE Conference, Rome. 1–2 October 2015.

Løken, E., 2007. Use of multicriteria decision analysis methods for energy planning problems. *Renewable & Sustainable Energy Reviews* **11**, 1584–95. https://doi.org/10.1016/j.rser.2005.11.005 (accessed 4 June 2018).

Macharis, C., Crompvoets, J., 2014. A stakeholder-based assessment framework applied to evaluate development scenarios for the spatial data infrastructure for Flanders. *Computers, Environment and Urban Systems* **46**, 45–56. https://doi.org/10.1016/j.compenvurbsys.2014.04.001 (accessed 4 June 2018).

Macharis, C., de Witte, A., Ampe, J., 2009. The multi-actor, multi-criteria analysis methodology (MAMCA) for the evaluation of transport projects: theory and practice. *Journal of Advanced Transportation* **43**, 183–202. https://doi.org/10.100 2/atr.5670430206 (accessed 4 June 2018).

Macharis, C., de Witte, A., Turcksin, L., 2010. The Multi Actor Multi Criteria Analysis (MAMCA) application in the Flemish long-term decision making process on mobility and logistics. *Transport Policy* **17**, 303–11. https://doi.org/10.1016 /j.tranpol.2010.02.004 (accessed 4 June 2018).

Macharis, C., Turcksin, L., Lebeau, K., 2012. Multi actor multi criteria analysis (MAMCA) as a tool to support sustainable decisions: state of use. *Decision Support Systems* **54**, 610–20. https://doi.org/10.1016/j.dss.2012.08.008 (accessed 4 June 2018).

Marttunen, M., Lienert, J., Belton, V., 2017. Structuring problems for Multi-Criteria Decision Analysis in practice: a literature review of method combinations. *European Journal of Operational Research*. https://doi.org/10.1016/j.ejor .2017.04.041 (accessed 4 June 2018).

Mayer, A.L., 2008. Strengths and weaknesses of common sustainability indices for multidimensional systems. *Environment International* **34**, 277–91. https://doi. org/10.1016/j.envint.2007.09.004 (accessed 4 June 2018).

Munda, G., 2004. Social multi-criteria evaluation: methodological foundations and operational consequences. *European Journal of Operational Research* **158**, 662–77. https://doi.org/10.1016/S0377-2217(03)00369-2 (accessed 4 June 2018).

Nijkamp, P., Rietveld, P., Voogd, H., 2013. *Multicriteria Evaluation in Physical Planning*. Amsterdam: Elsevier.

Parris, T.M., Kates, R.W., 2003. Characterizing and measuring sustainable development. *Annual Review of Environment and Resources* **28**, 559–86. https://doi. org/10.1146/annurev.energy.28.050302.105551 (accessed 4 June 2018).

Pohekar, S.D., Ramachandran, M., 2004. Application of multi-criteria decision making to sustainable energy planning – a review. *Renewable & Sustainable Energy Reviews* **8**, 365–81. https://doi.org/10.1016/j.rser.2003.12.007 (accessed 4 June 2018).

Pope, J., Annandale, D., Morrison-Saunders, A., 2004. Conceptualising sustainability assessment. *Environmental Impact Assessment Review* **24**, 595–616. https://doi.org/10.1016/j.eiar.2004.03.001 (accessed 4 June 2018).

Roy, B., 1985. *Méthodologie multicritère d'aide à la décision*. Paris: Economica.

Roy, B., 1991. The outranking approach and the foundations of ELECTRE methods. *Theory and Decision* **31**, 49–73. https://doi.org/10.1007/BF00134132 (accessed 4 June 2018).

Saaty, T.L., 2008. Decision making with the analytic hierarchy process. *International Journal of Services Sciences* **1**, 83–98. https://doi.org/10.1504/IJSSci.2008.01759 (accessed 4 June 2018).

Sala, S., Ciuffo, B., Nijkamp, P., 2015. A systemic framework for sustainability assessment. *Ecological Economics* **119**, 314–25. https://doi.org/10.1016/j.ecoleco n.2015.09.015 (accessed 4 June 2018).

Salo, A., Hämäläinen, R.P., 2010. Multicriteria decision analysis in group decision processes. In Kilgour, D.M., Eden, C. (eds), *Handbook of Group Decision and Negotiation, Advances in Group Decision and Negotiation*. Dordrecht: Springer Netherlands, pp. 269–83.

Savage, G.T., Nix, T.W., Whitehead, C.J., Blair, J.D., 1991. Strategies for assessing and managing organizational stakeholders. *The Executive* **5**, 61–75. https://doi. org/10.5465/AME.1991.4274682 (accessed 4 June 2018).

Turcksin, L., Macharis, C., Lebeau, K., Boureima, F., Van Mierlo, J., Bram, S., De Ruyck, J., Mertens, L., Jossart, J.-M., Gorissen, L., Pelkmans, L., 2011. A Multi Actor Multi Criteria framework to assess the stakeholder support for different biofuel options: The case of Belgium. *Energy Policy* **39**, 200–14. https://doi.or g/10.1016/j.enpol.2010.09.033 (accessed 4 June 2018).

van Dam, J., Junginger, M., 2011. Striving to further harmonization of sustainability criteria for bioenergy in Europe: recommendations from a stakeholder questionnaire. *Energy Policy*, Special section: Renewable Energy Policy and Development **39**, 4051–66. https://doi.org/10.1016/j.enpol.2011.03.022 (accessed 4 June 2018).

Verlinde, S., Macharis, C., 2016. Who is in favor of off-hour deliveries to Brussels supermarkets? Applying Multi Actor Multi Criteria Analysis (MAMCA) to measure stakeholder support. *Transportation Research Procedia*, Tenth International Conference on City Logistics, 17–19 June 2015, Tenerife, Spain, pp. 522–32. https://doi.org/10.1016/j.trpro.2016.02.008 (accessed 4 June 2018).

Verlinde, S., Macharis, C., Milan, L., Kin, B., 2014. Does a mobile depot make urban deliveries faster, more sustainable and more economically viable: results of a pilot test in Brussels. *Transportation Research Procedia*, Special issue: Sustainable Mobility in Metropolitan Regions. mobil.TUM 2014. International Scientific Conference on Mobility and Transport. Conference Proceedings Vol. 4, pp. 361–73. https://doi.org/10.1016/j.trpro.2014.11.027 (accessed 4 June 2018).

Vermote, L., Macharis, C., Putman, K., 2013. A road network for freight transport in Flanders: Multi Actor Multi Criteria assessment of alternative ring ways. *Sustainability* **5**, 4222–46. https://doi.org/10.3390/su5104222 (accessed 4 June 2018).

Wang, M., Yang, J., 1998. A multi-criterion experimental comparison of three multi-attribute weight measurement methods. Journal of Multi-Criteria Decision Analysis 7, 340–50. https://doi.org/10.1002/(SICI)1099-1360(199811)7:6<340::AI D-MCDA206>3.0.CO;2-S (accessed 4 June 2018).

Wang, J.-J., Jing, Y.-Y., Zhang, C.-F., Zhao, J.-H., 2009. Review on multi-criteria decision analysis aid in sustainable energy decision-making. *Renewable & Sustainable Energy Reviews* **13**, 2263–78. https://doi.org/10.1016/j.rser.2009.06.021 (accessed 4 June 2018).

Weiner, E., Brown, A., 1986. Stakeholder analysis for effective issues management, *Planning Review* **14**(3), 27–31.

Williamson, O.E., 1991. Strategizing, economizing, and economic organization. *Strategic Management Journal* **12**, 75–94. https://doi.org/10.1002/smj.4250121007 (accessed 4 June 2018).

Zhu, S.-H., Anderson, N.H., 1991. Self-estimation of weight parameter in multiattribute analysis. *Organizational Behavior and Human Decision Processes* **48**, 36–54.

2. When to use Multi Actor Multi Criteria Analysis or other evaluation methods?

Cathy Macharis, Klaas De Brucker and Koen Van Raemdonck

2.1 INTRODUCTION

Evaluation is a broad concept. It concerns the systematic analysis of the conceptualisation, design, implementation and utility of a social intervention programme by using socio-economic evaluation procedures (Rossi and Freeman, 1993). In addition, major transport projects require high capital investment and generate a variety of economic, social and environmental impacts, which are not always positive (Flyvbjerg et al., 2003). Several evaluation tools can be used to evaluate transport measures, such as Cost-Effectiveness Analysis (CEA), Social Cost-Benefit Analysis (SCBA), Regional Economic Impact Study (REIS), Multi Criteria Analysis (MCA) and Multi Actor Multi Criteria Analysis (MAMCA). As these methods have their specific basic assumptions and objectives, it is not surprising that conclusions differ when different evaluation methods are used (De Brucker et al., 2011). In the past, economists and policy analysts sharply disagreed on which method was to be preferred (e.g., Janssen and Munda, 1999; Adler and Posner, 2006; Tudela et al., 2006; Polak, 2007). The intensity of this discussion has, however, diminished now. Generally, economists and policy analysts now agree that there is no clear answer to this question and that the actual choice to be made depends on the decision-making (DM) context and the desire to consider other elements than purely economic ones (e.g., strategic or political issues).

The evaluation tools can be classified according to the perspective of the evaluation (business versus social, i.e., the vertical dimension in Table 2.1) as well as the characteristics of the evaluation tool in terms of the number of criteria that can be taken into account, for example, uni-criterion methods (such as Private Investment Analysis or PIA) or multi-criteria methods (such as MCA) (i.e., the horizontal dimension in Table 2.1). A

Table 2.1   Classification of decision-making tools

	Uni-criterion Methods	Multi-criteria Methods One Value Tree	Multi-criteria Methods Separate Value Trees
Business	PIA, CEA	Most of the methods (amongst others MCA)	MAMCA
Social	SCBA, CEA, REIS	SEA, SMCA, EMCA, REIS	MAMCA

Source: Designed by the authors.

second distinction can be made, namely, whether the multiple criteria are integrated into a single value tree (e.g., SMCA) or clustered into separate value trees per stakeholder (e.g., MAMCA). Social MCA (SMCA) studies societal DM problems as a whole (i.e., using a single value tree) and can be considered part of public choice. MAMCA, on the other hand, uses separate value trees to study a DM problem. The aim of this chapter is not to describe all the existing methods in detail but to aid the decision maker in selecting the most appropriate tool.

2.2   DISCUSSION OF DECISION-MAKING METHODS

2.2.1   Cost-Effectiveness Analysis (CEA)

CEA evaluates an alternative in terms of its effectiveness in achieving a particular policy objective, as well as in terms of its efficiency in achieving that objective. In other words, CEA takes the political objective as given and selects the measure that enables achieving this objective at the lowest budgetary cost possible (Hakkert and Wesemann, 2005; De Brucker et al., 2011). The fundamental desirability of that policy objective is not evaluated in CEA, as there is no formal decision rule for accepting or rejecting a project. In fact, CEA is frequently used to determine the effectiveness of policy measures (such as those related to road safety). Here, CEA compares the effects of implementing a particular road safety measure with the cost of implementing that measure. This comparison is made on the basis of an effectiveness-cost ratio (ECR) (2.1), where O represents the outcome of a particular policy measure and C the unit cost of the implementation of this measure). To select the most appropriate measure, the ECRs of the various alternatives need to be compared. Finally, the measure with the highest ECR is preferred.

$$ECR = \frac{O}{C} \tag{2.1}$$

In a road safety context, the number of lives or accidents saved as a consequence of the implementation of a measure is often used as a parameter of its effectiveness (Weijermars and Wesemann, 2013). However, the number of lives saved can also be replaced by other parameters such as the number of accidents or casualties. The CEA thus examines which road safety measures can be implemented at the lowest cost to obtain a predefined objective (i.e., the cost-effectiveness or cost-minimisation perspective). Conversely, this method can also identify the best – that is, most cost-effective – measure to improve road safety within a limited budget (i.e., the effect-maximisation perspective) (Vlakveld et al., 2005; Boardman et al., 2011). It is important to convert all costs of implementation to an annual basis using discount rates in order to make measures with different lifespans comparable.

A major strength of CEA is the fact that intangible effects do not have to be monetised and that it gives the decision maker more insight into, for example, the cost of saving one statistical life. However, this tool can only assess one effect at a time. As a result, CEA cannot evaluate mobility, environmental and safety impacts simultaneously. Moreover, CEA does not facilitate comparing safety effects for different levels of accident severity. CEA remains, however, a sound evaluation method when there is only a single primary policy objective which is not subjected to a fundamental evaluation and where other policy objectives are absent or may be neglected. Furthermore, CEA does not take into account the various stakeholders' interests. CEA is classified (in Table 2.1) as a mono-criterion, mono-stakeholder evaluation method (Macharis, 2007). However, a mono-stakeholder may also be interested in multiple effects. Hence, this stakeholder will not always be satisfied with a CEA. Consequently, the CEA may result in an incomplete economic analysis, which may lead to the selection of a measure that would not be selected if more complete data were used.

2.2.2 Social Cost-Benefit Analysis (SCBA)

SCBA is a widely used technique in the context of transport evaluation (Mouter et al., 2013; Nogués and González-González, 2014) and has its roots in neoclassical welfare economics. As opposed to PIA, SCBA evaluates projects from a broader societal perspective. Principally, all project effects (i.e., costs and benefits) are taken into account irrespective of the identity of the actors affected. This means that a wide range of policy effects can be taken into account, such as effects on mobility, the environment, road safety and so on. CEA can itself be considered a partial form of SCBA, as it can be carried out with a mere subset of the data necessary for SCBA. As opposed to CEA, SCBA examines the fundamental desirability of realising a policy objective. This is done by comparing one or several project alternatives (always in reference to a baseline scenario or 'counterfactual') aimed at realising that objective. As the aim of SCBA is to maximise welfare, the scenario with the highest positive net present value (NPV) will be preferred. As shown in (2.2), the NPV of a project alternative (a) corresponds to the sum of all the net cash flows obtained by deducting the social costs (C) from social benefits (B) associated with the policy measure. The costs and benefits correspond to reductions or increases in utility levels, respectively. When applying SCBA each effect needs to be expressed in money values. These are subsequently converted into their present values in order to allow for time preference (Boardman et al., 2011). Therefore t (t = 1,. . .,T) represents the period of time within which the cash flow occurs and i corresponds to the discount rate. In addition to the NPV, other decision criteria can be used such as the benefit-cost ratio (BCR) (2.3) (Geudens et al., 2009). By carrying out an SCBA the measures are evaluated in a more comprehensive way as compared to CEA. Like CEA, SCBA will also look for the cheapest way of reaching a policy objective, but SCBA will do this by weighing social benefits and social costs of projects aimed at realizing the policy objective (De Brucker et al., 2011).

$$NPV(a) = \sum_{t=1}^{T} \frac{B(a)_t - C(a)_t}{(1 + i)^t} \tag{2.2}$$

$$BCR(a) = \frac{\sum_{t=1}^{T} \frac{B(a)_t}{(1 + i)^t}}{\sum_{t=1}^{T} \frac{C(a)_t}{(1 + i)^t}} \tag{2.3}$$

In (2.3), the denominator refers to the 'implementation cost', that is, the budgetary cost of a measure. The benefits (i.e., the nominator in formula 2.3) comprise all social benefits. Negative benefits (i.e., social cost), such as for example increased travel time, if these were to be estimated, are subtracted from the benefits.

An important strength of the SCBA is the possibility of converting future values into present values using a discount rate. The selection of an appropriate discount rate has, however, a strong influence on the results of the evaluation method. Higher discount rates favour short-term projects as they reduce the present value of long-term effects heavily. Lower discount rates, on the other hand, favour long-term projects such as irrigation works or forestry. Here, some argue in favour of one discount rate for all effects, others for multiple discount rates depending on the effect studied (Elvik and Veisten, 2004). SCBA is a relatively simple evaluation method when the necessary data are available and there is sufficient understanding of the effects, especially regarding the monetisation of the effects. The basic principle underlying SCBA, as made explicit in the NPV formula (2.2), is the Hicks-Kaldor (H-K) compensation criterion (Hicks, 1939; Kaldor, 1939). This criterion states that persons whose welfare levels have increased (i.e., the winners) should be able to compensate those whose welfare level have decreased (i.e., the losers). In other words, welfare is assumed to increase when winners win more than losers lose, that is, when benefits are higher than costs as made explicit in the NPV formula (2.2). Although distributional issues are inherent in the H-K principle, these are not studied explicitly in SCBA. It is assumed that income redistribution can be realised more easily (and at lower cost) by government as part of macro-economic tax and income transfer policy. Another corollary is that SCBA does not follow a utilitarian approach, since utility changes are not directly expressed in terms of utility changes in the H-K criterion, but in terms of a proxy such as prices or income levels (Boardman et al., 2011). One euro accruing to a poor person is assumed to have the same utility value as one euro accruing to a rich person. Hence, SCBA disregards equity issues.

SCBA is also associated with some other weaknesses. Monetisation of intangible effects (such as the value of human life or biodiversity) is sometimes problematic. Market prices cannot be applied to determine the money value of these effects. There are, however, a number of methods for calculating the value of intangible effects (Elvik and Veisten, 2004). The willingness-to-pay (WTP) method is widely used. Here, two approaches exist, namely, 'revealed preference' and 'stated preference' (or 'contingent evaluation'). The former derives consumer preferences from choices consumers make (or 'reveal') when they allocate their scarce resources among competing alternatives. The latter constructs a hypothetical market using questionnaires. Stated-preference methods are fraught with problems (Sen, 2000), in particular when the questions asked are hypothetical. Then, respondents do not clearly grasp the effects that are surveyed as they lack the experience of trading these in their daily lives. Within each approach several techniques exist (Pearce and Howarth, 2000; Boardman et al., 2011). However, these often yield results that are significantly different.

Also, methods based on willingness-to-accept (WTA) often lead to results that are different from WTP methods. The choice of a particular valuation method may, therefore, affect the level of benefits and costs and influence the final result of the evaluation. When evaluations are carried out on a global scale, an additional problem is that welfare levels differ among countries. WTP depends on people's ability to pay, which is determined by income levels (Elvik, 2001). Therefore, it becomes difficult to compare costs and benefits for projects implemented in an international context.

2.2.3 Multi Criteria Analysis (MCA)

MCA is an ex ante DM tool, which has its roots in operations research (Charnes and Cooper, 1961), developed for solving complex DM problems. MCA is used when several alternatives have to be prioritised in terms of multiple, often conflicting criteria, as measured by indicators (Pomerol and Barba-Romero, 2000; Belton and Stewart, 2002). In MCA, values (i.e., criteria, scores, weights etc.) are derived from policymakers' objectives and not from consumer WTP, as was the case in SCBA (De Brucker et al., 2013). MCA makes it possible for the decision maker to take into account all known aspects of a given problem simultaneously, in a structured and transparent way (Geudens et al., 2009). MCA is, therefore, an appropriate tool for evaluating mobility projects where different effects and goals such as safety, mobility, environment, implementation issues and so on are to be taken into account. In most DM problems, the decision maker has to deal with several (conflicting) goals which he or she may want to trade off. This is in contrast with CEA, where only one objective is evaluated. In MCA, each alternative is scored using different criteria. Each criterion is given a weight, reflecting its importance. The scores for the different criteria are finally aggregated. Here, several methods can be used such as Saaty's (1995) analytic hierarchy process (AHP), ELECTRE[1] and PROMETHEE.[2] In a sensitivity analysis the effects of a change in the weight of one or more criteria can be simulated so as to inform the decision maker about the impact of this change on the final result (Geudens et al., 2009). MCA, often also called 'MCDA' (i.e., Multi Criteria Decision Aid), does not replace the decision maker, but will rather 'aid' the decision maker to make better decisions by providing information about the effects of the alternatives,

---

[1] ELECTRE is the abbreviation for *ÉLimination Et Choix Traduisant la Réalité* and was designed by Roy (1968) (see also Roy, 1996; Belton and Stewart, 2002).
[2] PROMETHEE is the abbreviation for PReference Ordering METHod for the Enrichment of Evaluations and was designed by Brans and Vincke (1985) and Brans et al. (1986).

as well as an interactive tool to process this information. As a result, the decision maker may be better informed and more able to justify the choices made to the public.

MCA has a number of advantages and disadvantages. In MCA the effects do not have to be based on (welfare) economic concepts such as consumer surplus or value added. The alternatives are compared using criteria which represent the (sub)objectives of the stakeholders. A major strength is that every effect (tangible or intangible) is measured either quantitatively or qualitatively, but not necessarily in money terms (e.g., Chen et al., 2014). As a result, heterogeneous information can be included in the evaluation process. In addition, the MCA makes low demands in terms of data requirements (Baum and Höhnsheid, 2001). A disadvantage of some MCA methods may, however, be related to rank reversal between alternatives when adding or deleting alternatives (Bana e Costa and Vansnick, 2008; Maleki and Zahir, 2013). However, rank reversal is only possible with some specific MCA methods and it only occurs rarely. In addition, rank reversal may be justified in specific decision contexts, for example, for ranking problems, that is, when the alternatives have to be prioritised based on their relative worth instead of selection problems where the main objective is to pick a single best alternative (Saaty, 1995). Another element of criticism is that MCA is usually applied when several alternatives need to be evaluated or prioritised, whereas SCBA can easily be applied to evaluate a single alternative. In the latter case, it is also easier to make a judgement about the fundamental desirability of projects. However, it needs to be said that in SCBA reference is always implicitly made to a baseline scenario or 'counterfactual' (see above). So, a positive NPV in SCBA merely means that the project scenario is better than the baseline scenario. Also, MCA can, theoretically, be applied to a single project to make judgements about the fundamental desirability of that project, when reference is made to a predefined baseline scenario. Practical applications of these are, however, scarce (Cascajo and Monzon, 2014). Here, MCA rather becomes a sort of satisfaction analysis. MCA may also sometimes cause concerns about preference and structural independence. First, the set of criteria should be constructed so that each criterion (or group of criteria) is preferentially independent. This means that it must be possible to express preferences (and trade-offs) with respect to a criterion (or group of criteria), independent of the level of one or more of the remaining criteria. The level of the latter must not influence the preference direction of the former (Belton and Stewart, 2002). Second, care should be taken that structural dependence does not result in double counting of effects (Fenton and Neil, 2001). The risk of double counting does not exist when the structurally dependent criteria contribute to different points of view, different stakeholder objectives or affect different pockets (Roy, 1996).

To conduct MCA, the analyst should have sufficient knowledge about the different aggregation methods. Another element of criticism may be related to the alleged subjectivity associated with the weighting procedure in MCA. This criticism, however, also applies to other evaluation methods such as SCBA. In the latter, all effects are evaluated, weighed and synthesised in the NPV based on evaluation in money terms (i.e., consumer WTP), which depends heavily upon income and consumer preferences (De Brucker et al., 2013). In fact, important decisions always entail multiple objectives and weighting these is subjective by nature. Therefore, objectivity is nothing more than 'agreed-upon subjectivity' or 'subjectivity made objective'. The only thing that is possible is to be 'as objective as possible' or to 'follow objective procedures' (Buchanan et al., 1998; Forman and Selly, 2001).

2.2.4   Eclectic MCA

The idea of the eclectic MCA (De Brucker and Saitua-Nistal, 2006; De Brucker and Verbeke, 2007; De Brucker et al., 2013) is that for large projects, it makes sense to perform both a SCBA and a MCA and often also an environmental impact assessment (EIA) as well as a regional economic impact study (REIS) (which focuses on value added and job creation for a region, as well as backflow to government via taxation). Other studies also argue for combining different methods including quantitative and qualitative ones (Howick and Ackermann, 2011; Ferretti, 2016). SCBA is then mainly used in the phase of analysis, whereas MCA is used in the phase of decision. Here, a multi-faceted evaluation framework is constructed in the form of a MCA ('eclectic MCA' or EMCA). This evaluation framework is called 'eclectic' since it aims at extracting from various theories/methods those elements that are relevant and compatible enough to constitute the building stones for a new, integrative theory/method. Indeed, in the phase of decision, other elements than purely monetisable effects may become relevant, such as effects for which the money value cannot be established in a reliable way (e.g., specific environmental effects, such as biodiversity, climate change, effects on landscape etc.) as well as strategic issues related to the implementation of a project. Depending on the proportion of non-monetised versus monetised effects, the EMCA may either tend towards a (pure) MCA or more towards a traditional SCBA. But the EMCA itself remains most useful for the so-called 'swollen middle'. EMCA makes it possible to order the complexity of DM processes and synthesise them using an interactive step-by-step procedure. The 'ordered complexity' of EMCA sharply contrasts with the 'false simplicity' of SCBA, where all effects are synthesised in the NPV, which may seem easier to interpret. Although criteria are not clustered per stakeholder, stakeholder concerns are implicitly present in the EMCA. They can be addressed by simulating the effects on the final ranking of a change in the weights of the criteria contributing to the objectives of a specific stakeholder in the DM process.

2.2.5   Multi Actor Multi Criteria Analysis (MAMCA)

The MAMCA can be seen as a further extension of MCA. It adds another layer to the value tree that includes the stakeholders. In fact, criteria are clustered together so that they contribute to specific stakeholder objectives. The interaction between stakeholders may become a sound basis for constructing innovative alternatives that better fit the needs of the entirety of stakeholders. MAMCA, like most other MCA methods, fully recognises the endogenous character of preferences and can, therefore, stimulate learning among stakeholders. As MAMCA is an MCA, the same benefits as for MCA apply to MAMCA, in particular the fact that it is not necessary to monetise all of the effects (Macharis, 2007). Furthermore, MAMCA can solve some weaknesses of traditional MCA, in particular the issue of structural dependence among criteria, because criteria are clustered together so that they contribute to separate stakeholder objectives. Finally, MAMCA may result in multiple solutions, in contrast to the CEA, SCBA and MCA. This is because MAMCA aims at selecting (and ranking) the best alternatives for each stakeholder separately. Sometimes there may be one alternative that is ranked at (or near) the top in terms of all stakeholders' objectives, but usually solutions differ per stakeholder. However, this constitutes a strength rather than a weakness. A solution is finally constructed by the group of stakeholders, based on a learning process.

Several procedures to construct this solution exist. One can assign (different) weights to the stakeholders to obtain an overall ranking in terms of all stakeholder points of view. This overall ranking can either be taken as the final one or can be used merely as a benchmark for making comparisons between the particular stakeholder rankings, on the one hand, and the overall ranking, on the other hand, to check how big the gap is. Another approach is to present the separate rankings to the decision maker, without using stakeholder weights. Still another approach consists of identifying within the set of stakeholders one central or 'hub' stakeholder representing the public policy point of view (e.g., society, government) and using the ranking in terms of this stakeholder's objectives as a starting base for discussion (as in the IN-SAFETY case study, De Brucker et al., 2015).

The rankings derived in terms of the other stakeholders' points of view are then used to test to what extent they are compatible (or not) with those derived in terms of the public policy point of view. If compatibility is high, public policy has momentum and will be facilitated by the actions of the other stakeholders. If compatibility is low, public policy may be hindered and extra incentives (e.g., government subsidies) may be necessary so as gradually to gather momentum. In fact, the dialogue among experts and stakeholders may foster a learning process that can finally lead to the construction of a solution, as expressed in the quote attributed to the French philosopher N. Boileau (1636–1711): 'du choc des idées jaillit la lumière' ('from the clash of ideas can spring true insight'). This way, (MA)MCA can be viewed as an 'institution in action' creating momentum to solve societal conflict (De Brucker et al., 2013).

The major strengths and weaknesses of the various socio-economic evaluation methods are synthesised in Table 2.2.

2.3   RESULTS AND DISCUSSION

Since a multitude of DM tools exist, the selection of the most appropriate tool for a specific DM problem is not straightforward. In addition, using multiple methods may produce multiple (and different) results. This is due to the fact that each method has its own specific objectives and characteristics. In fact, the most adequate evaluation method to be used depends on the DM context. Therefore, we develop in this section a decision tree. This decision tree has been developed based both on the discussion in Section 2.2 as well as on many years of expertise and research in this field with a wide range of case studies (e.g., De Brucker et al., 2014, 2015; Macharis et al., 2014, 2015; Vermote et al., 2014; Milan et al., 2015). The objectives of developing such a decision tree are twofold. First, the decision tree aims at assisting DMs to choose the most appropriate ex ante evaluation method. Second, the decision tree contributes to standardising evaluation processes by structuring the complexity of the DM process. In addition, and as a corollary, the decision tree also makes it possible to obtain better insight on how Operational Research (OR)-related tools (such as MCA) relate to non-OR methods (such as SCBA and other methods) and how these can be used in conjunction with each other.

2.3.1   A Decision Tree Based on the Evaluation Objectives

Since each evaluation method has its own specific basic assumptions and objectives, the choice of an appropriate evaluation method is determined

Table 2.2   Strengths and weaknesses of socio-economic evaluation methods

	Strengths	Weaknesses
CEA	• Easy to calculate the ECR • Inclusion of non-monetised effects • Explicit evaluation of the basic (but often partial) objective • Not time-consuming • Low demands in terms of data • Easy to interpret for policymakers (results formulated in a straightforward way)	• No formal decision criterion to accept/reject a project • No evaluation of the fundamental desirability of a project (i.e., in terms of economic efficiency) • Only one effect (or policy objective) can be evaluated at a time • Time horizon: short and medium term • Does not accommodate stakeholder interests
SCBA	• *Ex post* and *ex ante* evaluation is possible • Costs and benefits over a longer period of time are included through discounting • Sound evaluation method: can include multiple effects (including environmental effects) • Easy to interpret for policymakers (results formulated in a straightforward way)	• Monetisation of some intangible effects may pose a problem • Equity issues are waived • Decision makers do not play an active role • Lack of knowledge regarding some effects • The choice of appropriate discount rate(s) • High demands in terms of data • Results do not address the actual complexity of the DM process • Cross-border problems may exist
MCA	• Intangible effects do not need to be monetised • Sound evaluation method • Decision maker still plays an active role; MCA is a tool for 'decision aid', not 'decision making' • Low demands in terms of data (data do not necessarily have to be monetised)	• Rank reversal may occasionally occur in some specific methods • Dependence between criteria may sometimes occur • Mainly useful for *ex ante* evaluation

Table 2.2   (continued)

	Strengths	Weaknesses
	• In cross-border studies no conversions of money values are needed • Useful when dealing with conflicting objectives	• More than one alternative is usually needed
EMCA	• Makes it possible to integrate monetised effects (from SCBA) and non-monetised effects (from MCA) into a single evaluation framework • Makes it possible to split up DM process into a phase of analysis and a phase of decision • The underlying MCA methodology is a sound evaluation methodology • DM still plays an active role; like MCA, EMCA is a tool for 'decision aid', not 'decision making' • Lower demands in terms of data compared to SCBA • Useful when dealing with conflicting objectives ('structured complexity')	• Rank reversal may occasionally occur depending on the underlying MCA method used • Dependence between criteria may sometimes occur • Mainly useful for *ex ante* evaluation • More than one alternative is usually needed • A discount rate still needs to be chosen (for the SCBA component)
MAMCA	• Stakeholders are included explicitly in the DM process • Intangible effects do not need to be monetised • The underlying MCA methodology is a sound evaluation methodology • Decision maker still plays an active role; MCA (including MAMCA) is a tool for 'decision aid', not 'decision making' • In cross-border studies no conversions of money values are needed • Particularly useful when dealing with conflicting objectives	• Rank reversal may occasionally occur in some specific underlying MCA methods • Mainly useful for *ex ante* evaluation • More than one alternative is usually needed • Does not necessarily yield a single solution

Source: Designed by the authors.

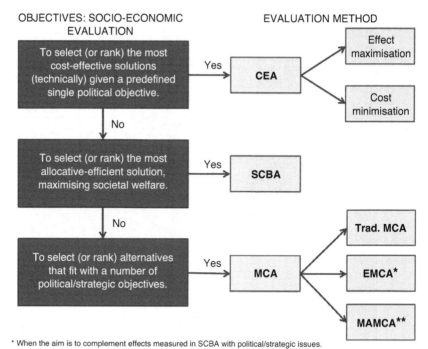

* When the aim is to complement effects measured in SCBA with political/strategic issues.
** When stakeholders play a prominent role in the decision-making process and criteria can be clustered so that they contribute to separate stakeholders' objectives.

Source: Designed by the authors.

Figure 2.1   Decision tree based on the objectives of the evaluation

in the first place by the objectives of the evaluation process, as shown in Figure 2.1. If the main objective is to find the most cost-effective way of implementing (technically) a predefined political objective (one not subject to fundamental evaluation in terms of economic efficiency), then CEA may be the most appropriate tool. If the focus is on evaluating the fundamental desirability of a project in terms of economic efficiency and societal welfare, then SCBA is the most appropriate tool. If the aim is to select measures that perform well in terms of specific (stakeholder) objectives that are often conflicting, then MCA (the traditional, the eclectic or the MAMCA) is the appropriate tool. When stakeholders are playing a prominent role in the DM process and one wants to assess to what extent the stakeholders will facilitate or obstruct the implementation of specific policy alternatives, then MAMCA becomes extremely useful. If the focus or objective of the evaluation is dual, then multiple methods may be applied, as explained below.

2.3.2   The Decision Tree Based on Other Characteristics

The objectives of the evaluation (discussed above) are, however, not the only elements that determine the actual choice of a method. There are a number of other, more practical, considerations that play an important role, such as the characteristics of the method, the feasibility of monetising the effects and the aspiration to involve stakeholders. These elements will play an important role in the final decision tree, presented in Figure 2.2.

The first-level parameter in the decision tree that determines the choice to be made is related to the number of available alternatives. If there are not multiple alternatives to be evaluated, it usually becomes less appropriate to apply MCA (or MAMCA). Then, SCBA, CEA or satisfaction analysis may be preferred (as shown in the lower part of Figure 2.2). The actual choice here depends on the possibility of monetising the effects as well as

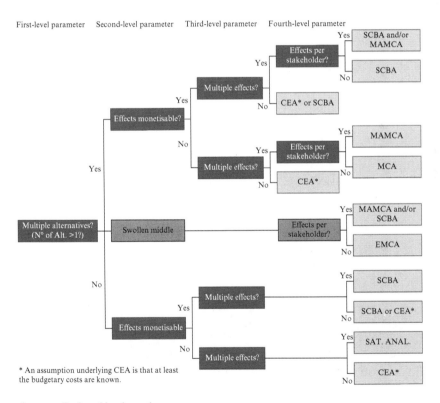

Source: Designed by the authors.

Figure 2.2   Decision tree based on the characteristics of the methods

the number of effects that are considered relevant, which are the second- and third-level parameters, respectively. In case effects are monetisable and at the same time multiple, then SCBA is the most appropriate tool (CEA is not possible because of the multiplicity of effects). But when the effects are single, both SCBA and CEA can be applied. In the latter case, CEA makes fewer demands in terms of data (only the budgetary cost needs to be monetised), but assumes that the fundamental desirability of a predefined policy objective (i.e., in terms of economic efficiency and social welfare) does not need to be evaluated (see also Figure 2.1). In case the effects are not monetisable, SCBA is not possible and CEA is the appropriate tool when the effects are single. But when the effects are multiple, one should rely on some sort of (MCA-like) satisfaction analysis. With only a single alternative to be studied, the presence of stakeholders in the DM process (which is the fourth-level parameter in the decision tree) does not a priori result in choosing another DM tool. Nevertheless (and in particular when multiple effects are to be evaluated), it may be advisable here to conduct some sort of stakeholder analysis, if only in terms of mapping the positive and negative impacts on the different stakeholders.

If there are multiple alternatives to be evaluated and the answer to the monetisation issue remains negative, then SCBA is not possible and it may be advisable to conduct MCA or MAMCA (or in particular cases CEA). Here, the actual choice to be made depends on whether stakeholders constitute a prominent actor in the DM process in such a way that one wants to assess to what extent the alternatives contribute to specific stakeholder objectives (e.g., to assess the implementation potential of the measures). If this is the case, MAMCA may be used (instead of traditional MCA). However, when there is only a single (basic) objective (measured by a single effect) and the costs of the measures contributing to that objective can be easily determined, then one can use CEA. Stakeholder concerns will be less of an issue here (or will have a lower level of complexity) because there is only a single effect to be studied (usually on a single stakeholder).

In case the answer to the monetisation issue is positive, one may opt to conduct SCBA (or in particular cases CEA) sometimes complemented with MAMCA. Here, the actual choice again depends on whether stakeholders play an important role in the DM process. If so, the SCBA should ideally be complemented with a MAMCA or at least with some sort of stakeholder analysis, if only in terms of mapping the positive and negative impacts on the different stakeholders. Here again, when there is only one effect to be evaluated, both SCBA and CEA can be applied. The latter again requires less data but does not evaluate the fundamental desirability of the policy objective. Also here, with only a single effect to be studied, stakeholder concerns will be less of an issue.

From the above explanation, it becomes clear that in specific circumstances different evaluation methods may be applied simultaneously (but separately), so as to obtain information from different perspectives. One particular approach involving integrating or combining different evaluation methods into a single framework is the eclectic MCA (EMCA) approach. This approach is suitable for the so-called 'swollen middle' in Figure 2.2, that is, when some of the effects are monetisable and others are not. In addition, it is possible to split up the DM process into a phase of analysis and a phase of decision. In the former, one can focus on welfare creation as measured by SCBA (which consists of monetised effects only). In the latter, the effects evaluated in money terms can be complemented by effects that are difficult to monetise, as well as implementation issues (distributional effects, political feasibility etc.). Moreover, in the EMCA it is possible to include stakeholder concerns. However, this is usually done in an implicit way, that is, by simulating the effects on the final ranking of a change in the weights corresponding to a particular stakeholder's objectives. However, if one wants to assess stakeholder concerns more explicitly, still in the 'swollen middle' case, then one can complement the SCBA by a MAMCA (instead of an EMCA) or rearrange the criteria into a MAMCA framework and conduct a conventional MAMCA.

2.4   CONCLUSIONS

In this chapter, we gave a brief overview of the differences between the main objectives and characteristics of a number of evaluation methods including Cost-Effectiveness Analysis (CEA), Social Cost-Benefit Analysis (SCBA) and Multi Actor Multi Criteria Analysis (MAMCA). Since these differences are quite substantial, applying different methods to the same DM problem may, in many case studies, produce different results. This finding should not be considered unnatural since the objectives and characteristics of the evaluation methods differ substantially. CEA focuses on (technical) cost-effectiveness to achieve a predefined political objective, SCBA on economic efficiency and societal welfare and MAMCA on stakeholder objectives (which are often conflicting) and implementation issues. The availability of a multitude of DM tools should not be viewed as a drawback. An evaluation from different perspectives becomes possible now. Indeed, quoting Maslow (1966, pp. 15–16) we can say, 'When your only tool is a hammer, everything looks like a nail.' The multitude of DM tools may, on the other hand, confuse the decision maker. In order to reduce complexity and standardise DM processes, we developed a decision tree. This decision tree not only makes it possible to guide decision makers in choosing the most appropriate method(s) in a particular DM context, but also provides policymakers and analysts with better insights on how OR methods (like MCA) relate to non-OR methods (like SCBA and other methods) and how these can be used in conjunction with each other.

REFERENCES

Adler, M.D. and Posner, E.A. 2006. *New Foundations of Cost-Benefit Analysis*. Cambridge, MA and London: Harvard University Press.

Bana e Costa, C.A. and Vansnick, J.C. 2008. A critical analysis of the eigenvalue method used to derive priorities in AHP. *European Journal of Operational Research* **187**, 1422–8.

Baum, H. and Höhnsheid, K.J. 2001. Economic evaluation of road traffic safety measures. Paper presented at the European Conference of Ministers of Transport. Paris, 26–27 October 2000.

Belton, V. and Stewart, T.J. 2002. *Multiple Criteria Decision Making: An Integrated Approach*. Boston, MA, Dordrecht and London: Kluwer Academic Publishers.

Boardman, A.E., Greenberg, D.H., Vining, A.R. and Weimer, D.L. 2011, *Cost-Benefit Analysis: Concepts and Practice*, Boston, MA: Prentice Hall/Pearson.

Brans, J.P. and Vincke, P. 1985. A preference ranking organisation method: the PROMETHEE method for multiple criteria decision-making. *Management Science* **31**(6), 647–56.

Brans, J.P., Vincke, P. and Mareschal, B. 1986. How to select and how to rank projects: the Promethee method. *European Journal of Operational Research* **24**, 228–38.

Buchanan, J.T., Henig, E.J. and Henig, M.I. 1998. Objectivity and subjectivity in the decision making process. *Annals of Operations Research* **80**, 333–45.

Cascajo, R. and Monzon, A. 2014. Assessment of innovative measures implemented in European bus systems using key performance indicators, *Public Transport* **6**(3), 257–82.

Charnes, A. and Cooper, W.W. 1961. *Management Models and Industrial Applications of Linear Programming*. New York: Wiley & Sons.

Chen, S., Leng, Y., Mao, B. and Liu, S. 2014. Integrated weight-based multi-criteria evaluation on transfer in large transport terminals: a case study of the Beijing South railway station. *Transportation Research Part A* **66**, 13–26.

De Brucker, K. and Saitua-Nistal, R. 2006. Naar een geïntegreerde methodiek voor de beoordeling van investeringsprojecten op vlak van grootstedenbeleid en mobiliteit: Een poging om de kloof tussen analysefase en beslissingsfase te dichten. In M. Despontin and C. Macharis (eds), *Mobiliteit en (groot)stedenbeleid, 27ste Vlaams Wetenschappelijk Economisch Congres*, Brussels, 19–20 October, pp. 307–48.

De Brucker, K. and Verbeke, A. 2007. The institutional theory approach to transport policy and evaluation. The collective benefits of a stakeholder's approach: towards an eclectic multi-criteria analysis. In E. Haezendonck (ed.), *Transport Project Evaluation: Extending the Social Cost-Benefit Approach*. Cheltenham, UK and Northampton, MA, USA: Edward Elgar, pp. 55–94.

De Brucker, K., Macharis, C. and Veisten, K. 2011. Structuring the way: a new approach on multi-criteria and cost-benefit analysis to be applied to road safety measures. In E. Bekiaris, M. Wiethoff and E. Gaitanidou (eds), *Infrastructure and Safety in a Collaborative World: Road Traffic Safety*. New York: Springer, pp. 15–22.

De Brucker, K., Verbeke, A. and Macharis, C. 2013. Multi-criteria analysis and the resolution of sustainable development dilemmas: a stakeholder management approach. *European Journal of Operational Research* **224**(1), 122–31.

De Brucker, K., Macharis, C., Wiethoff, M. and Marchau, V. 2014. Strategic analysis of stakeholder preferences regarding the design of ITS-based road safety measures. *IET Intelligent Transport Systems* **8**(3), 190–9.

De Brucker, K., Macharis, C. and Verbeke, A. 2015. Two-stage multi-criteria analysis and the future of intelligent transport systems-based safety innovation projects. *IET Intelligent Transport Systems* **9**(9), 842–50.

Elvik, R. 2001. Cost-benefit analysis of road safety measures: applicability and controversies. *Accident Analysis and Prevention* **33**, 9–17.

Elvik, R. and Veisten, K. 2004. *Barriers to the Use of Efficiency Assessment Tools in Road Safety Policy. Road Safety and Environmental Benefit-cost and Cost-effectiveness Analysis for Use in Decision-making*. ROSEBUD thematic network, Report D4, European Commission, DGET, 5th Framework Programme, http://ec.europa.eu/transport/roadsafety_library/publications/rosebud_report_wp2.pdf (accessed 27 December 2013).

Fenton, N. and Neil, M. 2001. Making decisions: using Bayesian nets and MCDA. *Knowledge Based Systems* **14**, 307–25.

Ferretti, V. 2016. From stakeholders' analysis to cognitive mapping and Multi-Attribute Value Theory: an integrated approach for policy support, *European Journal of Operational Research* **253**, 524–41.

Flyvbjerg, B., Bruzelius, N. and Rothengatter, W. 2003. *Megaprojects and Risk – an Anatomy of Ambition*. Cambridge: Cambridge University Press.

Forman, E.H. and Selly, M.A. 2001. *Decision by Objectives: How to Convince Others that You are Right*. New Jersey and London: World Scientific.

Geudens, T., Macharis, C., Plastria, F. and Crompvoets, J. 2009. Assessing spatial data infrastructure strategies using the Multi Actor Multi Criteria Analysis. *International Journal of Spatial Data Infrastructures Research* **4**, 265–97.

Hakkert, S. and Wesemann, P. 2005. *The Use of Efficiency Assessment Tools: Solutions to Barriers*. SWOV Report R-2005-02. Institute for Road Safety Research (SWOV), Leidschendam, http://library.swov.nl/action/front/fulltext?id=109255 (accessed 27 December 2013).

Hicks, J.R. (1939). The foundations of welfare economics. *Economic Journal 196*, 696–712.

Howick, S. and Ackermann, F. 2011, Mixing OR methods in practice: past, present and future directions. *European Journal of Operational Research* **215**, 503–11.

Janssen, R. and Munda, G. 1999. Multi-criteria methods for quantitative, qualitative and fuzzy evaluation problems. In J.C.J.M. van den Bergh (ed.), *Handbook of Environmental and Resource Economics*. Cheltenham, UK and Northampton, MA, USA: Edward Elgar, pp. 837–54.

Kaldor, N. 1939. Welfare comparisons of economics and interpersonal comparisons of utility. *Economic Journal* **195**, 549–52.

Macharis, C. 2007. Multi-Criteria Analysis as a tool to include stakeholders in project evaluation: the MAMCA method. In E. Haezendonck (ed.), *Transport*

Project Evaluation: Extending the Social Cost-Benefit Approach. Cheltenham, UK and Northampton, MA, USA: Edward Elgar, Chapter 5.

Macharis, C., Milan, L. and Verlinde, S. 2014. A stakeholder-based multicriteria evaluation framework for city distribution. *Research in Transportation Business & Management* **11**, 75–84.

Macharis, C., Meers, D. and van Lier, T. 2015. Modal choice in freight transport: combining multi-criteria decision analysis and geographic information systems. *International Journal of Multicriteria Decision Making* **5**(4), 355–71.

Maleki, H. and Zahir, S. 2013. A comprehensive literature review of the rank reversal phenomenon in the analytic hierarchy process. *Journal of Multi-Criteria Decision Analysis* **20**, 141–55.

Maslow, A.H. 1966. *The Psychology of Science: A Reconnaissance by Abraham H. Maslow.* New York: Harper & Row.

Milan, L., Kin, B., Verlinde, S. and Macharis, C. 2015. Multi Actor Multi Criteria Analysis for sustainable city distribution: a new assessment framework. *International Journal of Multicriteria Decision Making* **5**(4), 334–54.

Mouter, N., Annema, J.A. and van Wee, B. 2013. Attitudes towards the role of Cost-Benefit Analysis in the decision-making process for spatial-infrastructure projects: a Dutch case study. *Transportation Research Part A* **58**, 1–14.

Nogués, S. and González-González, E. 2014. Multi-criteria impact assessment for ranking highway projects in North Spain. *Transportation Research Part A* **65**, 80–91.

Pearce, D.W. and Howarth, A. 2000. *Technical Report on Methodology: Cost Benefit Analysis and Policy Responses.* RIVM Rapport 481505020, Rijksinstituut voor Volksgezondheid en Milieu, 82 pp., http://www.rivm.nl/dsresource?objectid =rivmp:14910&type=org&disposition=inline&ns_nc=1 (accessed 27 December 2013).

Polak, J.B. 2007. De multicriteria-analyse als alternatief voor de kosten-batenanalyse? Enkele welvaartstheoretische kanttekeningen. *Tijdschrift Vervoerswetenschap* **43**(2), 28–33.

Pomerol, J.C. and Barba-Romero, S. 2000. *Multicriterion Decision in Management: Principles and Practice.* Berlin: Springer.

Rossi, P.H. and Freeman, H.W. 1993. *Evaluation: A systematic approach.* Newbury Park, CA: Sage Publications.

Roy, B. 1968. Classement et choix en présence de points de vue multiples (la méthode Electre). *Revue française d'Informatique et de Recherche Opérationnelle* **8**, 57–75.

Roy, B. 1996. *Multicriteria Methodology for Decision Aiding.* Dordrecht : Kluwer Academic Publishers.

Saaty, T.L. 1995. *Decision Making for Leaders.* Pittsburgh, PA: RWS Publications.

Sen, A.K. 2000. The discipline of cost-benefit analysis. *Journal of Legal Studies* **29**, 931–52.

Tudela, A., Akiki, N. and Cisternas, R. 2006. Comparing the output of cost benefit and multi-criteria analysis. An application to urban transport investments. *Transportation Research Part A* **40**, 414–23.

Vermote, L., Macharis, C., Boeykens, F., Schoolmeester, C. and Putman, K. 2014. Traffic-restriction in Ramallah (Palestine): participatory sustainability assessment of pedestrian scenarios using a simplified transport model. *Land Use Policy* **41**, 453–64.

Vlakveld, W., Wesemann, P., Devillers, E., Elvik, R. and Veisten, K. 2005. *Detailed*

Cost-benefit Analysis of Potential Impairment Countermeasures. SWOV Report R-2005-10. Institute for Road Safety Research (SWOV), Leidschendam, http://www.swov.nl/rapport/R-2005-10.pdf (accessed 27 December 2013).

Weijermars, W. and Wesemann, P. 2013. Road safety forecasting and ex-ante evaluation of policy in the Netherlands. *Transportation Research Part A* **52**, 64–72.

3. The Multi Actor Multi Criteria Analysis software

Gino Baudry, Koen Van Raemdonck and Cathy Macharis

3.1 INTRODUCTION

With the Multi Actor Multi Criteria Analysis (MAMCA) software, it is possible to easily go through the seven steps of the MAMCA methodology. It can be used to support stakeholders going through these steps in a friendly way, during a workshop or as a stand-alone tool.

The software consists of the dashboard and six main tabs, namely: Alternatives, Actors, Criteria, Weights, Evaluation and Multi Actors. The dashboard enables the project manager to create new projects and to manage his project portfolio. The choice of the core decision-method of the MAMCA must be done from the dashboard. The software currently embeds the AHP (Analytic Hierarchy Process) and the PROMETHEE (Preference Ranking Organization METHod for Enriched Evaluation) methods. The choice of a method is prerequisite as the input requirement relies on the method used. When creating or selecting an existing project, the manager has access to the above-mentioned tabs, enabling the MAMCA to be performed step by step.

The objective of the chapter is to present the MAMCA software and guide future users in its use. Section 3.2 presents the two decision-methods that are included in the software. Section 3.3 presents the different tabs and their associated commands by means of an illustrative case. Section 3.4 concludes.

3.2 THE CHOICE FOR A DECISION-METHOD

When creating a new project, defining the name and selecting a decision-method is required (Figure 3.1).

The literature provides a wide range of decision-methods among which AHP and PROMETHEE are the most popular when it

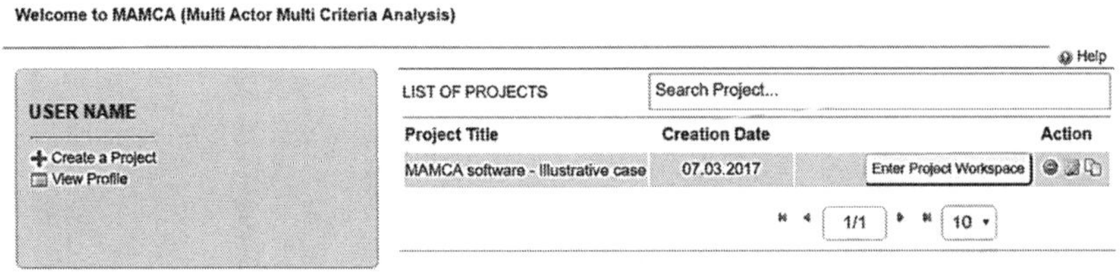
Welcome to MAMCA (Multi Actor Multi Criteria Analysis)
Help
USER NAME
Create a Project
View Profile
LIST OF PROJECTS
Search Project...
Project Title
Creation Date
Action
MAMCA software - Illustrative case
07.03.2017
Enter Project Workspace
1/1
10

Source: Extracted from the MAMCA software.

Figure 3.1 Project management tab

comes to addressing sustainability issues (Løken, 2007; Pohekar and Ramachandran, 2004; Wang et al., 2009). Nevertheless, there is no absolute best method to address decision-making problems (Lahdelma et al., 2014; Salo and Hämäläinen, 2010). Various factors may influence the choice for a method, for example, the number of participants, the participants' background, the project manager's preference, the availability of a user-friendly software and so on. This section presents the details of AHP and PROMETHEE to make transparent the software data computation.

3.2.1 AHP

AHP is a pairwise comparison method based on the Saaty nine-level scale (Saaty, 1977; Table 3.1). AHP can be used to elicit weights and in assessing the performance of the alternatives. It is one of the most popular Multi Criteria Decision Aid (MCDA) methods in the context of sustainable mobility and transport problems (Macharis et al., 2012). Based on the MAMCA application history record (see Chapter 1), we recommend using AHP method in MAMCA when there are many qualitative data. Thanks to the pairwise comparison mechanism, weights and evaluations can be obtained in a structured way.

The Saaty scale enables the expression of stakeholder intensity preferences between each pair of criteria (for weight elicitation) or each pair of alternatives (for the performance assessment). The whole scores allocated by the stakeholders though the scale constitute the elements of the pairwise comparison matrix, (PCM) which enables one to compute the weights or performance of the alternatives.

Several approaches can be used to compute the data, such as the arithmetic mean method, the least squares method or though the eigenvectors. The latter requires using some more mathematics. The following approach

Table 3.1   Description of the Saaty scale

Decision maker statements	Saaty scale	
Both elements* have equal importance	*1*	*1*
Intermediate	*2*	*1/2*
Moderately higher importance of C1 compared with C2	*3*	*1/3*
Intermediate	*4*	*1/4*
Higher importance of C1 compared with C2	*5*	*1/5*
Intermediate	*6*	*1/6*
Much higher importance of C1 compared with C2	*7*	*1/7*
Intermediate	*8*	*1/8*
Complete dominance of C1 compared with C2	*9*	*1/9*
	score	*reciprocal*

Note: * Elements refer to criteria or alternatives.

Source: Saaty (1977).

enables one to evaluate a very close approximation of the weights with simple mathematics. In the following example, AHP is assumed to be used to elicit weights, but one could just replace the mention of criteria by alternatives to illustrate the computation of alternative performance assessment.

Let us consider a three-criteria decision-problem in which the decision maker expresses equal importance between criteria 2 and 3 and a moderate preference for criteria 2 and 3 compared with criterion 1.

Using the Saaty scale, the pairwise comparison matrix PCM_{AHP} can be expressed:

Numeric illustration:

$$PCM_{AHP} = \begin{bmatrix} 1 & 1/3 & 1/3 \\ \mathbf{3} & 1 & 1 \\ 3 & 1 & 1 \end{bmatrix}$$

In bold, given the Saaty scale, a moderately higher preference refers to three:
"criterion 2 is moderately preferred compared with criterion 1;

Theory:

$$PCM_{AHP} =$$

$$\begin{bmatrix} C_1/C_1 & C_1/C_2 & \cdots & C_1/C_n \\ C_2/C_1 & C_2/C_2 & \cdots & C_2/C_n \\ \vdots & \vdots & \ddots & \vdots \\ C_n/C_1 & C_n/C_2 & \cdots & C_n/C_n \end{bmatrix}$$

With C_i/C_j representing the preference of criterion C_i compared with criterion C_j
With n being the number of criteria.

Step 1 consists in constructing a vector S_1 by adding up each of the PCM columns:

Numeric illustration:	*Theory:*
$S_1 = [7 \ \ 7/3 \ \ 7/3]$	$S_1 = \begin{bmatrix} C_1/C_1 & C_1/C_2 & \dots & C_1/C_n \\ + & + & \dots & + \\ C_2/C_1 & C_2/C_2 & \dots & C_2/C_n \\ + & + & \dots & + \\ \vdots & \vdots & \ddots & \dots \\ + & + & \dots & + \\ C_n/C_1 & C_n/C_2 & \dots & C_n/C_n \end{bmatrix}$ $= [s_1 \ \ s_2 \ \ \dots \ \ s_n]$

Step 2 consists in constructing a matrix S_2 by dividing each of the PCM elements with the sum of its column obtained in S_1:

Numeric illustration:	*Theory:*
$S_2 = \begin{bmatrix} 1/7 & 1/7 & 1/7 \\ 3/7 & 3/7 & 3/7 \\ 3/7 & 3/7 & 3/7 \end{bmatrix}$	$S_2 = \begin{bmatrix} \frac{C_1}{C_1}/s_1 & \frac{C_1}{C_2}/s_2 & \dots & \frac{C_1}{C_n}/s_n \\ \frac{C_2}{C_1}/s_1 & \frac{C_2}{C_2}/s_2 & \dots & \frac{C_2}{C_n}/s_n \\ \vdots & \vdots & \ddots & \vdots \\ \frac{C_n}{C_1}/s_1 & \frac{C_n}{C_2}/s_2 & \dots & \frac{C_n}{C_n}/s_n \end{bmatrix}$

Step 3 consists in constructing a vector S_3 by adding up each of the PCM rows:

Numeric illustration:	*Theory:*
$S_3 = \begin{bmatrix} 3/7 \\ 9/7 \\ 9/7 \end{bmatrix}$	$S_3 = \begin{bmatrix} \frac{\frac{C_1}{C_1}/s_1}{s_1} + \frac{\frac{C_1}{C_2}}{s_2} + \dots + \frac{C_1}{C_n}/s_n \\ \frac{\frac{C_2}{C_1}/s_1}{s_1} + \frac{\frac{C_2}{C_2}}{s_2} + \dots + \frac{C_2}{C_n}/s_n \\ \vdots & \vdots & \ddots & \vdots \\ \frac{\frac{C_n}{C_1}}{s_1} + \frac{\frac{C_n}{C_2}}{s_2} + \dots + \frac{C_n}{C_n}/s_n \end{bmatrix} = \begin{bmatrix} s'_1 \\ s'_2 \\ \vdots \\ s'_n \end{bmatrix}$

Step 4 enables one to compute the weights vector W_{AHP}:

Numeric illustration: | ***Theoretical:***

$$W_{AHP} = 1/3. \begin{bmatrix} 3/7 \\ 9/7 \\ 9/7 \end{bmatrix} = \begin{bmatrix} 1/7 \\ 3/7 \\ 3/7 \end{bmatrix} = \begin{bmatrix} 0.14 \\ 0.43 \\ 0.43 \end{bmatrix} \qquad W_{AHP} = \frac{1}{n}.S_3 = \begin{bmatrix} s'_1/n \\ s'_2/n \\ \vdots \\ s'_n/n \end{bmatrix} = \begin{bmatrix} w_1 \\ w_2 \\ \vdots \\ w_n \end{bmatrix}$$

With $\sum_{i=1}^{n=3} w_i = 0.14 + 0.43 + 0.43 = 1$ $\qquad\qquad$ with $\sum_{i=1}^{n} w_i = 1$

When using AHP, the consistency of the PCM needs to be checked. In other words, if A is two times preferred to B, and if B is of equal preference with C, A should be twice preferred compared with C. The software automatically informs the user in case of inconsistency. In such case, the AHP process needs to be re-performed starting from the building of the PCM (the consistency test mathematics is provided in Appendix 3A.1).

3.2.2 PROMETHEE

PROMETHEE was developed by Brans and Vincke (1985). The methodology is based on the computation of the preference degrees which aim at enriching the evaluation process by means of the decision maker's preference information. Various variants of the method have been developed such as PROMETHEE II, III, IV and V. PROMETHEE is an outranking approach, which means that one alternative is preferred compared with another one when it is at least as good as the other on most criteria, without being much worse on the other criteria. The present subsection will focus on PROMETHEE II which is implemented in the software. The PROMETHEE theory is presented, followed by a numerical example. Based on the MAMCA application history record (see Chapter 1), it is recommended that PROMETHEE is used in the MAMCA when one may have to deal with many hard data.

Step 1: the unicriterion preference degrees
In PROMETHEE, the evaluation process depends on how the decision maker perceives the difference in performance between two alternatives regarding each of his decision-criteria:

$$d_j(A_i, A_k) = f_j(A_i) - f_j(A_k)$$

$d_j(A_i, A_k)$ being the performance differential between the alternatives A_i and A_k regarding the criterion j;

$f_j(A_i)$ being the performance of the alternative A_i regarding the criterion j.

For each pair of alternatives (A_i, A_k), a unicriterion preference degree P_{ik}^j can be computed to express the extent of which a decision maker prefers the alternative A_i compared with A_k regarding the criterion j. The unicriterion preference degree P_{ik}^j is a function of the performance differential between two alternatives $d_j(A_i, A_k)$ regarding the criterion j. The unicriterion preference degree is computed by means of a preference function (Figure 3.2).

By hypothesis, the preference function ranges between zero and one, with one expressing a total preference for an alternative over another and zero expressing indifference. Functions are positive and non-decreasing in PROMETHEE ($P^j: \mathbb{R} \rightarrow [0,1]$). The unicriterion preference degree P_{ik}^j can take various forms to express the decision maker's preference.

Assuming a linear preference function (Figure 3.2a, b), the unicriterion preference degrees are obtained as follows:

$$P_{ik}^j = \begin{cases} 0 & if & d_j(A_i, A_k) \le q \\ [d_j(A_i, A_k) - q]/(p - q) & if & q < d_j(A_i, A_k) < p \\ 1 & if & d_j(A_i, A_k) \ge p \end{cases}$$

Assuming a Gaussian preference function (Figure 3.2d), the unicriterion preference degrees can be computed as follows:

$$P_{ik}^j = 1 - \exp\left(\frac{-d_j(A_i, A_k)^2}{2s^2}\right) \text{ if } d_j(A_i, A_k) \ge P_{ik}^j = 0 \text{ otherwise}$$

With:

P_{ik}^j being the unicriterion preference degree regarding the criterion j;

q being the indifference threshold, that is, the threshold for which the decision maker is indifferent between the alternatives A_i and A_k;

p being the preference threshold, that is, the threshold for which the decision maker has an absolute preference for A_i compared with A_k;

s being the inflection point (see Figure 3.2).

As shown in Table 3.2, the unicriterion preference degree of an alternative compared to itself is always zero ($P_{kk}^j = 0$).

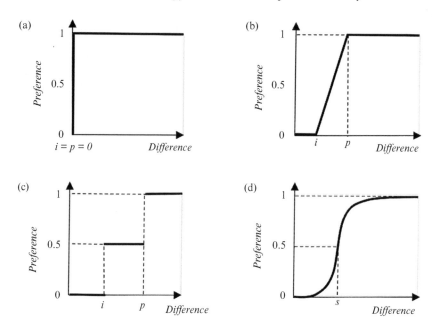

Source: Designed by the authors. Adapted from Ishizaka and Nemery (2013).

Figure 3.2   Example of different types of preference functions

Table 3.2   Unicriterion preference degrees for the criterion j

Criterion j	A_1	A_2	...	A_k
A_1	$P^j_{11} = 0$	P^j_{12}	...	P^j_{1k}
A_2	P^j_{21}	$P^j_{22} = 0$	...	P^j_{2k}
...	...	...	...	...
A_k	P^j_{k1}	P^j_{k2}	...	$P^j_{kk} = 0$

Step 2: the global preference degrees

Based on the unicriterion preference degrees, the global preference degrees can be computed to express the decision maker's global preference (π_{ik}) for the alternative A_i compared with A_k regarding the whole criteria and – eventually – their associated weights w_j:

$$\pi(A_i, A_k) = \pi_{ik} = \sum_{j=1}^{j=n} P^j_{ik} \cdot w_j$$

With:

$$\sum_{j=1}^{n} w_j = 1 \text{ for } j=1, \ldots, n$$

$$\pi_{ii} = 0 \text{ and } 0 \leq \pi_{ik} + \pi_{ki} \leq 1$$

The preference degrees π_{ik} can be presented as a matrix:

$$\begin{bmatrix} 0 & \pi(A_1, A_2) & \ldots & \pi(A_1, A_k) \\ \pi(A_2, A_1) & 0 & \ldots & \pi(A_2, A_k) \\ \ldots & \ldots & 0 & \ldots \\ \pi(A_k, A_1) & \pi(A_k, A_2) & \ldots & 0 \end{bmatrix}$$

Step 3: the global positive, negative and net flows

The positive flow is a score that ranges between zero and one that expresses the mean preference degree of the decision maker for an alternative compared with all others. The positive flow $\varnothing^+$ of each alternative A_i consists of the normalized sum of the preference matrix rows:

$$\varnothing^+(A_i) = \frac{1}{(m-1)} \sum_{k=1}^{k=m} \pi_j(A_i, A_k) \text{ for } k=1, \ldots, m$$

The negative flow also ranges between zero and one. It is the mean preference degree of the decision maker for an alternative compared with another one. The negative flow $\varnothing^-$ of each alternative A_i consists of the normalized sum of the preference matrix columns:

$$\varnothing^-(A_i) = \frac{1}{(m-1)} \sum_{k=1}^{k=m} \pi_j(A_k, A_i) \text{ for } k=1, \ldots, m$$

The net flow $\varnothing(A_i)$ ranges between minus one and one. It considers both the negative and positive aspects of the alternatives and is the difference between the positive and negative flows:

$$\varnothing(A_i) = \varnothing^+(A_i) - \varnothing^-(A_i)$$

Step 4: the PROMETHEE ranking

When using PROMETHEE II, trade-offs are allowed, and the ranking depends on the global net flows: the higher the score, the better the alternative.

- An alternative outperforms the other if its global net flow score is higher than the other:

$$A_i > A_k \text{ if } \varnothing(A_i) > \varnothing(A_k)$$

- An alternative is outperformed by the other if its global net flow scores is lower than the other:

$$A_i < A_k \text{ if } \varnothing(A_i) < \varnothing(A_k)$$

- Two alternatives can be considered equivalent if both have an equal global net flow score:

$$A_i \sim A_k \text{ if } \varnothing(A_i) < \varnothing(A_k)$$

Let us consider a simple problem setting: the choice of a transport mode for two people who travel from Paris to Rome (Table 3.3).

Table 3.4 presents a possible setting concerning the required PROMETHEE inputs.

Let us illustrate the PROMETHEE mechanics by focusing on the cost criterion. Let us assume a linear function to express the decision maker's preference regarding the cost criterion, with a preference threshold $q = 50$ and an indifference threshold $p = 175$ as shown in Figure 3.3.

When comparing an alternative to itself, the preference degree is 0 (Table 3.5). The car option is the most expensive option, which means that

Table 3.3   Problem setting to illustrate PROMETHEE methodology

Criteria	Cost (to minimize)	GHG[a] emission (to minimize)	Convenience (to maximize)
Car	710€[b]	192	High[c]
Train	560€	4.5	Medium
Plane	360€	430	Low
Unit	Quantitative (€)	Quantitative (kgeqCO$_2$)	Qualitative scale

Notes:
a. GHG is greenhouse gas.
b. Per-kilometer running costs, including the total cost of ownership of a traditional grand tourism car (insurance, fuel, car wear, maintenance costs etc.), that is, 0.5€ per km.
c. Assuming a three-level scale: High preference: 1, Medium preference: 1, High preference: 1.

Source: Designed by the authors.

Table 3.4   Preference function inputs

Criteria	Unit	Function type	q threshold	p threshold
Cost	€	Linear (b)	145	230
GHG	KgeqCO$_2$	Linear (b)*	50	175
Convenience	Qualitative	Gaussian (c)	Medium	High

Note: * See Figure 3.3.

Source: Designed by the authors.

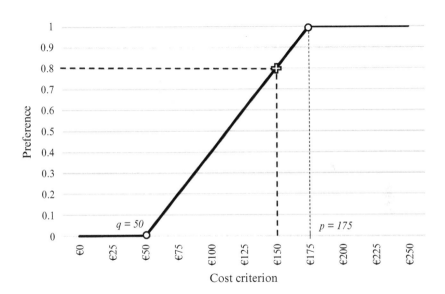

Source: Designed by the authors.

Figure 3.3   Illustration of a preference function for the cost criterion

$\pi_{cost}(A_{car}, A_{train}) = \pi_{cost}(A_{car}, A_{plane}) = 0$. When focusing on the train option, it is 350€ more expensive than the plane, which is above the preference threshold, consequently, $\pi_{cost}(A_{train}, A_{plane}) = 0$ and $\pi_{cost}(A_{plane}, A_{train}) = 1$, which means an absolute preference for the plane option compared with the train regarding the cost criterion. The same goes for the car and plane options: $\pi_{cost}(A_{car}, A_{plane}) = 0$ and $\pi_{cost}(A_{plane}, A_{car}) = 1$.

The car option is more expensive than the train one, which means that

Table 3.5   Unicriterion preference degrees for the illustration case

Cost	Car	Train	Plane	GHG	Car	Train	Plane	Conv.	Car	Train	Plane
Car	0	0	0	Car	0	0.5	1	Car	0	1	1
Train	0.8	0	0	Train	1	0	1	Train	0	0	1
Plane	1	1	0	Plane	0	0	0	Plane	0	0	0

Source: Designed by the authors.

$\pi_{cost}(A_{car}, A_{train}) = 0$. Nevertheless, the cost differential is included between the indifference and preference threshold:

$$q_{cost} = 50 < d_{cost}(A_{train}, A_{car}) = 150 < p_{cost} = 175$$

Consequently, as illustrated by Figure 3.3:

$$\pi_{cost}(A_{train}, A_{car}) = \frac{|d_{cost}(A_{train}, A_{car})| - q}{p - q} = \frac{150 - 50}{175 - 50} = 0.8$$

Based on the preference degrees, Table 3.6 presents the global positive, negative and net flows of the alternatives, assuming two different sets of weights. Weight set 1 assumes an equal preference between the different criteria (all weights are equal to 1/3). Weight set 2 assumes a higher preference for cost and GHG criteria such as $w_{cost} = w_{GHG} = 0.4$ and $w_{convenience} = 0.2$.

Given Table 3.6, the global positive, negative and net flows can be computed (Table 3.7).

As shown in Table 3.7, the final ranking remains unchanged whatever the weight set: the train option is preferred, followed by the car and plane options. However, the change in our decision maker's priorities has an impact on the final option scores.

Following the method choice, the MAMCA software is set to enable the collection of the different inputs and to yield the different outputs. The following section thus presents the different software tabs and commands by means of an illustrative case study.

3.3   ILLUSTRATIVE CASE STUDY

Let us consider a transport planning problem: a public authority who wants to improve city center mobility while also improving its environmental sustainability.

Table 3.6   Preference matrices considering two different weight sets

Weight set	Weights 1			Weights 2		
Options	Car	Train	Plane	Car	Train	Plane
Car	0	0.50	0.67	0	0.6	0.8
Train	0.60	0	0.67	0.72	0	0.8
Plane	0.33	0.33	0	0.2	0.2	0

Source: Designed by the authors.

Table 3.7   Preference matrices considering two different weight sets

Weight set	Weights 1			Weights 2		
Flows	Positive	Negative	Net	Positive	Negative	Net
Car	0.58	0.47	0.12	0.7	0.46	0.24
Train	0.63	0.42	0.22	0.76	0.4	0.36
Plane	0.33	0.67	−0.33	0.2	0.8	−0.60

Source: Designed by the authors.

3.3.1   Step 1: Decision-problem and Alternatives

In the project workspace, the user has access to the six tabs, the first one (Figure 3.4) enables the user to add information about the alternatives.

Let us consider the following alternatives (Figure 3.4):

1. *Road infrastructure.* Opening a new road lane may help in increasing the traffic speed, reducing traffic jams and associated pollution. Nevertheless, it may not help in moving towards a low-carbon mobility, it may even foster more car usage, which may increase the overall pollution. Adapting the infrastructure may represent a heavy cost for the municipality.
2. *Public transport.* Implementing a bus lane may foster a modal shift from car to public transport and reduce air pollutant emissions. Drawbacks may lie in the cost for the municipality concerning the infrastructure and the human resources required to implement this option.
3. *Cycle path.* Implementing a cycle path may foster a modal shift from car to bike and thus reduce pollution. The modal shift may, however, be limited because of the lack of convenience for end-users. The cost

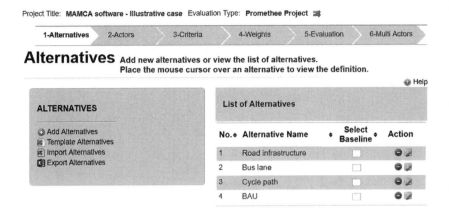

Source: Extracted from the MAMCA software.

Figure 3.4   Tab 1: alternatives

for the municipality is much cheaper compared with the previously mentioned options.

4. *Business as Usual (BAU).* This provides a benchmark to assess whether the other options can be considered an improvement or a degradation regarding the different objectives compared with the current situation.

Alternatives can be added through the "Add alternatives" command (Figure 3.4). An alternative name is required, and a short description can be added. The description may help the participants in interpreting the inputs to limit language vagueness and ambiguity issues. The data can also be imported/exported from/to Microsoft Excel by means of the commands "Import/Export Alternatives" (Figure 3.4). An Excel sheet template can be downloaded from the MAMCA software to ensure the compatibility of the inputs between the two softwares. A "baseline" command is also available which will be further detailed in Subsection 3.3.6.

3.3.2   Step 2: Stakeholder Analysis

The Actor tab allows the users to add stakeholder groups ("Add Actor Group" command, Figure 3.6). Stakeholder group data may either be added by the users or imported from an Excel file. A specific command enables the project manager to invite actors to participate in the project through email (Figure 3.5). Different user profiles can be assigned to the participants by the project manager. Each profile enables a different access (Table 3.8).

Table 3.8   User profile and access

User profile	Project manager	Actors	Surveyors	Experts
Tab 0-Dashboard	x			
Tab 1-Alternatives	x			
Tab 2-Actors	x			
Tab 3-Criteria	x	(x)		
Tab 4-Weights	x	x	x	
Tab 5-Evaluation	x	(x)		x
Tab 6-Multi Actors	x	x	x	x

Note: (x) depending on the parameters set by the project manager.

Source: Designed by the authors.

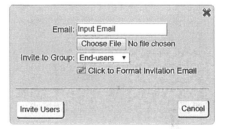

Source: Extracted from the MAMCA software.

Figure 3.5   (a) Actor group parameters; (b) actor invitation

Actors have personal logins and they can fill their criteria and weights in order to perform the evaluation of the alternatives and to see the multi actors' visuals. The surveyor profile can be assigned to many participants, without requiring the creation of accounts. The surveyor role is limited to the weight elicitation. It enables many participants to express their priorities in terms of criteria. The *expert* profile enables the participants to evaluate the perform-ance of the alternatives. These can be experts who are invited to evaluate certain criteria, for example, air quality. Each participant must be affiliated to one of the actor groups to be allowed to participate (Figure 3.5b).

When adding an actor group, the project manager can set the parameters concerning the different participants' roles (Figure 3.5). Criteria can be defined by the project manager or by the actors. The project manager may

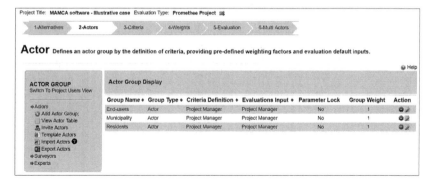

Source: Extracted from the MAMCA software.

Figure 3.6   Tab 2: actors

himself perform the evaluation or enable the actors or the experts to do so. In our illustrative case, the project manager will be selected (Figure 3.5). Such a choice depends on the decision-making context; for example, it may be more suitable for independent experts to perform the evaluation when objective evaluation is required. In another context, such as assessing the support of actors for a different alternative, it may be interesting to enable actors to perform the evaluation.

Considering each group equally is the common approach in the MAMCA. Nevertheless, the "Group Weight" command enables the project manager to prioritize the stakeholder groups against each other if necessary. The "Parameter Lock" command enables the project manager to disable the parameter modification of the Evaluation tab for the other users (decision-method parameters).

Let us consider three stakeholder groups for the illustration case:

1.   *End-users*. End-users are key actors through their modal choices, which itself may depend on the transport policy and available infrastructures. End-users represent a large population. Consequently, in a real case study, involving representatives such as end-users' associations may be relevant to aid data collection.
2.   *Residents*. Residents near the road will be affected by the consequences of the implementation of any alternative. For example, fostering public transport or cycling mobility should reduce pollution and improve air quality. Residents represent many people but are geographically concentrated. Representatives can be used to capture their inputs but local meetings and workshops can also be relevant.

3. *Municipality*. The public authority is a key stakeholder group when addressing urban mobility issues. The municipality will be considered the decision maker in our illustrative case. Contrary to residents and end-users, the number of actors to consider is limited. Consequently, face to face meetings can be relevant to capture the municipality's concerns.

3.3.3   Step 3a: Criteria Definition

The third tab enables the participants to add their criteria. The project manager may display each of the group data by clicking on the name of the stakeholder group (Figure 3.7).

Let us consider the following criteria in our illustrative case:

1. The end-users' criteria consist of the price attractiveness (price to minimize), the air quality (to maximize) and the convenience of the mobility mode (to maximize). The price attractiveness represents the cost of traveling. The air quality depends on the local emission of air pollutants. The convenience refers to the friendliness and flexibility of the different transport modes.
2. The residents' concerns focus on the traffic safety and the air quality. Traffic safety nearby the neighborhood refers to the risks of accidents. Air quality is a common criterion between residents and end-users,

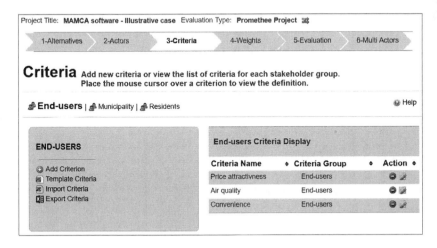

Source: Extracted from the MAMCA software.

Figure 3.7   Tab 3: criteria

which is allowed on the MAMCA framework as long as it represents a real value at stake for the different groups.

3. The municipality's criteria include the modal shift, the budget impact and the air quality. As for the other groups, the lower the emission of pollutant, the higher the option desirability. The budget impact refers to the required spending to implement an alternative. The modal shift criterion refers to the capacity of the alternative to foster people moving towards low-carbon transport modes.

3.3.4   Step 3b: Weights

The fourth tab enables actors to express their priorities between their criteria. In the software, weights can be elicited through three different approaches (Figure 3.8): (1) by considering each criterion of equal importance ("Equalize Weights" command; see Appendix 3A.2); (2) by using AHP ("Pairwise Comparison" command); (3) by manually filling the weight values ("Enter Weights Manually" command). Given the wide range of possible weighting methods, this last command enables one to elicit weights through another method and to enter the results in the software. Weights have, however, to be included between zero and one while their sum must be equal to one.

Weights can be expressed by each actor separately, for example, when using the surveyor profile. The software will then compute the arithmetic mean of the different actors' weights for each stakeholder group. Otherwise, each stakeholder group may come to a consensus, for example, during a workshop, and only provide a unique set of weights per group. When the actors' weights are collected separately without using the surveyor profile, the project manager must ensure that every participant is using the same weighting method for consistency.

As shown by Figure 3.8, the "Pairwise Comparison" command opens a window that enables actors to express their preferences. Let us consider the following weights for our example.

The air quality and the modal shift are considered of equal importance by the municipality, which corresponds to the assignment of a score of one in the Saaty scale. The budget impact is moderately more important than the air quality and the modal shift, which correspond to a score of three. By computing these values (Saaty, 2008), the software obtains the following weights (see Subsection 3.2.1): air budget impact (60 percent), quality (20 percent), modal shift (20 percent). For the end-users, the convenience is the most important criterion (73 percent), followed by price attractiveness (19 percent) and air quality (8 percent). For the residents, air quality and traffic safety are considered of equal importance.

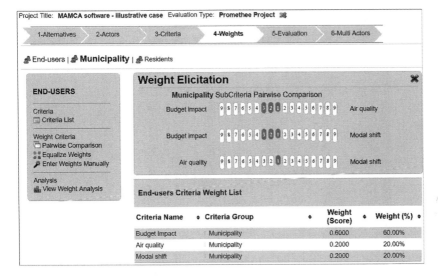

Figure 3.8   Tab 4: weights using AHP

For each stakeholder group, the MAMCA software checks the consistency[1] of the pairwise comparison matrix (see Appendix 3A.1). In case of inconsistency, the software displays the following alert: "*Criteria elicitation steps seem to be inconsistent*". The procedure has thus to be re-performed until the consistency requirement is fulfilled.

The weight chart may also be displayed ("View Weight Analysis" command) and downloaded (gray box in the right upper corner of Figure 3.9).

3.3.5   Step 4: Option Performance

The fifth tab enables the assessment of the option performances either though quantitative or qualitative scales that express the extent to which an alternative can comply with each of the criteria. The choice between the qualitative and quantitative indicators can be done by using the "Set Parameters" command. The participants will also be able to set the parameters relative to the PROMETHEE method.

In our present illustration, PROMETHEE is used. Consequently,

---

[1]   Consistency ratio (CR) is 0.1 in the MAMCA software (see Appendix 3A.1).

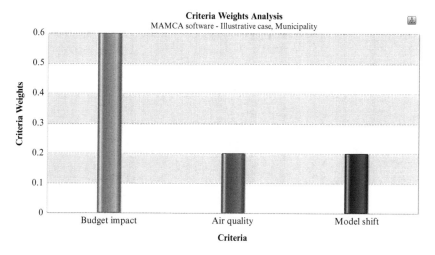

Source: Extracted from the MAMCA software.

Figure 3.9   Municipality's weight chart

parameters can be set (Figure 3.10): the function shape, the i and p threshold values, the type of scale and the indicator unit (see Section 3.2.2). When using a quantitative scale, the user can choose if the criterion must be maximized or minimized.

In our illustrative case, we will use the qualitative scale, presented in Table 3.9.

On this basis, the participants, experts or project manager can evaluate whether the implementation of an alternative constitutes an improvement or a degradation compared with the BAU regarding each criterion. The BAU performance is considered neutral for every criterion as it is the benchmark. Figure 3.11 illustrates the assessment of the different alternatives regarding the municipality's criteria.

In our example, the project manager performs the alternative assessment. Nevertheless, external experts or even stakeholders themselves may be invited to evaluate the alternatives depending on the problem setting.

Let us, for example, focus on the modal shift criterion. The softer the transport mode, the better the alternative regarding the modal shift criterion. Consequently, the bus lane and cycle path will have a positive and a very positive impact, respectively, compared with the BAU. On the contrary, a new road infrastructure will have a very negative impact, fostering car usage, compared with the BAU.

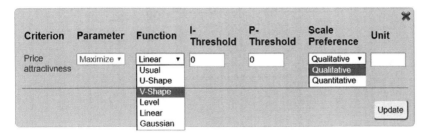

Source: Extracted from the MAMCA software.

Figure 3.10   PROMETHEE parameters

Table 3.9   The MAMCA software qualitative scale (seven levels)

Score	The option has . . .
Very negative	. . . a very negative impact compared with the BAU
Negative	. . . a negative impact compared with the BAU
Slightly negative	. . . a slightly negative impact compared with the BAU
Neutral	. . . no positive nor negative impact compared with the BAU
Slightly positive	. . . a slightly positive impact compared with the BAU
Positive	. . . a positive impact compared with the BAU
Very Positive	. . . a very positive impact compared with the BAU

Source: Extracted from the MAMCA software.

Source: Extracted from the MAMCA software.

Figure 3.11   Evaluation tab

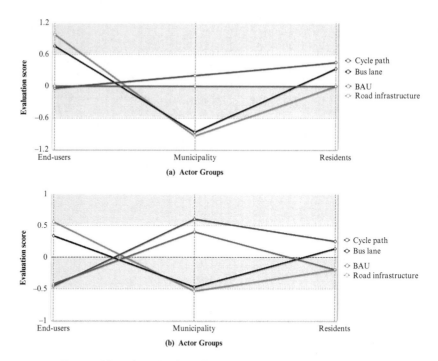

Source: Extracted from the MAMCA software.

*Figure 3.12   Multi actor charts: (a) baseline command on (BAU);
                (b) baseline command off*

The Evaluation tab enables one to display charts which are also available in the Multi Actor tab (see the next subsection).

3.3.6   Steps 5 and 6: Data Computation and Result Analysis

The software provides multiple visuals and tools to facilitate the dialogue and consensus-building process between the stakeholders.

Figure 3.12 presents the multi actor line charts which represent the alternative scores (Y-axis) for each actor group (X-axis).

For the end-users, all the alternatives represent a better option than the BAU, which means that the implementation of any alternative represents an amelioration from their perspective. The bus lane and road-widening alternatives constitute the most suited options with the same score. Thanks to the "baseline command" (cf. Subsection 3.3.1), an alternative can be used as a BAU when displaying the charts

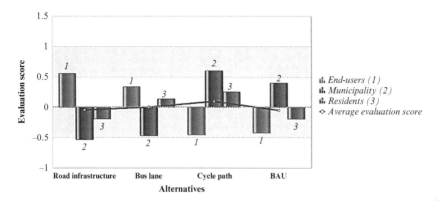

Source: Extracted from the MAMCA software.

Figure 3.13   Multi actor alternative analysis chart II

(Figure 3.12a). The command enables one to yield intuitive visuals to help in the discussion. For example, Figure 3.12b clearly shows that the cycle path option is the only alternative that outperforms the BAU for all the stakeholder groups.

Figure 3.13 illustrates another visual output that presents the alternative scores (Y-axis) for each alternative (X-axis). For example, the cycle path option is the most suited alternative for the municipality and the residents whereas it is not for the end-users.

Figure 3.14 presents the chart displayed through the command *"Criteria evaluation radar chart"*. The radar chart axes provide the alternatives' scores regarding each criterion.

Given the end-users' weights, the bus lane option outperforms the road infrastructure alternative concerning air quality and price attractiveness criteria whereas it is the opposite regarding the convenience. The strengths and weaknesses of the bus lane and road infrastructure alternatives compensate each other leading to an equal overall score. Despite its performance regarding air quality and price attractiveness, the cycle path is the least preferred option because of a lack of convenience.

For the municipality, even if the bus lane option contributes to lower the emissions of air pollutants and to foster the modal shift, the high budget impact compensates for these benefits. Consequently, the bus lane is less suited than the BAU. The cycle path option also fosters the modal shift while improving air quality but for an acceptable cost regarding the municipality's concerns.

For residents, the cycle path and bus lane options represent an

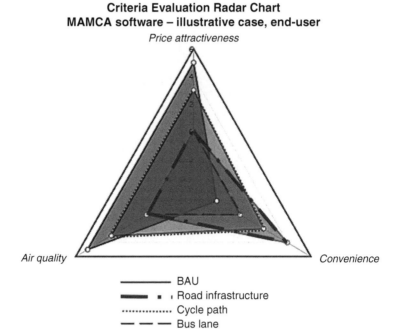

Criteria Evaluation Radar Chart
MAMCA software – illustrative case, end-user

Source: Extracted from the MAMCA software.

Figure 3 14   Radar charts

improvement compared with the BAU concerning the air quality and traffic safety. The cycle path especially contributes to lower the emissions of air pollutants. At the opposite end, the road infrastructure does not enable improvement compared with the BAU in terms of air quality and traffic safety.

The "Sensitivity Analysis" command enables one to visualize in real time the impact of changing the set of weights or the alternative evaluation in the group outputs (Figure 3.15). First, the participant can choose one of the group inputs, whether weights or evaluation. Second, the participant may manually increase or decrease an input value. Third, the software computes the data while considering the new setting and it displays the actualized multi actor chart. When focusing on the weights, decreasing a value will proportionally increase the weights of the others. When changing the performance of alternatives, the software will compute the new results by re-performing the MCA method (AHP or PROMETHEE). Finally, the "Restore" command allows the participant to come back to the initial setting.

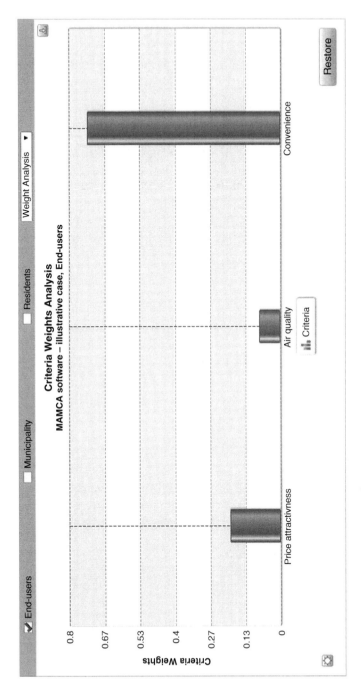

Source: Extracted from the MAMCA software.

Figure 3.15   Sensitivity analysis chart

The "Download Project Report" command enables the participant to obtain a report that includes the inputs and outputs of the whole project.

3.3.7 Step 7: Recommendations

During the consensus-building phase, additional information may be added. For example, one may evaluate the impact of an additional policy measure to compensate a negative impact on an actor group. Consequently, the user may modify at any time the inputs in the software. In our illustrative case, even if the cycle path is better than the BAU for the end-users, the municipality may develop additional measures to facilitate its implementation.

For example, given the end-users' perspective, specific measures can be deployed to cope with the lack of convenience of the cycle path option. The municipality may develop relay parking – park-and-ride – facilities to foster inter-modality and convenience for end-users. Obviously, this additional measure may generate additional budget spending which requires one to update option performances in terms of price attractiveness and/or budget impact. The park-and-ride facility may require a small contribution from end-users (park tickets), slightly holding back the option performance in terms of price attractiveness, and so on. Through this feedback loop, new insights – even inputs – will be provided to help in building and reaching a consensus.

3.4 CONCLUSION

The MAMCA software offers a user-friendly interface to address complex problems featuring multiple stakeholders and a wide range of data. It helps in collecting, structuring, computing and visualizing the data to support the participative decision-making process. The software can be easily explained and used in workshops but it can also be used to collect stakeholders' data from a distance, thanks to its actor invitation system. The MAMCA software is continuously upgraded.

REFERENCES

Brans, J.P., Vincke, P., 1985. Note – a preference ranking organisation method. *Management Science* 31, 647–56. https://doi.org/10.1287/mnsc.31.6.647 (accessed June 4, 2018).

Ishizaka, A., Nemery, P., 2013. *Multi-criteria Decision Analysis: Methods and Software*. New York: John Wiley & Sons.

Lahdelma, R., Salminen, P., Hokkanen, J., 2014. Using multicriteria methods in environmental planning and management. *Environmental Management* **26**, 595–605. https://doi.org/10.1007/s002670010118 (accessed June 4, 2018).

Løken, E., 2007. Use of multicriteria decision analysis methods for energy planning problems. *Renewable & Sustainable Energy Reviews* **11**, 1584–95. https://doi.org/10.1016/j.rser.2005.11.005 (accessed June 4, 2018).

Macharis, C., Turcksin, L., Lebeau, K., 2012. Multi actor multi criteria analysis (MAMCA) as a tool to support sustainable decisions: state of use. *Decision Support Systems* **54**, 610–20. https://doi.org/10.1016/j.dss.2012.08.008 (accessed June 4, 2018).

Pohekar, S.D., Ramachandran, M., 2004. Application of multi-criteria decision making to sustainable energy planning – a review. *Renewable & Sustainable Energy Reviews* **8**, 365–81. https://doi.org/10.1016/j.rser.2003.12.007 (accessed June 4, 2018).

Saaty, T.L., 1977. A scaling method for priorities in hierarchical structures. *Journal of Mathematical Psychology* **15**, 234–81. https://doi.org/10.1016/0022-2496(77)90033-5 (accessed June 4, 2018).

Saaty, T.L., 2008. Decision making with the analytic hierarchy process. *International Journal of Services Sciences* **1**, 83–98. https://doi.org/10.1504/IJSSci.2008.01759 (accessed June 4, 2018).

Salo, A., Hämäläinen, R.P., 2010. Multicriteria decision analysis in group decision processes. In Kilgour, D.M., Eden, C. (eds), *Handbook of Group Decision and Negotiation, Advances in Group Decision and Negotiation*. Amsterdam: Springer Netherlands, pp. 269–83.

Wang, J.-J., Jing, Y.-Y., Zhang, C.-F., Zhao, J.-H., 2009. Review on multi-criteria decision analysis aid in sustainable energy decision-making. *Renewable & Sustainable Energy Reviews* **13**, 2263–78. https://doi.org/10.1016/j.rser.2009.06.021 (accessed June 4, 2018).

APPENDIX

3A.1   AHP Consistency Test

The consistency ratio (CR) enables one to measure the inconsistency in the PCM (Saaty, 2008) through the random consistency index (RI) and the consistency index (CI), as illustrated below:

$$CR = CI/RI$$

Step 1: evaluating the principal eigenvalue λ_{max}

Given our illustrative case with three criteria ($n = 3$), let us assume three different PCM for which criteria 2 and 3 are considered of equal importance:

$$PCM^1_{AHP} = \begin{bmatrix} 1 & 1/3 & 1/3 \\ 3 & 1 & 1 \\ 3 & 1 & 1 \end{bmatrix} \quad PCM^2_{AHP} = \begin{bmatrix} 1 & 1/3 & 1/4 \\ 3 & 1 & 1 \\ 4 & 1 & 1 \end{bmatrix}$$

$$PCM^3_{AHP} = \begin{bmatrix} 1 & 1/3 & 1/5 \\ 3 & 1 & 1 \\ 5 & 1 & 1 \end{bmatrix}$$

The principal eigenvalue is obtained from the addition of products between each element of the eigenvector W_{AHP} and each element of the vector S_1:

$$\lambda_{max} = \sum_{i=1}^{n} s_i . w_i \text{ for } i = 1,...,n$$

Thus:

$$\lambda^1_{max} = \sum_{i=1}^{n=3} s_i . w_i = 0.14*7 + 0.43*\frac{7}{3} + 0.43*\frac{7}{3} = 3$$

$$\lambda^2_{max} = 0.14*8 + 0.43*\frac{7}{3} + 0.43*\frac{9}{4} = 3.09$$

$$\lambda^3_{max} = 0.14*9 + 0.43*\frac{7}{3} + 0.43*\frac{11}{5} = 3.21$$

Table A3.1   Random consistency index table

Number of criteria	1	2	3	4	5	6	7	8	9	10
RI values	0	0	0.58	0.9	1.12	1.24	1.32	1.41	1.45	1.51

Step 2: evaluating CI

$$CI = \frac{(\lambda_{max} - n)}{(n - 1)}$$

Numerically:

$$CI^1 = \frac{(3 - 3)}{(3 - 1)} = 0$$

$$CI^2 = \frac{(3.09 - 3)}{(3 - 1)} = 0.045$$

$$CI^3 = \frac{(3.21 - 3)}{(3 - 1)} = 0.104$$

Step 3: identifying RI
The RI value depends on the number of criteria of the decision-problem as shown in Table 3A.1. In our illustrative case, there are three criteria which correspond to $RI_{n=3} = 0.58$.

Step 4: evaluating CR
The higher the problem complexity, the higher the risk of inconstancy in the preferences. According to Saaty (2008), a PCM can be considered consistent if:

$$CR = \frac{CI}{RI} \leq 10\% \text{ means that the PCM is consistent}$$

Numerically:

$$CR^1 = \frac{0}{0.58} = 0 < 0.1 \qquad CR^2 = \frac{0.045}{0.58} = 0.078 < 0.1$$

$$CR^3 = \frac{0.104}{0.58} = 0.18 > 0.1$$

PCM^1_{AHP} is perfectly consistent: criteria 2 and 3 are of equal importance; criterion 2 is moderately preferred than criterion 1; criterion 3 is moderately preferred than criterion 1.

PCM^2_{AHP} is reasonably consistent: criteria 2 and 3 are of equal importance; criterion 2 is moderately preferred than criterion 1 but criterion 3 is more than moderately preferred than criterion 1 (with a score of four). This inconsistency is, nevertheless, at an acceptable level.

PCM^3_{AHP} is inconsistent: criteria 2 and 3 are of equal importance; criterion 2 is moderately preferred than criterion 1 but criterion 3 is highly preferred than criterion 1 (with a score of five). Regarding this score, criteria 2 and 3 cannot be considered of equal importance. The matrix is thus considered inconsistent. In such case, the pairwise comparison must be re-performed. In the MAMCA software, the consistency is automatically checked.

3A.2 Equal Weights Method

When addressing sustainability problems, one may say that each of the sustainability criteria is of equal importance. The command is thus available in the MAMCA software in the Tab 4 (Step 3b, Subsection 3.3.4). The expression of this equal importance can be written:

$$w_i = \frac{1}{n}, i = 1, 2, \ldots, n$$

The weight w_i of the criterion i is the same for all the n criteria. As an illustration, let us consider a decision-problem with four criteria ($n = 4$). The weight assignment would be:

$$w_1 = w_2 = w_3 = w_4 = \frac{1}{4}$$

This method is popular because it requires minimal knowledge and input from the stakeholders. Other assets lie in its simplicity, the process is transparent and require minimal time availability from the decision maker(s).

4. From desirable to feasible: fostering inter-institutional cooperation with Competence-based Multi Criteria Analysis (COMCA)

Geert te Boveldt, Koen Van Raemdonck and Cathy Macharis

4.1 INTRODUCTION

In many situations decision makers are faced with problems that stretch beyond their institutional boundaries or fields of competence. Typical examples include global challenges that cannot be dealt with by single states, such as financial market regulation, climate policy, migration policy and others. Inter-institutional cooperation is also needed in smaller-scale issues, such as metropolitan transport infrastructure between cities and surrounding commuter municipalities.

This chapter presents a novel group decision-making tool that aims to foster inter-institutional cooperation: Competence-based Multi Criteria Analysis (COMCA). Its use is explained in helping face two challenges associated with inter-institutional cooperation: (1) political transaction costs and (2) the non-internalisation of externalities.

The chapter first explains COMCA and its origins in Multi Criteria Decision Aid (MCDA). Then, the challenges of political transaction costs and the non-internalisation of externalities are discussed together with the role COMCA can play to tackle these challenges. Next, ongoing research for the application of COMCA in the planning of metropolitan infrastructure is discussed before the chapter concludes.

4.2 WHAT IS COMCA?

In short, COMCA is a group evaluation and decision-making tool for problems with multiple actors with different tasks or levels of responsibility. It indicates which decision alternatives best meet the priorities of individual actors, but it also indicates the feasibility of decision alternatives by showing the support for each alternative among each of the actor groups that are accountable for each of the tasks needed for implementing the decision alternatives.

COMCA is a means for applying MCDA in a multi-actor, multi-level context and builds on the Multi Actor Multi Criteria Analysis (MAMCA). The focus, however, here is on the institutional actors and the different institutional levels that are involved. Its principle is to provide the decision maker with an indication of the desirability of several decision alternatives, usually in the form of a preference ranking, based on multiple, often conflicting, criteria.

However, many real-world decision problems do not concern just one but several decision makers. For this reason, several methods have been developed for involving multiple stakeholders or actors in the process. MAMCA (Macharis, 2005; Macharis et al., 2012), for instance, juxtaposes the preference rankings of a common set of alternatives by multiple actors, each using an individual set of criteria.

In MAMCA, aggregation of individual preference rankings into a common preference ranking is usually omitted and the focus is put on critical actors or critical criteria regarding a common decision (Macharis et al., 2012). Indeed, aggregation of individual preference rankings only makes sense in cases where (1) a single group judgement is required rather than an indication of obstructing factors and (2) actors are interchangeable or are considered equivalent.

These conditions might be met in situations with a large number of actors, of whom no one's individual judgement is crucial (e.g., customers co-deciding on the launch of a new product) or in situations where MAMCA is adopted as a group decision-making method by actors who consider each other equivalent, that is, when it is applied using a constructive approach (Roy, 1993), rather than a prescriptive or descriptive approach (Bell et al., 1988).

Thus, simple aggregation of individual preferences is not appropriate in most real-world policy-making situations. In certain decision problems, however, the number of actors is so high (e.g., citizens or customers) and the degree of influence so different (e.g., national versus local government or citizens) that a mere juxtaposition of preference rankings would play down the preferences of crucial actors and leave too much complexity for decision makers to deal with. In such situations, differentiation between actors is needed in order to structure their preferences.

Several methods differentiate between actors by assigning weights to stakeholders. This typically implies actors assigning each other relative degrees of influence (Hosseini and Brenner, 1992; Ramanathan and Ganesh, 1994; Van Den Honert, 2001). While this might be sensible in a constructive approach, with all actors adopting 'the rules of the game', again, it is less likely to accurately reflect real-world power relations. Moreover, when actors evaluate each other, there is a risk of coalition formation (Bogetoft, 1992; Van Den Honert, 2001).

In COMCA, the actors' degree of influence is not expressed with an absolute value. On the contrary, the actors' influence depends on their role in the implementation of the decision in question, that is, their competence. Accordingly, actors are classified in competence domains; the smallest subsets of actors of which support as a group is essential for the decision's implementation. From this classification one can derive if actors constitute a competence domain on their own and are therefore to be considered as veto players (such as permit-granting authorities) or as belonging to a group of whom only a substantial amount but no individual support is required (customers, citizens in participatory processes) and whose preferences are therefore eligible for aggregation.

Through preference ranking by competence domain one can derive the desirability of the different project alternatives for each of the actor groups accountable for implementing the decision. This also provides an indication for the feasibility of each decision alternative as a whole.

4.3   HOW DOES COMCA WORK?

In theory, within COMCA, any existing MCDA technique can be used, such as MAUT (von Neumann and Morgenstern, 1947), ELECTRE (Roy, 1968), AHP (Saaty, 1980), PROMETHEE (Brans and Vincke, 1985) or Verbal Decision Analysis (Larichev and Moshkovich, 1997).[1] The social context of COMCA, however, requires maximum transparency, rather than mathematical sophistication. For this reason, in many cases, Simple Additive Weighting might be the most appropriate technique (Mayer and Stirling, 2004; Stirling and Mayer, 1999).

In summary, COMCA consists of the following steps: (1) determination of the planning problem and project alternatives; (2) determination of required competences; (3) identification of actors; (4) determination of criteria; (5) assessment of criteria alternatives; (6) assignment of relative priorities for criteria; (7) determination of individual actor preferences;

---

[1]   MAUT: Multi Attribute Utility Theory; ELECTRE: ELimination Et Choix Traduisant la REalité (ELimination and Choice Expressing REality); AHP: Analytic Hierarchy Process; PROMETHEE: Preference Ranking Organization METHod for Enrichment Evaluation.

(8) determination of group preferences per competence domain; and (9) determination of overall group preferences (Figure 4.1). These steps do not have to follow each other in the stated order as more often than not decision making is not a linear but rather a circular or chaotic process with multiple feedback loops.

4.3.1 Alleviating Political Transaction Costs

For institutions such as local or regional governments, cooperation can be advantageous in many different ways, especially when the social-economic functioning of their respective jurisdictions is spatially entangled. However, even when potentially beneficial for all actors involved, inter-institutional cooperation can be hampered by political transaction costs. North (1990) defines transaction costs as the costs of 'measuring and enforcing agreements'. In inter-institutional cooperation the concept can be used to refer to the non-monetary costs of obtaining information on which issue to cooperate with which actors, but also the burden of negotiation on which decision to take might be perceived as too high a cost for making cooperation attractive.

COMCA can help to alleviate political transaction costs. Any actor can initiate a process to explore the social-political feasibility of an inter-institutional project. COMCA provides information on which actors are likely to provide support for which project alternatives. Using this method helps actors to reveal previously unknown mutual interests. Negotiation costs are brought down as well, as actors stipulate the criteria that make decisions, in their perspective, acceptable or not.

4.3.2 Internalising Externalities

Alleviating political transaction costs leads to win-win situations in projects that are beneficial to all actors. However, many inter-institutional projects do not generate equal benefits and costs for all. Infrastructure, for instance, is beneficial to those who use it to reach their destination, but disadvantageous for those who experience environmental nuisance. A waste incineration plant is indispensable, but undesirable for those living nearby. In other words, some actors have to bear sacrifices in favour of the common good.

This, however, is unlikely to happen in situations where each actor has a de facto veto right; a common sight in international politics (e.g., European Union, United Nations) or within federalised states (e.g., Belgium). Rationally acting actors have no incentive to act in favour of the common good when it is not beneficial to their own situation. The problem

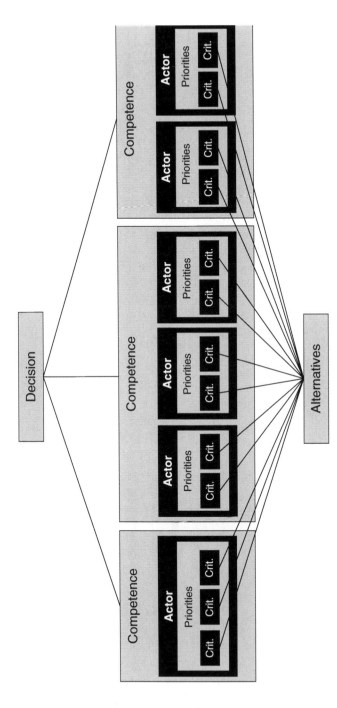

Source: Designed by the authors.

Figure 4.1 Structuring multi-actor multi-level decision making with COMCA

is, indeed, that when the territories of jurisdictions do not correspond to the spatial functions they host, institutions do not experience the full impact of their decisions. As Hooghe and Marks (2003) put it: institutions do not internalise the negative or positive externalities of their decisions.

This situation leads to what Scharpf (1988) calls the joint decision trap; inter-institutional decisions do not reflect the social optimum, but rather the lowest common denominator, that is, the decision accepted by all. Solutions that are desirable from a group perspective are not feasible because they are not desirable for each individual. Likewise, feasible solutions are unlikely to be the most desirable for the group as a whole.

In multi-level governance contexts, such as occur in federal or European Union politics, a higher-level institution cannot overrule a lower-level institution's veto. This implies that in prescriptive decision analysis methods (Bell et al., 1988), their respective preferences should be held in equal regard.

Figure 4.2 shows the juxtaposed preference rankings of a hypothetical project straddling the border between two regions. Even if alternative A, the social optimum, is preferred by most actors, it is not a feasible alternative because certain actors (municipality 2 and to a lesser extent, region 2) are unlikely to accept.

COMCA, or any group decision-making method for that matter, cannot change the institutional set-up to remove an institution's veto right. Yet, in a constructive approach (Roy, 1993) where actors are incited to act beyond maximising local utility, COMCA can be used to reveal area-optimal

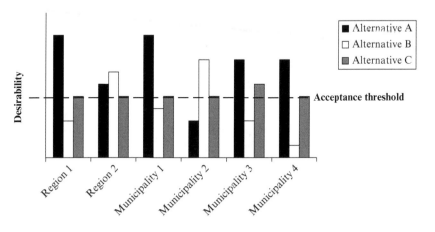

Source: Designed by the authors.

Figure 4.2   Desirable versus feasible decision alternatives

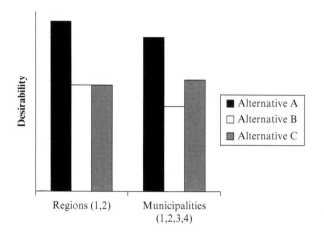

Figure 4.3 Preferences aggregated by institutional level

solutions. That is, in inter-institutional projects with an uneven distribution of effects (as in any infrastructure project), institutions of the same level can be considered competitors for the project's amenities (and the avoidance of nuisance) and will favour different project alternatives. In a constructive COMCA approach, institutions of the same level can be considered equivalents, allowing for the aggregation of their preferences. The result reflects an area-optimal solution where local interests are compensated for by other local interests of the same level; externalities are internalised.

Figure 4.3 shows the aggregate preference rankings for each institutional level using the same project as for Figure 4.2. It shows that for the project area as a whole (which can either be divided into two regions or four municipalities) alternative A is the optimal solution. Yet, even if a constructive COMCA approach reveals group- or area-optimal solutions, the intermediary steps revealing critical actors and criteria remain useful for formulating compensation policies.

4.3.3 COMCA Applications

COMCA is currently applied in the metropolitan area of Brussels, Belgium, for the planning of several transport projects, such as highway feeder roads, suburban (light) rail and bus lines. This metropolitan area has the peculiarity that the central city (itself consisting of 19 municipalities) and its commuter belt belong to three different regions, each with a high degree of transport policy autonomy, without any coordination from a higher policy level. This has resulted in political deadlock and a virtual standstill of most metropolitan transport projects.

Applying COMCA, the authors aim to contribute in overcoming the institutional deadlock with innovative forms of cooperation and decision making. Simultaneously, experience is gathered for fine-tuning the method in terms of data input, stakeholder consultation, and modes of processing and aggregating stakeholder input.

4.4   CONCLUSION

Many contemporary policy issues demand an inter-institutional approach. Cooperation between institutions, however, is hampered by problems such as political transaction costs and the non-internationalisation of externalities. This chapter shows how a novel group and decision-making method, COMCA, can be applied to tackle these problems. It is potentially helpful in identifying feasible inter-institutional policy options and actor coalitions. Also, it helps to reveal which policy options are desirable for each actor individually, which options are feasible considering each actor's competence to make or break a decision, and which options are desirable from a global rather than a local point of view. Potentially, COMCA can be applied in any decision problem with actors that have different roles in the decision's implementation.

REFERENCES

Bell, D., Raiffa, H., and Tverski, A. (1988). *Decision Making: Descriptive, Normative and Prescriptive Interactions*. Cambridge: Cambridge University Press.

Bogetoft, P. (1992). A note on conflict resolution and truthtelling. *European Journal of Operational Research,* **60**(1), 109–16. http://doi.org/10.1016/0377-221 7(92)90338-A (accessed 4 June 2018).

Brans, J.P. and Vincke, P. (1985). A preference ranking organisation method: (the PROMETHEE method for multiple criteria decision-making). *Management Science,* **31**(6), 647–56.

Hooghe, L. and Marks, G. (2003). Unravelling the central state, but how? Types of multi-level governance. *Reihe Politikwissenschaft,* **97**(2), 233–43.

Hosseini, J.C. and Brenner, S.N. (1992). The stakeholder theory of the firm: a methodology to generate value matrix weights. *Business Ethics Quarterly,* **2**(2), 99–119. http://doi.org/https://doi.org/10.2307/3857566 (accessed 4 June 2018).

Larichev, O.I. and Moshkovich, H.M. (1997). *Verbal Decision Analysis for Unstructured Problems*. Boston, MA: Kluwer Academic Press.

Macharis, C. (2005). The importance of stakeholder analysis in freight transport. *European Transport/Trasporti Europei,* **25–6**, 114–26.

Macharis, C., Turcksin, L., and Lebeau, K. (2012). Multi actor multi criteria analysis (MAMCA) as a tool to support sustainable decisions: state of use. *Decision Support Systems,* **54**(1), 610–20. http://doi.org/10.1016/j.dss.2012.08.008 (accessed 4 June 2018).

Mayer, S. and Stirling, A. (2004). GM crops: good or bad? Those who choose the questions determine the answers. EMBO Reports 5(11). https://doi.org/10.1038/sj.embor.7400285 (accessed 30 May 2017).

North, D.C. (1990). A transaction cost theory of politics. *Journal of Theoretical Politics,* **2**(4), 355–67.

Ramanathan, R. and Ganesh, L.S. (1994). Group preference aggregation methods employed in AHP: an evaluation and an intrinsic process for deriving members' weightages. *European Journal of Operational Research,* **79**, 249–65.

Roy, B. 1968. Classement et choix en présence de points de vue multiples (la méthode Electre). *Revue française d'Informatique et de Recherche Opérationnelle* **8**, 57–75.

Roy, B. (1993). Decision science or decision-aid science? *European Journal of Operational Research,* **66**, 184–203.

Saaty, T.L. (1980). *The Analytic Hierarchy Process: Planning, Priority Setting, Resources Allocation.* New York: McGraw-Hill.

Scharpf, F.W. (1988). The joint-decision trap: lessons from German federalism and European integration. *Public Administration,* **66**(3), 239–78.

Stirling, A. and Mayer, S. (1999). Rethinking risk. A pilot multicriteria mapping of a genetically modified crop in agricultural systems in the UK. http://users.sussex.ac.uk/~prfh0/Rethinking Risk.pdf (accessed May 30, 2017).

Van Den Honert, R.C. (2001). Decisional power in group decision making: a note on the allocation of group members' weights in the multiplicative AHP and SMART. *Group Decision and Negotiation,* **10**, 275–86. http://doi.org/10.1023/A:1011201501379 (accessed 4 June 2018).

von Neumann, J. and Morgenstern, O. (1947). *Theory of Games and Economic Behavior.* Princeton, NJ: Princeton University Press.

5. Broadening the scope of Multi Actor Multi Criteria Analysis (MAMCA) by implementing an exploratory scenario approach to support participatory decision-making under uncertainty: the range-based MAMCA

Gino Baudry, Thomas Vallée and Cathy Macharis

5.1 INTRODUCTION

The decision-making context can be characterized by different types of uncertainty that may affect the decision-making process and its outcomes. Decision-making procedures often require one to cope with an evolving and partly uncertain context that no social actors can completely control or understand (Berkhout et al., 2002). Such uncertain contexts may lead decision-makers to take unsuited or at least non-optimal decisions (Van Der Kleij et al., 2003).

By implementing an exploratory scenario approach, using a Monte-Carlo simulation, the range-based Multi Actor Multi Criteria Analysis (MAMCA) (Baudry et al., 2018) generates a large variety of possible scenarios for which a MAMCA is performed for each scenario. The scope of the scenario possibilities is based on the identification and consideration of the various uncertainty factors that may affect the alternative performance assessment and thus the decision-making process. The chapter presents the range-based MAMCA methodology as well as the main rationales to deploy it.

Table 5.1   Types of uncertainty in MCDM processes

Types of uncertainty	Subcategory
• Knowledge uncertainty • Human judgement • Procedural uncertainty • Decision-making uncertainty	• Context knowledge • Model understanding • Linguistic vagueness • Language ambiguity • Communication • Available time and resources • Controversy • Alternative impact

Source: Based on Ascough et al. (2008) and Mirakyan and De Guio (2015).

5.2   DECISION-CONTEXT UNDER UNCERTAINTY

The transport and mobility decision settings may be characterized by high uncertainty. Table 5.1 presents the main types of uncertainty that may occur when applying Multi Criteria Decision-making (MCDM).

The previous chapters have already mentioned the uncertainty about knowledge and human judgement. Knowledge uncertainty describes the limited knowledge about the decision-makers and/or social actors and about the whole decision-problem setting: What is really at stake? How might it affect the different stakeholders? How is the collected data treated (model understanding)? And so on. Knowledge uncertainty can be limited (1) by promoting transparency concerning the MCDM tools and (2) though the learning process that enables stakeholders to learn about the decision-context, such as other social actors' concerns or the different possible alternatives.

Human judgement uncertainty refers to the language ambiguity and linguistic vagueness which may especially occur during the collection of the decision-makers' and/or stakeholders' inputs. Language vagueness arises from the natural semantic limitation in expressing precise quantities with words. Language ambiguity arises because some words have more than one meaning, which can potentially result in misinterpretation. Uncertainty can also affect the decision-making process because of the limited available time and resources. The determination of new or more detailed information or data might require additional and unplanned time or resources with no *ex ante* guarantee that the quality will increase.

When assessing the performance of an alternative, in other words, the extent of an alternative capacity to fulfill the stakeholders' objectives, uncertainty may occur. For example, the alternative performance may rely on an eventual technological breakthrough, the evolution of the legal context or the social acceptance. Uncertainty may also occur because experts/literature are not consensual about an alternative performance. In such cases, it may be better to consider a range of possible values to assess an alternative performance rather than a unique one. This is what the range-based MAMCA is all about, considering the wide range of uncertainty that may affect the performance of alternatives and thus the decision-making outcomes.

Scenario building has become increasingly popular in the literature to cope with such uncertainty, particularly when addressing sustainability issues (Comes et al., 2011; Kowalski et al., 2009). Based on Berkhout et al. (2002), three types of approaches may be distinguished:

- *Extrapolatory approaches* assume that the future is essentially defined as a continuation of the past. The strength of such approaches relies on its strong empirical basis. However, the approach does not consider qualitative changes in relationships, novelty or unexpected events.
- *Normative scenario approaches* are built from a settled vision and assume that social agents will be able to shape a pathway to reach that future through milestone setting. The advantage of such approaches is the assumption that social agents might be able to shape the future, but it may overestimate these agent capacities.
- *Exploratory scenario approaches* consist of generating a range of possible futures driven by underlying, evolving socio-economic conditions. By assuming a limited control of the social agents, such approaches seek to respond to the other approaches' limits. The method consists of generating a possible future, that is, a map of possibilities that are legitimately based on diverse expert opinions.

Fundamentally, the range-based MAMCA is the combination of the traditional MAMCA and a Monte-Carlo simulation (MC). MC makes it possible to capture the full range of possible alternative performances without requiring many assumptions about the model structure. In other words, it enables one to consider that the uncertainties about the alternatives' performance may be independent or occasionally related to one another through no clear and quantifiable interdependence but depend on a complex, evolving context that no social actors can completely control or understand (Madani and Lund, 2011; Mosadeghi et al., 2013). The next section will describe step by step the range-based MAMCA methodology and detail how it differs from the traditional MAMCA.

5.3   THE RANGE-BASED MAMCA METHODOLOGY

Figure 5.1 presents the range-based MAMCA methodology and Table 5.2 summarizes how social actors may be involved in the different steps.

In Table 5.2, the manager refers to the project manager; the stakeholders refer to the participants, including the decision-makers. Although they can help in defining the scope of the problem, the identification of criteria, stakeholders and alternatives, experts are not considered a stakeholder group as they have not their own criteria tree. Nevertheless, experts have a key role in the evaluation of the performance of alternatives as detailed in the following subsection.

5.3.1   Step 6.1: Alternative Performance Assessment

The first extra step consists of the identification of the relevant sources of uncertainty of the decision-context (Figure 5.2). In the range-based MAMCA, uncertainty factors can be (1) specific to a criterion/alternative or (2) common to multiple criteria/alternatives, (3) endogenous or (4) exogenous regarding the stakeholders' criteria (Table 5.3).

Based on a real case study, let us consider the economic competitiveness criterion regarding a biorefinery which aims to choose between different vegetable oil alternatives, one based on food crops, the other based on used cooking oil (UCO). Let us consider that the stakeholders' subcriteria are the price of the feedstock, including the Common Agricultural Policy (CAP) subsidies, and the processing cost. The economic competitiveness will thus rely on the cost of the raw material, which will be specific to each alternative. The economic competitiveness will also depend on the processing cost, which is common for both alternatives and which is partly endogenous (fixed cost of the biorefinery; Table 5.3), partly exogenous (variable costs, oil and/or energy processing costs). A specific and exogenous uncertainty factor may also affect an alternative performance without affecting others. For example, the uncertainty about the upcoming level of CAP subsidies may either lower or rise the economic competitiveness a food crop-based oils without affecting the performance of the UCO.

Given the procedural uncertainty, the extent of the in-depth analysis of the uncertainty factors depends on the outcomes that the project manager/ decision-makers want to obtain. For example, one may consider multiple factors to evaluate the feedstock price, such as the oil price, the feedstock producers' margin, the land yields and so on. One may consider that capturing the overall feedstock price uncertainty is more suited to the decision setting and requirements.

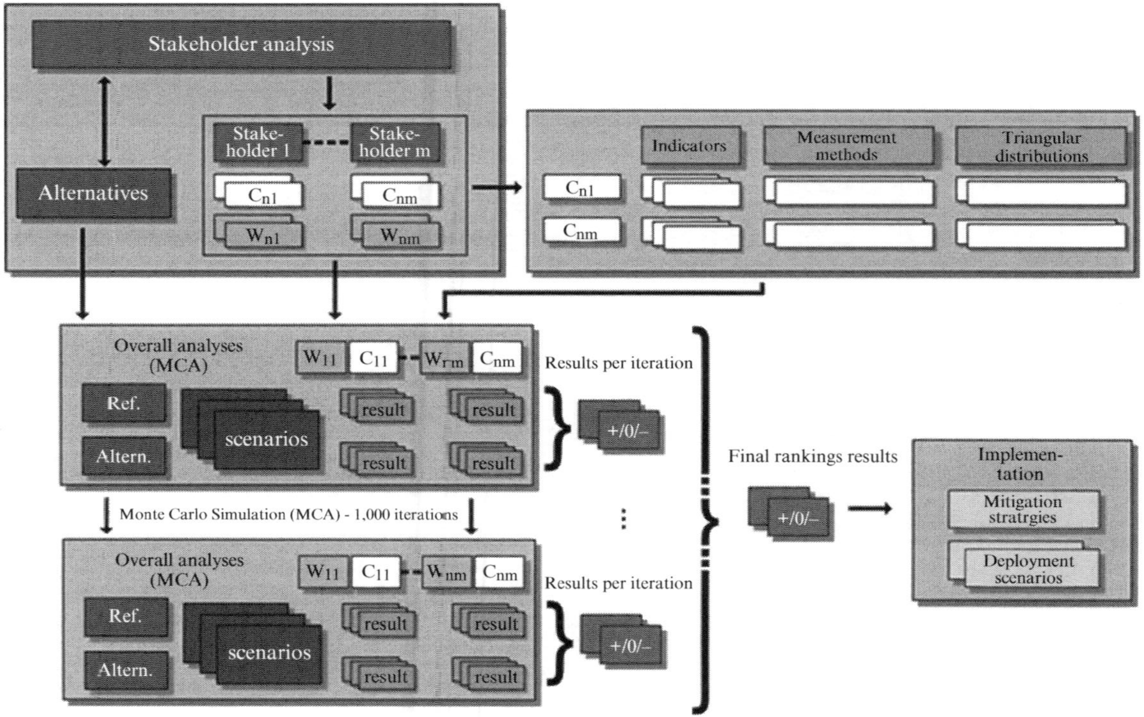

Source: Baudry et al. (2018).

Figure 5.1 Overview of the range-based MAMCA

Table 5.2   How are social actors involved in the range-based MAMCA?

Range-based MAMCA steps	Manager	Stakeholders	Experts
1. Defining the scope of the problem	x	x	x
2. Alternatives identification	x	x	x
3. Stakeholder groups identification	x	x	x
4. Criteria definition	x	x	(x)
5. Weighting	x	x	–
6. Alternative performance assessment	x	(x)	x
6.1 Defining the uncertainty factors	x	(x)	x
6.2 Design of the EBDLs	x	(x)	x
7. Data computation	x	–	–
7.1 Combing MC with MCDM	x	–	–
8. Results analysis & Recommendation	x	x	x

Note: x: direct involvement; (x): indirect involvement; – not involved, EBDL: expert-based distribution laws.

Source: Designed by the authors.

5.3.2   Step 6.2: Designing the EBDLs

Each of the identified uncertainty factors can be expressed as a range of possible values, discrete or continuous, using different distributions (EBDLs). EBDLs (or expert-based distribution laws) enable one to define the boundaries of the scenario-building process into the range-based MAMCA. EBDLs are legitimately based on the literature, empirical data and/or expert consultations (Berkhout et al., 2002; Lahdelma et al., 2014). We suggest that EBDLs are checked and validated by both independent experts and stakeholders to ensure the reliability and acceptance of the data.

Figure 5.3 presents examples of EBDLs:

- Continuous and uniform laws enable one to equally consider every value that lies in between the pessimistic and optimistic values.
- Triangular distributions enable one to consider the values that lie in between the pessimistic and optimistic values while considering a most probable one.
- Open triangular distributions enable one to consider a margin of error compared with the literature and/or exerts' inputs, especially when uncertainty is very high (Hillson and Simon, 2012).
- Discrete laws enable one to consider discrete choices between different values.

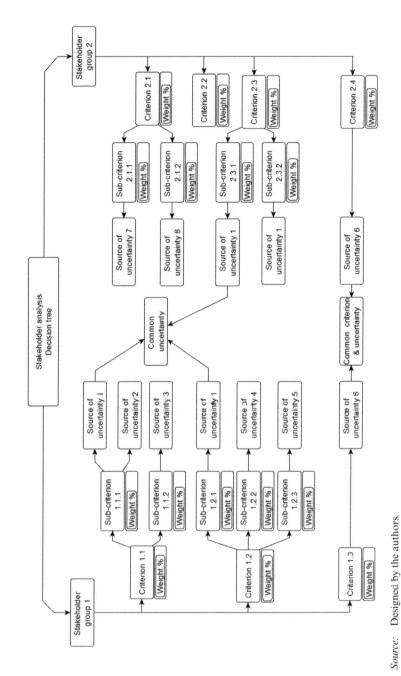

Source: Designed by the authors.

Figure 5.2   Focus on the uncertainty factors

Table 5.3   Illustration of the uncertainty factors

Uncertainty factors	Specific uncertainty	Common uncertainty
Endogenous uncertainty	Feedstock price	Processing fixed cost
Exogenous uncertainty	Legal scheme – CAP	Energy processing cost

Source: Designed by the authors.

EBDLs can take various forms, but we suggest limiting them to the following to keep the methodology as simple as possible. Triangular distributions are particularly well suited to measure sustainability impacts (del Socorro García Cascales et al., 2014). Obviously, multiple alternative performances may be certain and thus they do not require design of EBDLs.

5.3.3   Step 7: the Monte Carlo Simulation

The Monte-Carlo simulation is a powerful tool that enables one to capture different types of uncertainty in MCA methods without requiring many assumptions (Carmone et al., 1997; Madani and Lund, 2011; Mosadeghi et al., 2013). The procedure consists of (1) randomly picking a value from each EBDL to constitute a possible state of the world or scenario; (2) performing the MAMCA analysis; (3) repeating the procedure from (1) to cover the wide range of scenario possibilities. Though this procedure, the different uncertainty factors are considered but also how the different combination of uncertainty factors may affect the decision-making process and outcomes.

Figure 5.4 illustrates the expected performances of nine biofuel options compared with the oil-based fuels reference. The X-axis presents the different options and the Y-axis presents the scores of the biofuel options, using the weighted sum method (Wang et al., 2009). The box plots present the range of possible scores that can characterize a biofuel option given the uncertainty factors. For example, the score of Ethanol 1G–1/2G stands for first/second generation – it may range between 0.09 and 0.12. When two box plots are not overlapping, it means that whatever the uncertainty factors, the option with the higher score will always outperform the other one. When two box plots are overlapping, it means that a ranking reversal may occur between two options depending on the uncertainty factors. The range-based MAMCA also provides information about the probability that an option outperforms the other ones (Table 5.4).

Table 5.4 can be read as: "microalgae biodiesel RW outperforms the Ethanol 1G alternative in 43.5 percent of the Monte Carlo iterations",

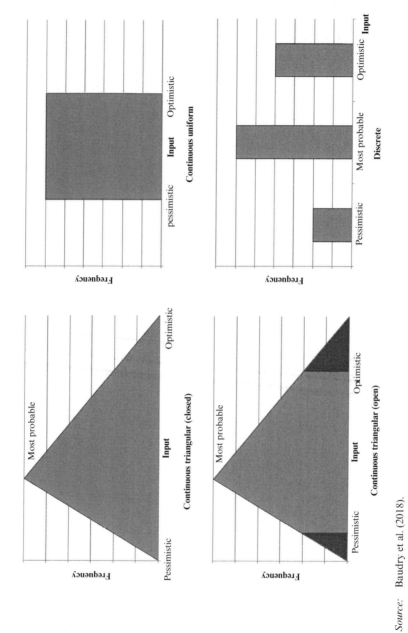

Source: Baudry et al. (2018).

Figure 5.3 Examples of EBDLs

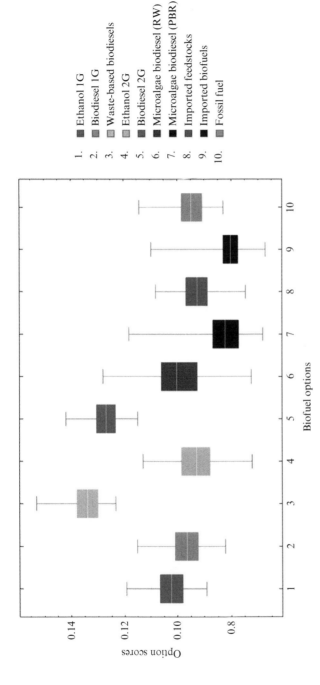

Legend:
1. ■ Ethanol 1G
2. ■ Biodiesel 1G
3. ■ Waste-based biodiesels
4. ■ Ethanol 2G
5. ■ Biodiesel 2G
6. ■ Microalgae biodiesel (RW)
7. ■ Microalgae biodiesel (PBR)
8. ■ Imported feedstocks
9. ■ Imported biofuels
10. ■ Fossil fuel

Source: Designed by the authors.

Figure 5.4   Illustration of the range-based MAMCA outcome

Table 5.4   Probability that microalgae biodiesels outperform the other options

Biofuel options	Microalgae biodiesel (PBR*) (%)	Microalgae biodiesel (RW*) (%)
Ethanol 1G	3.5	43.5
Biodiesel 1G	9.3	59.1
Waste-based biodiesel	0.0	0.0
Ethanol 2G	21.2	72.1
Biodiesel 2G	0.0	0.3
Microalgae biodiesel (RW)	13.5	–
Microalgae biodiesel (PBR)	–	86.5
Imported feedstock	16.9	72.5
Imported biofuels	58.9	94.4
Fossil-fuel reference	9.4	64.7

Note: A photobioreactor (PBR) is a closed system which provides a controlled environment and enables high productivity of microorganisms, such as microalgae in the present case. PBR enables one to control the growing environment of algae according to their requirements. A raceway (RW) is either an open or a closed pond that can be used for algae cultivation (for more information, see Delrue et al., 2012).

Source: Designed by the authors.

or else, "whatever the uncertainty factors, waste-based biodiesel always outperforms microalgae biodiesels options". The larger the range of scores, the higher the risk that the uncertainty factors may affect the actual suitability of an option.

5.3.4   Step 7: Results and Recommendations

The range-based MAMCA provides outcomes (such as Figure 5.4 and Table 5.4) at the overall, stakeholder group and criterion levels. Added to the traditional MAMCA outcomes, information about the uncertainty factors may help in developing complementary measures to reduce the extent of the uncertainty effects to aid the design of more suitable implementation pathways for the different alternatives.

5.4   CONCLUSION

The range-based MAMCA methodology is especially suited to address evolving decision-contexts characterized by various uncertainty factors that no social actors can completely control or understand. Based on the stakeholders' and experts' inputs, the methodology enables one to identify and consider the various uncertainty factors regarding the decision-context without requiring many additional inputs. Using this additional information, the decision-makers may limit the risk of making mistaken or at least not optimal decisions because of uncertainty (Van Der Kleij et al., 2003). Depending on individual preferences, stakeholders may prefer alternatives with possibly high scores regardless of the uncertainty or, at the opposite end, they may prefer a lower ranked alternative for which the performance is less uncertain. Consequently, further research is currently being carried out on the range-based MAMCA to enable this risk aversion of the stakeholders to be considered in the alternative scores.

REFERENCES

Ascough II, J.C., Maier, H.R., Ravalico, J.K., Strudley, M.W., 2008. Future research challenges for incorporation of uncertainty in environmental and ecological decision-making. *Ecological Modelling* **219**(3–4), 383–99. Part of Special issue: The Importance of Uncertainty and Sensitivity Analysis in Process-based Models of Carbon and Nitrogen Cycling in Terrestrial Ecosystems with Particular Emphasis on Forest Ecosystems: Selected Papers from a Workshop Organized by the International Society for Ecological Modelling (ISEM) at the Third Biennal Meeting of the International Environmental Modelling and Software Society (IEMSS) in Burlington, Vermont, USA, August 9–13, 2006. https://doi.org/10.1016/j.ecolmodel.2008.07.015 (accessed June 4, 2018).

Baudry, G., Macharis, C., Vallée, T., 2018. Range-based Multi-Actor Multi-Criteria Analysis: a combined method of Multi-Actor Multi-Criteria Analysis and Monte Carlo simulation to support participatory decision making under uncertainty. *European Journal of Operational Research* **264**, 257–69. https://doi.org/10.1016/j.ejor.2017.06.036 (accessed June 4, 2018).

Berkhout, F., Hertin, J., Jordan, A., 2002. Socio-economic futures in climate change impact assessment: using scenarios as "learning machines". *Global Environmental Change* **12**, 83–95. https://doi.org/10.1016/S0959-3780(02)00006-7 (accessed June 4, 2018).

Carmone Jr, F.J., Kara, A., Zanakis, S.H., 1997. A Monte Carlo investigation of incomplete pairwise comparison matrices in AHP. *European Journal of Operational Research* **102**, 538–53. https://doi.org/10.1016/S0377-2217(96)00250-0 (accessed June 4, 2018).

Comes, T., Hiete, M., Wijngaards, N., Schultmann, F., 2011. Decision maps: a framework for multi-criteria decision support under severe uncertainty. *Decision Support Systems* **52**, 108–18. https://doi.org/10.1016/j.dss.2011.05.008 (accessed June 4, 2018).

del Socorro García Cascales, M., Sánchez Lozano, J.M., Masegosa Arredondo, A.D., Cruz Corona, C., 2014. *Soft Computing Applications for Renewable Energy and Energy Efficiency*, Engineering and Green Technologies. IGI Global: Hershey, PA.

Delrue, F., Setier, P.-A., Sahut, C., Cournac, L., Roubaud, A., Peltier, G., Froment, A.-K., 2012. An economic, sustainability, and energetic model of biodiesel production from microalgae. *Bioresource Technology* **111**, 191–200. doi:10.1016/j. biortech.2012.02.020 (accessed June 4, 2018).

Hillson, D., Simon, P., 2012. *Practical Project Risk Management: The ATOM Methodology*. Tysons Corner, VA: Virginia Management Concepts Press

Kowalski, K., Stagl, S., Madlener, R., Omann, I., 2009. Sustainable energy futures: methodological challenges in combining scenarios and participatory multi-criteria analysis. *European Journal of Operational Research* **197**, 1063–74. https:// doi.org/10.1016/j.ejor.2007.12.049 (accessed June 4, 2018).

Lahdelma, R., Salminen, P., Hokkanen, J., 2014. Using multicriteria methods in environmental planning and management. *Environmental Management* **26**, 595–605. https://doi.org/10.1007/s002670010118 (accessed June 4, 2018).

Madani, K., Lund, J.R., 2011. A Monte-Carlo game theoretic approach for Multi-Criteria Decision Making under uncertainty. *Advances in Water Resources* **34**, 607–16. https://doi.org/10.1016/j.advwatres.2011.02.009 (accessed June 4, 2018).

Mirakyan, A., De Guio, R., 2015. Modelling and uncertainties in integrated energy planning. *Renewable & Sustainable Energy Reviews* **46**, 62–9. https://doi. org/10.1016/j.rser.2015.02.028 (accessed June 4, 2018).

Mosadeghi, R., Warnken, J., Tomlinson, R., Mirfenderesk, H., 2013. Uncertainty analysis in the application of multi-criteria decision-making methods in Australian strategic environmental decisions. *Journal of Environmental Planning and Management* **56**, 1097–124. https://doi.org/10.1080/09640568.2012.717886 (accessed June 4, 2018).

Van Der Kleij, C., Hulscher, S., Louters, T., 2003. Comparing uncertain alternatives for a possible airport island location in the North Sea. *Ocean & Coastal Management* **46**, 1031–47.

Wang, J.-J., Jing, Y.-Y., Zhang, C.-F., Zhao, J.-H., 2009. Review on multi-criteria decision analysis aid in sustainable energy decision-making. *Renewable & Sustainable Energy Reviews* **13**, 2263–78. https://doi.org/10.1016/j.rser.2009.06.021 (accessed June 4, 2018).

PART II

Case studies

6. Comparing Cost-Benefit Analysis and Multi Actor Multi Criteria Analysis: the case of Blackpool and the South Fylde Line

Marco Dean and Robin Hickman

6.1 INTRODUCTION

Transport infrastructure investments can have a 'catalytic' role in promoting the development of a territory (Banister and Berechman, 2000; Hickman et al. 2015) – the type and shape of new transport infrastructure can have a critical impact on how a new development is designed and used. Major transport projects require high capital investment costs and generate multiple economic, social and environmental impacts, which are not always positive (Flyvbjerg et al., 2003; Hickman et al., 2010; Lucas, 2012). Such impacts are likely to be distributed unevenly over space and time, and consequently amongst population groups (Gellert and Lynch, 2003). This therefore calls for detailed and careful *ex ante* (before the project) appraisal analyses before any decision can be made to proceed.

Though progress has been made in appraisal practice in recent years (Goodman and Hastak, 2006), how transport projects should be most appropriately appraised continues to generate debate amongst academics, infrastructure specialists, investors and governments alike (Dimitriou, 2016). In particular, a large number of scholars have expressed concern about primacy given to economic-centric tools such as Cost-Benefit Analysis (CBA) (see Næss, 2006; Metz, 2008; Dimitriou et al., 2010; Hickman and Dean, 2017) and the exclusion of important project stakeholders from the process (see Haezendonck, 2007; Dimitriou et al., 2012; Dean et al., 2018). Over the past decades, many have started to regard participatory Multi Criteria Analysis (MCA) methodologies as a valuable approach to the appraisal of transport projects (see, amongst others, Macharis et al., 2009; Leleur, 2012; Jensen et al., 2013; Barfod and Salling, 2015; Dimitriou et al., 2016; Ward et al., 2016; Dean et al., 2018), adding much to the CBA process. According to their proponents, participatory MCA approaches can help to capture varied impacts more accurately than traditional CBA (and also relative to purely analyst-led MCA techniques), be more participatory in assessing multiple actor views, and lead to greater deliberation in decision-making. It is contended that the inclusion of different points of views in the analysis may enhance the transparency of the process and increase the possibility for the legitimation of outcomes. However, MCA approaches are not immune to criticism and doubts over their effective applicability have been raised (see Annema et al., 2015).

This chapter has two objectives: first, to compare the application of CBA and Multi Actor Multi Criteria Analysis (MAMCA), using a case study project, to test whether there are different results in using different appraisal approaches; second, to test and comment on the applicability of participatory MCA approaches with specific reference to the selected case study. The work draws from the European Union (EU) INTERREG IVB SINTROPHER project,[1] carried out between 2009 and 2015. The case study examined is from Blackpool, a large town and coastal resort in North West England which has been ranked as one of the most deprived towns in England. SINTROPHER has examined the role that transport may have in supporting regeneration and considered the potential beneficial effects of the improvement of the South Fylde line, a railway line linking Blackpool, the Fylde Coast and the city of Preston. Three different options for improvements of the line are appraised using conventional CBA and MAMCA approaches.

The chapter consists of the following sections. Initially, there is a brief overview of transport appraisal practice, with particular reference to the UK context; and the case study and project options are described. This is followed by the main empirical analysis, comparing CBA and MAMCA approaches for the project options. The application of the MAMCA framework is critically discussed. Finally, the main findings of the analysis are discussed and some reflections developed for practice and research.

---

[1] SINTROPHER (Sustainable Integrated Tram-Based Transport Options for Peripheral European Regions) is a EU Interreg IVB project, funded by € 23 million from the European Regional Development Fund's (ERDF) Interreg IVB programme and national match funding (including the UK's Department for Transport or DfT), running from 2009 to 2015. It involves 13 partners in five European Regions in five Member States: Fylde Coast (UK), West Flanders (Belgium), Valenciennes (France), Nijmegen (Netherlands) and Kassel (Germany). The lead partner is University College London (UCL).

6.2   TRANSPORT APPRAISAL IN THE UK

In the UK, and in many other countries, CBA has constituted one of the most widely used methods to help prioritize transport investment over recent decades (Bristow and Nellthorp, 2000; Vickerman, 2000). This technique, in particular, seeks to establish the desirability of undertaking a given project, mainly from the economic point of view (Sinden and Thampapillai, 1995), by quantifying in monetary terms the value of all the positive (benefits) and negative (costs) consequences of a project for all members of society (Boardman et al., 2006). In the case of transport projects, for instance, the key benefits may comprise travel time saving, reduced vehicle operating costs, reduced accident costs as well as reduced emissions due to modal shift (for example, from road to rail). The main costs may include capital costs, costs of disruption during construction (for example, noise, delays and so on), maintenance and operating costs. The potential benefits of a project proposal are evaluated in terms of willingness to pay, namely, a metric for estimating a person's welfare change, derived from a certain action, which is aggregated across people to obtain the overall net benefit of the outcome. The costs of the project are estimated in terms of resource costs. In order to make the costs and benefits occurring at different points during the project life cycle comparable, CBA uses a discounting procedure to converts all future costs and benefits into their present value. The results of CBA are often presented in summary, using the Net Present Value (NPV), which is obtained by subtracting the sum of the discounted costs from the sum of the discounted benefits, and the Benefit-Cost Ratio (BCR), which is produced by dividing the sum of the discounted costs into the sum of the discounted benefits. The idea behind CBA is that scarce resources should be allocated to where there is most value, namely, projects whose benefits outweigh their costs (projects whose NPV is positive and whose BCR exceeds the value of one).

Notwithstanding its wide use, the use and application of CBA has been highly debated. The critiques, spanning from technical problems to the theoretical foundations of the approach, include: lack of consideration to different policy objectives beside economic efficiency (Dimitriou et al., 2010); excessive importance given to travel time savings in the calculation of the total benefits of a transport project (Metz, 2008); adoption of highly disputable techniques for monetizing impacts, especially social and environmental impacts (Mackie and Preston, 1998); dismissal of many important effects, particularly where these are not easily quantifiable in monetary terms (Ackerman and Heinzerling, 2004); disregard of the distribution of impacts (Van Wee, 2012); underestimation of the potential long-term negative environmental consequences of a project proposal due to discounting procedures (Næss, 2006); poor incorporation of uncertainties (Salling and Leleur, 2009); and lack of stakeholder involvement during the analysis (Macharis and Bernardini, 2015). In the end, there is often much partiality in terms of what can be included in the CBA (Hickman and Dean, 2017).

In the attempt to address the limitations of CBA, while also responding to emerging global issues and challenges, new appraisal methodologies and frameworks have been continually developed and proposed in different countries (Goodman and Hastak, 2006). The UK Department of the Environment, Transport and the Regions (DETR) adopted the New Approach to Appraisal (NATA) in the late 1990s with the view to developing a wider and more transparent assessment framework (DETR, 1998a, 1998b). The framework is summarized in an Appraisal Summary Table (AST), which gives the traditional economic indicators (for example, user benefits), together with environmental, social and other wider criteria which had been frequently omitted in the past (Vickerman, 2000). As illustrated in Table 6.1, in the AST, these different items are clustered around five dimensions, namely, the economy, environment, safety, accessibility and integration, which represented the government's objectives for transport as outlined in the 1998 White Paper (DETR, 1998c). Initially adopted only for informing the prioritization of trunk road investment proposals (DETR, 1998a, 1998b), NATA has progressively evolved and has been included into WebTAG (Web-based Transport Analysis Guidance), namely, the DfT's transport appraisal guidance and toolkit (DfT, 2014). NATA and the AST now form the basis for the appraisal of multi-modal studies, Highway Agency road schemes, major road and public transport proposals developed as part of local transport plans, the strategic Rail Authority's appraisal criteria, airports and also ports (DfT, 2014) – hence provides the framework for appraisal of all major transport projects in the UK.

While some practitioners perceive the UK as being at the forefront of contemporary transport appraisal internationally (Worsley and Mackie, 2015), others have criticized NATA and WebTAG. Sayers and colleagues (2003), for instance, claim that the absence of any guidance on which objectives matter most may result in a reduction of the transparency of the process and lack of coherence in decision-making. According to Dimitriou et al. (2010), the appraisal framework adopted in the UK still includes a rather narrow range of objectives and, within it, CBA metrics appear to carry too much importance. Further, Hickman (2018) argues that three pillar-based interpretations of sustainability is problematic in transport appraisal, and leads to the primacy of economic goals when all objectives cannot be met. Hickman and Dean (2017) suggest that a

Table 6.1   NATA Appraisal Summary Table

Dimensions	Objectives
Environment	Noise
	Local air quality
	Landscape
	Biodiversity
	Heritage
	Water
	Physical fitness
	Journey Ambience
Safety	Accidents
	Security
Economy	Journey times and vehicle
	operating costs
	Journey time reliability
	Scheme costs
	Regeneration
	Journey times and vehicle
Accessibility	Access to public transport
	Community severance
	Pedestrians and others
Integration	Transport interchange
	Land-use policy
	Other government policies

Source: Adapted from DfT (2014).

wider participatory and deliberative process is required to better identify appraisal criteria against local objectives, assess impacts against different views, and improve participation in the decision-making process.

6.3   CASE STUDY: BLACKPOOL AND THE SOUTH FYLDE LINE

With a resident population of 140,000 and 13 million tourism visits per annum, Blackpool is the Fylde Coast peninsula's largest settlement and economic centre. However, in recent years, the town has suffered from competition from package holidays to foreign destinations. This has produced severe socio-economic consequences, with high levels of social deprivation amongst residents. The situation is further exacerbated by a relatively poor transport connectivity, which makes it difficult for Blackpool and the Fylde Coast peninsula to maintain links with neighbouring urban areas. The EU INTERREG IVB SINTROPHER project (Hickman and Osborne, 2017) examined the role that transport may have in supporting regeneration in the area and in particular the potential beneficial effects of the improvement of the South Fylde Line, namely, a 19 kilometre non-electrified and single-tracked railway line linking the Fylde Coast with the city of Preston. Several possible alternative improvements of the South Fylde Line were considered, and the following options were shortlisted (Jacobs, 2015; Figure 6.1):

- Option 1: improvement of the existing regional rail services, with an increase in service frequency of the existing services on the South Fylde Line, from one train per hour to two trains per hour. This option includes an extension of the service to Manchester and Manchester Airport, but no new stations will be created along the line.
- Option 2: introduction of a tram-train service in place of the existing regional rail service. A tram-train service will replace the existing regional rail service between Blackpool South and Preston. The service will be extended to Blackpool North and ten new stations will be added along the line.
- Option 3: combination of regional rail services and a tram-train service. This is a compromise between the first two options. It entails the doubling of the service frequency of the existing regional rail services and the introduction of a tram service from Saltcotes to Blackpool North. This implies an overlap between tram and train services between Lytham St Anne's and Saltcotes. It also entails the provision of 13 new stations along the line.

6.4 CBA OF OPTIONS

A CBA was carried out as part of the outline business case for the project options, commissioned and co-funded by Lancashire County Council and the EU SINTROPHER project (Table 6.2). According to the CBA analysis, Option 1 constitutes the most economically efficient allocation of resources, followed by Option 3 and Option 2. This was an unexpected result and led us to query the components of the CBA (Hickman and Dean, 2017). Most of the user benefits for all options arise from estimated time savings, and little else is quantified. There is some attempt to estimate regeneration impacts, but these remain small. Environmental issues such

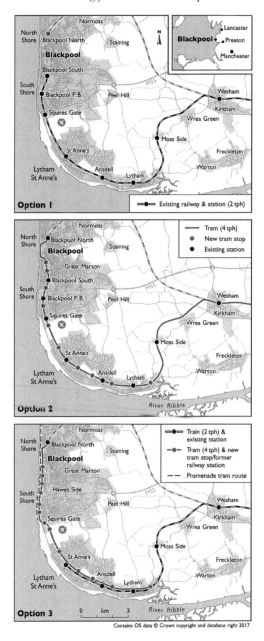

Source: Based on Jacobs (2015).

Figure 6.1   South Fylde Line investment options

Table 6.2   CBA for the project options

Options	Option 1	Option 2	Option 3
Cost-Benefit Analysis			
PVB	£ 281.5 m	£ 277.1 m	£ 329–462 m
PVC	£ 77.1 m	£ 399.7 m	£ 223–240m
NPV	£ 204.5 m	–£ 122.6 m	£ 106–222m
BCR	3.70	0.70	1.5–1.9
Wider Economic Benefits (WEB)			
Agglomeration	£ 37 m	£ 68 m	£ 60 m
Labour supply and productivity	£ 28 m	£ 64 m	£ 40 m
Sub-total	£ 65 m	£ 132 m	£ 100 m
CBA + WEB			
PVB	£ 346.5 m	£ 409 m	£ 429–562 m
PVC	£ 77.1 m	£ 399.7 m	£ 223 m
NPV	£ 269.5 m	£ 9.4 m	£ 206–322 m
BCR	4.5	1	1.9

Note: PVB – Present Value of Benefits; PVC – Present Value of Costs.

Source: Jacobs (2015).

as carbon dioxide (CO2) emissions are estimated at such a small level that they have no bearing on the BCR. There are no effective attempts to incorporate wider environmental, social or built environment impacts into the CBA, which would be the real benefits of the tram-train options. The costs of the tram-train options mean that the partial nature of the CBA exercise leads to favouring the relatively minor rail enhancement scheme. Though CBA is considered part of the multi-criteria WebTAG process, the weight given to the MCA, particularly the non-quantified elements, is low, and the BCR dominates the process.

6.5   MAMCA OF OPTIONS

6.5.1   Problem Setting

To further examine options, a MAMCA exercise was undertaken to test different ways of appraising the possibilities for the South Fylde Line.

The framework and project options are set within the context of a masterplan for the local area – hence the urban planning framework sets the strategic developmental vision, and the transport options are developed to support this. Without this, the transport projects developed can be very poorly integrated with the planning strategy for an area. Funding availability is used to constrain option consideration – only the projects likely to be affordable are included. The idea is to develop a deliberative process for decision-making, where a consensus can be reached on the most appropriate investments. Different actors present and understand each other's positions. A voting mechanism could feasibly be used to help support the making of the final decision.

Six different stakeholder groups, encompassing a wide range of institutional interests and views, were involved in the process:

- Group 1: local authorities (district-level government)
- Group 2: Lancashire County Council (county-level government)
- Group 3: local communities
- Group 4: business groups
- Group 5: environmental groups
- Group 6: transport planners.

Each group consisted of three to five participants, with a total of 26 participants who were deemed to hold (albeit from different perspectives) a good knowledge of the problem under investigation. The discussion was held during a one-day workshop at Lancashire County Council's offices in Preston in July 2015. In the first part of the workshop, participants were exposed to a series of short presentations and panel discussions focusing on the key principles of the MAMCA exercise, the issues affecting Blackpool and the South Fylde Line, and the possible alternative solutions and their features.

The stakeholder groups were asked to assess the project options against a preliminary list of policy objectives developed by the research team on the basis of analysis of key transport, planning and policy documents. Sixteen project objectives belonging to four different appraisal dimensions, namely, transport and development, economic, environmental and social were identified (Table 6.3). The criteria more closely map onto the UK sustainable development indicators (DEFRA, 2013) than WebTAG, and are related to local policy priorities rather than national. There are no criteria based on time savings for users – this was not seen as a policy objective. Stakeholders were given the freedom to choose objectives from the list as well as to identify entirely new project objectives.

Once an agreed set of objectives was established, stakeholders were invited to weight the different objectives to reflect their relative importance. The point allocation method was adopted. Each stakeholder group was asked to allocate a budget of 100 points over the selected criteria to reflect their relative importance. Participants were required, first of all, to

Table 6.3 Preliminary objectives

Themes	Objectives	Description
Transport and development	Increased non-car mode share	Contribution to an increased usage of public transport, walking and cycling.
	Improved journey integration, comfort and convenience	Integration of services between different modes, including reduction of interchanges and improvement of transfer, journey comfort and convenience.
	Improved regeneration potential	Integration with the urban planning strategy and the potential for redevelopment around the catchment areas along the route and around the transport nodes. The redevelopment could be for residence, employment or other mixed use development and support regeneration objectives.
Economic	Increased economic prosperity	The potential to support economic growth, such as higher productivity in higher value-added activities associated with transport improvement.
	Reduced unemployment	Job creation with investment from the public and private sectors.
	Reduced poverty	Increase in income and spending power.
	Increased diversity of local economies	Wider range of economic activities associated with the transport investment.
Environmental	Reduced greenhouse gas emissions	Changed mode share and trip distribution; a better public transport system is likely to reduce the reliance on private cars.
	Reduced noise, pollution and vibration	Promotion of clean and efficient energy of transport systems which can significantly address noise, pollution and vibration issues.
	Improved safety	Reliable and safe transport systems and facilities which can reduce casualties and crime rates.
	Improved urban realm	Better quality of urban public space around the stations and along the transport routes.
Social	Improved healthy life expectancy	Increased use of active modes such as walking and cycling to integrate with public transport systems. This can improve healthy life expectancy, reduce obesity and other non-communicable diseases.
	Improved access to social and community facilities, enhanced social capital	A better connected society which facilitates communication and social interaction.
	Improved social mobility	Better employment opportunities and incomes for all, increased social mobility.
	Improved housing provision	Improved housing provision in development lands around the South Fylde Line nodes and along routes.

Source: Dean et al. (2018).

allocate these 100 points over the four appraisal dimensions (transport and regeneration, economic, environmental and social) and, successively, to further split these amounts within the different objectives selected within each dimension.

Stakeholders were then required to score the performance of the three different project options against their own list of project objectives. In MCA, different interval scales can be employed for scoring the performances of the options. Following Macharis et al. (2010), a five-point scale was adopted, ranging from minus two (severe negative effects) to two (important positive effects) where zero represents a neutral value (no significant effects). The outcomes of the process, which will be discussed in the following section, were expressed in the form of tables illustrating both the performances of the different options according to the viewpoint of the different stakeholder groups and a multi-actor view, which represents a synthesis of the individual viewpoints. These outcomes were also compared with the results of the traditional CBA of the same project options.

6.5.2   MAMCA Results

Table 6.4 shows the objectives identified by the various project stakeholders and experts. All the stakeholder groups employed a low number of objectives for their analysis, far fewer than the preliminary list of 16 project objectives proposed by the research team. Local communities, for instance, selected only six objectives. Transport planners, by comparison, chose seven objectives, while all the other groups adopted eight objectives.

All the objectives included in the preliminary list were selected once by at least one stakeholder group. Nonetheless, only one objective, namely, 'improved journey integration, comfort, and convenience', was included by all the different parties within their own MCA framework. Stakeholders had the possibility to propose their own objectives in addition to the ones included in the preliminary list, but no new objectives were identified. The majority of stakeholder groups selected objectives relating to all of the four appraisal themes. The exception was environmental groups and transport planners who, in their analysis, considered objectives only belonging to two or three themes. Specifically, environmental groups did not adopt any economic objective, whereas transport planners carried out their assessment without including any objective related to the environmental theme.

Table 6.5 shows the weights given by the different groups to the four appraisal themes. All of the groups, with the exclusion of the transport planners, ascribed the highest level of importance to transport and development objectives. Transport planners, conversely, assigned the highest weight to economic objectives.

Table 6.4 *Objectives adopted by the stakeholder groups*

Themes	Objectives	Description					
		Group 1: Local Authorities	Group 2: Lancashire County Council	Group 3: Local Community	Group 4: Business Community	Group 5: Environmental Groups	Group 6: Transport Planners
Transport and development	Increased non-car mode share	•				•	•
	Improved journey integration, comfort, and convenience	•	•	•	•	•	
	Improved regeneration potential	•	•	•	•		•
Economic	Increased economic prosperity	•	•	•	•		•
	Reduced unemployment	•	•	•	•		•
	Reduced poverty	•					•
	Increased diversity of local economies						•
Environmental	Reduced greenhouse gas emissions	•	•	•	•	•	
	Reduced noise, pollution and vibration					•	
	Improved safety					•	
	Improved urban quality		•		•	•	
Social	Improved healthy life expectancy	•	•	•			
	Improved social and community facilities and social capital				•		
	Improved social mobility	•	•		•	•	•
	Improved housing provision				•		

Source: Dean et al. (2018).

Table 6.5   Weights ascribed by stakeholder groups to the appraisal themes

Stakeholder groups	Themes			
	Transport and development	Economic	Environmental	Social
Group 1: *Local Authorities*	40	30	10	20
Group 2: *Lancashire County Council*	40	20	20	20
Group 3: *Local Communities*	50	20	20	10
Group 4: *Business Communities*	40	20	20	20
Group 5: *Environmental Groups*	50	0	40	10
Group 6: *Transport Planners*	23	57	0	20

Source: Dean et al. (2018).

Figure 6.2 displays the overall performance of the different options according to the viewpoints of the different actors. The overall performances of each project option were computed as the weighted sum of its single performances against the different objectives. Option 2 turned out to be the preferred option for Lancashire County Council and the local communities. By comparison, Option 3 ranked first amongst the environmental groups and the transport planners. Options 2 and 3 performed equally well for the business groups, slightly better than Option 1. Local authorities did not complete the scoring procedure for the third option, mainly due to time constraints. This group seemed to prefer Option 2 over Option 1. The global ranking was obtained by using the average of the overall performances of the single project options according to the point of view of the different groups. In the multi-actor view, Option 2 ranked first, followed by Option 3 and Option 1.

6.6   COMMENTS

A number of issues have emerged from applying MAMCA in practice and are worthy of critical discussion. MAMCA is a useful process and

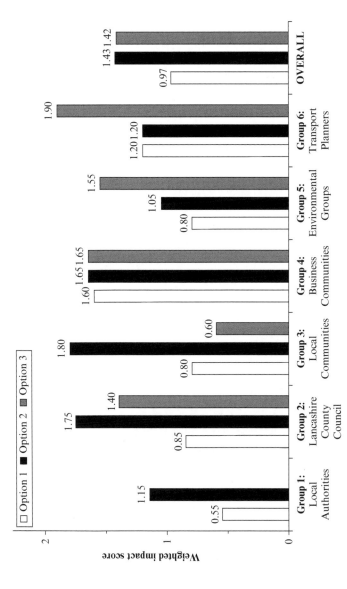

Multi-actor scoring

Note: If Group 1 is discounted as being incomplete, Option scores 1.05, Option 2 scores 1.49 and Option 3 scores 1.42.

Source: Dean et al. (2018).

Figure 6.2   Multi-actor and overall performance of the options

helps incorporate wider views and actors into the decision-making process. The promotion of dialogue between participants can be very positive, allowing an understanding of different views, and even leading to a modification of views during the process. This is a step forward from a purely analyst-led, desktop CBA process, which can be very difficult to understand for those outside the 'blackboxed' process. When considering options for the South Fylde Line, MAMCA led to a different project option being chosen by participants relative to the CBA, with a preference for Option 2 Tram-Train, as this aligned best to local policy goals. This was an interesting finding and should be tested further with different case studies, comparing the outcomes from different appraisal approaches. It suggests something rather fundamental: that the type of appraisal process adopted is important to the projects that are prioritized, and that perhaps we are not using the appropriate techniques to help fund effective public transport projects.

However, a number of issues can be raised with the process of participatory MCA (Dean et al., 2018). The process is difficult to run and requires skilled facilitation. The experience from the workshop run in Preston was that the type of facilitation and actor involvement is also very likely to influence results. The experience and knowledge of participants is critical to the success of the process, and there are many issues here around who is invited, how groups are formed, how views are mediated and progress towards a common end goal maintained. Participants with different levels of knowledge can be difficult to manage and include within the process. Often, the voices heard may be those which are given through conventional consultation processes, and that there is still a lack of participation by particular groups. Indeed, the participation of different groups does not ensure legitimacy or transparency for others – the process may still reflect particular views within society and remain relatively closed.

It is sometimes contended that MCA is even more arbitrary than CBA. Indeed, CBA entails well-established principles for the selection of the benefits and costs to consider as well as for their measurement. While, with MCA, there are no accepted rules concerning the number and types of criteria to be included in the appraisal, scoring and weighting procedures, aggregation method through which all the elements of the MCA framework (criteria, scores and weights) are ultimately brought together, as well as other parameters. All of these issues can strongly affect the results of the analysis. Furthermore, in participatory MCA processes, the identification of the stakeholder groups to be involved is also likely to have substantial impacts on the final results. In the specific case study used in this chapter, for instance, it is possible to argue that had more economists or transport engineers been involved in the process, the criteria related to project costs and other more 'hard' information would have received more consideration.

For simplicity reasons, a linear MCA model was employed to calculate the performance scores of the project options. According to this, the overall performance of each option was computed as the weighted sum of its single performances against the different criteria. It is evident that this model does not differ substantially from the structure of CBA, where a single indicator (NPV and/or BCR) is used to express the conclusions of the analysis from calculation in monetary terms. Whereas a single index approach responds to the needs of arriving at a final judgement over the desirability of the various alternative options, it may result in excessive over-simplification of the decision situation and loss of important information, especially concerning equity issues and distributional effects.

Finally, people taking part in a participatory MCA exercise may not be informed enough to correctly assess the consequences of the project proposals under examination, or may not be able to abstract or conceptualize issues, impacts and preferences according to a multi-criteria framework. For example, during the workshop in Preston, some participants experienced difficulties in understanding the basic principles of the MCA exercise and the differences in scope and impacts of the project options. This unavoidably raises doubts over the reliability of the outcomes of the process. Stakeholder groups may thus be required to increase their knowledge of MCA processes before they can begin to approach their task – hence the process needs to be a deliberative exercise.

But, in the end, there is much promise in participatory MCA, with increased potential for debate and deliberation, and learning while carrying out the process – and perhaps it is a matter of a very careful planning required of the process to ensure the potential problems are avoided.

6.7   CONCLUSIONS

The shape of the appraisal framework appears important to the projects that can be prioritized and supported with investment. MAMCA offers a way forward for transport appraisal in allowing projects to be better matched to local policy priorities and for a deliberative process to be developed. Different perspectives can be considered, levels of awareness can be improved amongst project stakeholders, including potentially the public, and a consensus can be developed over the future strategy and investment. Critically, a stronger integration can be developed with urban planning objectives, as these form part of the assessment criteria.

The process is very flexible, and can be modified to different projects and contexts.

The contribution of this chapter is to compare the different outputs from CBA and MAMCA in relation to options for public transport investment. Different results were evident from two approaches to appraisal, and this calls into question which is giving us the 'right' result. If we are keen on funding projects that are aligned to policy objectives, then the optimum approach has to be through MCA, and ideally this is carried out in a participatory manner to ensure greater ownership of the process. CBA gives us only an alignment to a rather abstract 'economic efficiency' goal, and this itself is heavily loaded to time savings against cost (Hickman and Dean, 2017). When the process of CBA is partial, in other words, when many impacts cannot be quantified and are not included in the CBA, then the BCR becomes quite an arbitrary figure.

We argue that prioritizing public transport investment needs a different form of project appraisal to the one we have, particularly where there are severe social deprivation problems in the context studied. In many of these cases, it seems better to use a participatory MCA process such as MAMCA. Participatory MCA may be particularly effective at the early stage of the planning and decision-making process (from the problem structuring phase) as it can capture, better than CBA, the full spectrum of interests and values in dispute. Yet, it is also evident that participatory MCA techniques cannot be considered a panacea to conflicts and controversies surrounding the decision-making process of major transport projects. MCA itself can, of course, be arbitrarily applied and the process can be unreliable. Any multi-actor MCA process must deal with the difficult questions of who should be involved in the process, how and at which stage. However, withstanding these issues, participatory MCA allows the inclusion of different point of view in the analysis, enhancing the transparency of the process and increasing the possibility for the legitimation of its outcomes. In this way, we might start to invest in an effective public transport system for areas such as Blackpool and the South Fylde coast.

ACKNOWLEDGEMENT

Thanks to Jamie Quinn for images and mapping.

REFERENCES

Ackerman, F. and Heinzerling, L. 2004. *Priceless: On Knowing the Price of Everything and the Value of Nothing*. New York, New Press.

Annema, J.A., Mouter, N. and Razaei, J. 2015. Cost-benefit analysis (CBA), or multi-criteria decision-making (MCDM) or both: politicians' perspective in transport policy appraisal. *Transportation Research Procedia*, **10**, 788–97.

Banister, D. and Berechmann, J. 2000. *Transport Investment and Economic Development*. London: UCL Press.

Barfod, M.B. and Salling, K.B. 2015. A new composite decision support framework for strategic and sustainable transport appraisals. *Transportation Research Part A*, **72**(1), 1–15

Boardman, A.E., Greenberg, D.H., Vining, A.R. and Weimer, D.L. 2006. *Cost-Benefit Analysis: Concept and Practice*, third edn. Upper Saddle River, NJ: Prentice Hall.

Bristow, A.L. and Nellthorp, J., 2000. Transport project appraisal in the European Union. *Transport Policy*, **7**, 51–60.

Dean, M., Hickman, R. and Chen, C.-L. 2018. Testing the effectiveness of participatory MCA: the case of the South Fylde Line. UCL Working Paper, under review.

DEFRA (Department for Food and Rural Affairs) 2013. *Sustainable Development Indicators*. London: DEFRA.

DETR (Department of the Environment, Transport and the Regions) 1998a. *A New Deal for Trunk Roads in England: Understanding the New Approach to Appraisal*. London: DETR.

DETR (Department of the Environment, Transport and the Regions) 1998b. *A New Deal for Trunk Roads in England: Guidance on the New Approach to Appraisal*. London: DETR.

DETR (Department of the Environment, Transport and the Regions) 1998c. *A New Deal for Transport: The Government's White Paper on the Future of Transport*. London: HMSO.

DfT (Department for Transport) 2014. Transport Analysis Guidance (TAG). http://www.webtag.org.uk (accessed 1 August 2015).

Dimitriou, H. 2016. Editorial. *Research in Transportation Economics*, Special Edition, **58**, 1–6.

Dimitriou, H., Wright, P. and Ward, E. 2010. *Incorporating Principles of Sustainable Development within the Design and Delivery of Major Projects: An International Study with particular reference to Major Infrastructure Projects for the Institution of Civil Engineering and the Actuarial Profession*. London: University College London.

Dimitriou, H., Wright, P. and Ward, E. 2012. *Lessons for Decision-makers: A Comparative Analysis of Selected Large-scale Transport Infrastructure Projects in Europe, USA and Asia-Pacific*. Executive Summary. London: University College London.

Dimitriou, H., Ward, E. and Dean, M. 2016. Presenting the case for the application of multi-criteria analysis to mega transport infrastructure appraisal. *Research in Transportation Economics*, Special Edition, **58**, 7–20.

Flyvbjerg, B., Bruzelius, N. and Rothengatter, W. 2003. *Megaprojects and Risk – an Anatomy of Ambition*. Cambridge: Cambridge University Press.

Gellert, P. and Lynch, B. 2003. Mega-projects as displacements. *International Social Science Journal*, **55**(175), 15–25.

Goodman, A. and Hastak, M., 2006. *Infrastructure Planning Handbook – Planning, Engineering, and Economics*. New York: ASCE Press.

Haezendonck, E. (ed.) 2007. *Transport Project Evaluation: Extending the Social Cost–Benefit Approach*. Cheltenham, UK and Northampton, MA, USA: Edward Elgar.

Hickman, R. 2018. Transport appraisal: thinking beyond the CBA? In I. Docherty and J. Shaw (eds), *The Inside Track: Why Transport Matters and How We Can Make it Better*. Bristol: Policy Press, forthcoming.

Hickman, R. and Dean, M. 2017. Incomplete cost-incomplete benefit analysis in transport appraisal. *Transport Reviews*, doi: 10.1080/01441647.2017.1407377.

Hickman, R. and Osborne, C. 2017. Sintropher Executive Summary, Interreg IVB. University College London.

Hickman, R., Ashiru, O. and Banister, D. 2010. Transport and climate change: simulating the options for carbon reduction in London. *Transport Policy*, **17**, 110–25.

Hickman, R., Givoni, M., Bonilla, D. and Banister, D. (eds) 2015. *An International Handbook on Transport and Development*. Cheltenham, UK and Northampton, MA, USA: Edward Elgar.

Jacobs Consultancy, 2015. South Fylde Rail Connectivity Study. Stage 2 Results. Lancashire County Council, Preston.

Jensen, A.V., Salling, K. and Leleur, S. 2013. The Sustain Appraisal Framework: flexible decision support for national sustainable transport planning. Paper presented at the 13th World Conference of Transport Research, Rio de Janeiro, 15–18 July.

Leleur, S. 2012. *Complex Strategic Choices: Applying Systemic Planning for Strategic Decision Making*. London: Springer.

Lucas, K. 2012. Transport and social exclusion: where are we now? *Transport Policy*, **20**, 105–13.

Macharis, C. and Bernardini, A. 2015. Reviewing the use of Multi-Criteria Decision Analysis for the evaluation of transport projects: time for a multi-actor approach. *Transport Policy*, **37**, 177–86

Macharis, C., De Witte, A. and Ampe, J. 2009. The Multi-Actor Multi-Criteria Analysis methodology (MAMCA) for the evaluation of transport projects: theory and practice. *Journal of Advanced Transportation*, **43**(2), 183–202.

Macharis, C., De Witte, A. and Turcksin, L. 2010. The Multi-Actor Multi Criteria Analysis (MAMCA) application in the Flemish long-term decision making process on mobility and logistics. *Transport Policy*, **17**, 303–11

Mackie, P. and Preston, J. 1998. Twenty-one sources of error and bias in transport appraisal. *Transport Policy*, **5**, 1–7.

Metz, D. 2008. The myth of travel time saving. *Transport Reviews*, **28**(3), 321–36,

Næss, P. 2006. Cost-Benefit Analyses of transportation investments: neither critical nor realistic. *Journal of Critical Realism*, **5**(1), 32–60.

Salling, K. and Leleur, S. 2009. Transport appraisal and Monte Carlo simulation by use of the CBA-DK model. *Transport Policy*, **18**(1), 236–45.

Sayers, T.M., Jessop, A. and Hills, P. 2003. Multi-criteria evaluation of transport options – flexible, transparent and user-friendly? *Transport Policy*, **10**(1), 95–105.

Sinden, J. and Thampapillai, D. 1995. *Introduction to Benefit-Cost Analysis*. New York: Longman.

Van Wee, B. 2012. How suitable is CBA for the ex-ante evaluation of transport projects and policies? A discussion from the perspective of ethics. *Transport Policy*, **19**(1), 1–7.

Vickerman, R. 2000. Evaluation methodologies for transport projects in the United Kingdom. *Transport Policy*, **7**(1), 7–16.

Ward, E., Dimitriou, H. and Dean, M. (2016). Theory and background of Multi-Criteria Analysis: toward a policy-led approach to mega transport infrastructure project appraisal. *Research in Transportation Economics*, Special Edition, **58**, 21–45.

Worsley, T. and Mackie, P. 2015. *Transport Policy, Appraisal and Decision-making.* RAC Foundation and Institute for Transport Studies, London and University of Leeds.

7. Evaluation of Value Capture Financing schemes for urban transportation infrastructure with the aid of Multi Actor Multi Criteria Analysis focusing on a Greek city

Anastasia Roukouni, Cathy Macharis and Socrates Basbas

7.1 INTRODUCTION

A sustainable urban mobility system is one that is capable of meeting the existing mobility needs of citizens without threatening the opportunity of future generations to fulfill their own needs. The creation of new transportation infrastructure increases accessibility levels, having an impact on the value of land and nearby properties. During recent years, public transport systems all over the world confront severe financial challenges due to continuously diminishing public resources dedicated to them, an outcome of the global economic crisis. A family of innovative financial mechanisms and tools for public transport is coming to the forefront in helping find alternative solutions to the development and expansion of transport infrastructure in cities. These mechanisms fall under the umbrella name "Value Capture Finance" (VCF) and rely on the value increment caused by the aforementioned enhanced accessibility (Coyle, 2011; Cidell and Prytherch, 2015; Sclar et al., 2014; UN-HABITAT, 2013).

At the same time, in terms of designing and implementing successful transport policies, achieving smooth collaboration and consensus among stakeholders is a key factor for the majority of cases. The essential role of active stakeholders' participation is increasingly emphasized in the literature related to the *ex ante* evaluation of transportation projects and policies (Coeck and Haezendonck, 2007).

The research presented herein uses the Multi Actor Multi Criteria Analysis developed by Macharis (2004, 2005) to assess alternative financing options for urban public transportation which are based on the value capture concept, focusing on the second largest city in Greece, Thessaloniki, and specifically on its metro system, which is still under construction while this chapter is being written.

7.2   LITERATURE REVIEW

Between transportation systems and land market there is unquestionable interaction, which is interpreted through the concept of accessibility, in other words, the ability to access activities and goods that are in demand (Geurs and Van Wee, 2004; Iacono et al., 2009). Rich literature on the relationship between transport systems and land value exists worldwide; the majority of studies have shown that land value increases as accessibility increases due to new or improved transportation infrastructure, *ceteris paribus* (Bowes and Ihlanfeldt, 2001; Cervero and Duncan, 2002; Cervero and Landis, 1993; Gibbons and Machin, 2004; Hess and Almeida, 2007; Smith et al., 2015). The basic notion of value capture is that the value increment that results from urban investment in infrastructure could be "captured" (partially or totally) to recover the capital costs of the investment or reinvest in the area (Medda, 2012). Although initially the term value capture referred to pure "land value capture", over the years it has been given a broader meaning, including today all the strategies which aim at financing through location-based value (Salon, 2014). There are numerous variations of financial instruments based on the notion of value capture worldwide; often different terminology is used in different countries/regions and by different researchers to describe very similar or even identical methods (Roukouni et al., 2015).

VCF mechanisms are increasingly used for urban public transportation systems. Some of the most ambitious and large-scale transportation projects recently completed or currently under construction are partially financed through a value capture program. Examples include the following: Denver Union Station redevelopment project, Colorado; Atlanta BeltLine project, Atlanta; Washington DC Metro expansion to Dulles Airport, Virginia; Portland's Cascade Station and Light Rail to PDX Airport, Oregon; Red Line, Los Angeles Metro, California (all in the USA); Crossrail project and Northern Line Extension (NLE), London, UK; Mass Transit (MTR), Hong Kong.

In the VCF world, no "magical recipes" promising a successful result exist; every case has its own unique characteristics, and therefore local circumstances can greatly affect the final result. As a non-trivial, multifaceted issue, it requires a multilevel and multi-actor approach. The choice of the most suitable VCF mechanism(s) to use involves a large variety of criteria which have to be considered. Moreover, a large number of actors are involved in the decision-making process; these actors usually come from diverse backgrounds and often have different goals, perspectives and aspirations (Macharis and Bernardini, 2015). Many researchers have underlined the increasing significance of stakeholder engagement in planning and evaluation of transportation infrastructure and policies (Banville et al., 1998; Dooms et al., 2013; Stough and Rietveld, 1997). According to Freeman (1984), stakeholder refers to every individual or group of individuals that can be affected by the achievement of the goals of an organization. With a focus on urban transportation issues, stakeholder is everyone who has a specific interest regarding a policy or measure in the field of transportation (Taschner and Fiedler, 2009). Stakeholder engagement refers to the inclusion of their needs, views and system of values in the decision-making process (Cascetta et al., 2015). In the European Union (EU) "Guidelines: Developing and Implementing a Sustainable Urban Mobility Plan" (2013), it is suggested that in urban mobility issues, identifying the stakeholders and their crucial role can truly contribute in achieving the goals of sustainable urban mobility. This in turn helps in finding possible conflicts and/or alliances among them and in realizing how their existence can influence the planning process regarding the geographical coverage, the combination of different policies, the availability of resources and so on. (Wefering et al., 2013). The literature review reveals that acceptance and support from stakeholders is repeatedly mentioned in different research studies (see Langley, 2013; Mathur, 2014; Medda, 2012) as a very important factor influencing successful implementation of VCF. Nevertheless, stakeholders have not yet been investigated in depth in the context of VCF research. In addition, the evaluation attempts (GVA Grimley, 2004; Iacono et al., 2009; Mathur, 2014) of VCF mechanisms are also are rather scarce to date, and there is a lack of comprehensive and established research in this direction (Roukouni et al., 2018).

The methodology to be used to aid *ex ante* evaluation of financing policies for transportation infrastructure should be selected very carefully The traditional methods used for *ex ante* evaluation of transport policies are not capable of explicitly incorporating stakeholders' views and usually restrict the analysis to specific criteria measured in monetary terms (Macharis et al., 2012). The main ones are: Cost-Benefit Analysis (CBA); Cost-Effectiveness Analysis (CEA); Economic-Effects Analysis (EEA)/Economic Impact Analysis (EIA); Social-Cost Benefit Analysis (SCBA). CBA in particular, which has been used – and is still being used – widely all over the world for decisions related to transportation investments (Annema et al., 2015; Berechman, 2009), has lately been subject to strong criticism regarding many aspects, and notably its weakness to effectively include non-quantifiable criteria in the analysis (see Banister and Thurstain-Goodwin, 2011; Beria et al., 2012; Iniestra and Gutierrez, 2009; Tsamboulas, 2007; Van Wee, 2012; Worsley and Mackie, 2015).

Multi Criteria Decision Aid (MCDA) methods have gained wide acceptance as they embody many quantitative and qualitative variables and different scenarios can be evaluated at the same time (Thomopoulos et al., 2009). The use of MCDA in transportation planning has shown a steadily increasing trend in recent years (Macharis and Bernardini, 2015). The suitability of each MCDA method and/or technique strongly depends on the research objectives and the scope of the analysis (De Brucker et al., 2013; Lami, 2014; Tsamboulas et al., 1999). The outcome of a MCDA process should not be interpreted as the only solution to the decision-making problem being discussed; it is more an indication of the potential consequences that could follow a particular set of actions (Riabacke, 2012).

An *ex ante* evaluation framework for assessing the suitability of different VCF mechanisms should be comprehensive and at the same time flexible, aiming at incorporating stakeholders as extensively as possible in the decision-making process (Roukouni et al., 2018). There are many different ways in which stakeholders could be involved in a MCDA (Marttunen et al., 2015). Nevertheless, in the majority of cases, stakeholders' participation does not take place in all stages of the analysis, nor is it a main and integral part of it (Macharis and Bernardini, 2015). The Multi Actor Multi Criteria Analysis (MAMCA) was deployed to address this issue.

7.3 CASE ANALYSIS: APPLICATION OF THE MAMCA, RESULTS AND DISCUSSION

The MAMCA was used to address a real-world case study, the metro system under construction in Thessaloniki. Thessaloniki is the second largest city in Greece, the second major economic, industrial, commercial and political center in the country, and a transportation hub for southeastern Europe and the Balkans. The metro is an on-going project, having started in 2006. After its completion, the basic metro line will run for 9.6 kilometers through the city and have 13 stations. It is worth mentioning that it is a rather irregular case; the construction of the metro was supposed to be completed years ago, but due to several reported issues (financial problems, archaeological findings and so on) a big delay on project delivery has occurred and there is still ambiguity concerning the expected opening, with the latest available information placing it in the year 2020.

An interesting fact is that the metro line is going to pass through one of the densest areas of the city in terms of population. The whole area is characterized by the existence of mixed land use, especially across the road axes, and there is also a mix of social groups: households of different sizes and varying income classes, as well as a noteworthy number of students (two university campuses are located across the metro route; one of them, the Aristotle University of Thessaloniki Campus, being the largest in Greece) and immigrants (Roukouni, 2016).

In 2003, it was decided that the construction of the project was to be financed by means of national and EU funds. The contract with the contracting joint venture AEGEK–IMPREGILO–ANSALDO T.S.F–SELI–ANSALDOBREDA was signed in 2006 and the construction of the project commenced. The basic metro line has an estimated portfolio of 1.36 billion euros. By 2009, 196.5 million euros from the 3rd Cofinanced Development Programme had already been used for its construction, in addition to the 33 million euros coming from national resources. Financing of the Thessaloniki metro project continues within the context of the National Strategic Reference Framework (NSRF) 2007–13 and NSRF 2014–20 (ATTIKO METRO S.A., 2016).

All the steps of the MAMCA for this specific case are addressed and discussed in this section, except for Step 7 (implementation of the results), as this is beyond the scope of the chapter.

7.3.1   MAMCA Step 1: Definition of the Problem and Identification of the Alternatives

The decision problem in this case is the *ex ante* assessment of the suitability of various financing mechanisms for urban transportation infrastructure which belong to the value capture family, for implementation in Greece, a country with no previous experience with VCF tools for this purpose. More specifically, the evaluation of potential VCF variants for the partial financing of the construction and/or operation costs of the Thessaloniki metro project is investigated. As described earlier in the literature review section of the chapter, there is a great variety of VCF mechanisms and tools worldwide. This chapter examines three alternative urban transportation financing scenarios, each one based on one of the three most widely used value capture tools in the context of urban public transport systems. These alternative scenarios are briefly presented below.

Scenario 1: betterment tax/benefit assessment
This refers to a tax/levy on properties which benefit from increased accessibility, by experiencing a rise in their value. Often, but not always, it is applied within a specific geographical zone. It can be directed either to

property owners (land-based levy) or businesses (economic prosperity-based levy), or both. Moreover, it can be either flat (same for all properties regardless of their location) or distance-based (Fogarty et al., 2008; Roukouni and Medda, 2012).

Scenario 2: Tax Increment Financing (TIF)
The term TIF refers to a financial instrument that attempts to remove physical blight and encourage economic development. Its implementation includes the creation of a geographical district, where the tax base (the property values) is "frozen" for a long period of time, usually 10 to 25 years, under the assumption that the area would not develop but for the planned intervention and therefore the creation of the TIF district (known as the "but for" requirement). As investments begin to take place within the TIF area, property values increase, and so does the tax revenue. The new property tax minus the tax on the frozen property values (tax increment) is collected by the TIF authority and used either to repay the capital costs of the investments or to support further development (Mathur, 2014; Rybeck, 2004).

Scenario 3: joint development
This refers to the establishment of cooperation between public and private entities, usually public transport authorities and real estate developers, in order to develop an urban project under transit-oriented development (TOD) principles. The basic principles of this method are that the private entity is responsible for compensating the public entity through payments or cost-sharing agreements and that all parties are involved in the process voluntarily, although the result is a legally binding agreement. A main difference between joint development and betterment tax and TIF is that identifying the direct and indirect impact of the transportation infrastructure to be implemented is not required, as in the case of the two aforementioned mechanisms. Despite the fact that in some cases there are similarities between joint development and Public Private Partnerships (PPPs), the two terms do not coincide (Medda, 2012; Zhao et al., 2012).

7.3.2 MAMCA Step 2: Stakeholder Analysis

In this step, the stakeholder analysis took place, under the objective of selecting the most suitable stakeholders to be involved in the decision-making processes concerning the implementation of innovative financing tools. Following this, categorization of the stakeholders into six groups was accomplished, aiming to achieve the maximum possible homogeneity within the groups regarding the stakeholders' objectives. The six groups are the following:

- Group A: Government/Local Authorities
- Group B: Transport Authorities
- Group C: Universities/Research Institutions
- Group D: Private Sector
- Group E: Society
- Group F: Professional Associations.

More specifically, the critical decision makers in most cases of *ex ante* transportation policies' evaluation worldwide are the country's elected government. Even when the policy is directed towards a specific city or area, central government is in charge of making the final key decisions when facing multidimensional and multidisciplinary issues. VCF is certainly a multifaceted issue, and its implementation is usually associated with essential institutional and legal settings.

Therefore, it is necessary to include governmental actors from three policy levels in the first stakeholder group: country, region, city (municipality). The second group comprises transport authorities responsible for the operation of the different transport modes/lines. It is important to record the views of representatives of as many transport authorities as possible, regardless of which transport mode the VCF policy is planned to affect; the feedback could provide the analyst with crucial information regarding potential expansion of the policy to other modes/target groups. The literature review also indicated the importance of including experts with an academic and/or research background in the decision-making process for transport-related problems. Based on the complex nature of VCF policies, special attention should be paid to selecting actors with diverse academic/research interests in order to gain insight into the different dimensions of the problem and, through this interdisciplinary approach, reveal aspects that would not be easily perceived, for instance, if only transportation engineers took part in the analysis. It is thus suggested that urban and regional planners, transportation economists, land-use planners, real-estate experts and so on should also be included in the third group. The private sector indisputably has a major role in the successful implementation of policies based on the value capture notion, as many variants of the existing VCF tools focus on developers and non-residential properties. The fourth group therefore consists of representatives of leading transport companies and consultancies, as well as the banks' real-estate departments. Society, which follows as the fifth group of stakeholders, is a very broad term; here it refers to organized social groups formed by citizens who share common interests/aspirations (for example, cyclists' community, environmental groups, student associations). The last group is titled professional associations and includes representatives of associations/chambers of relevant fields such as transportation engineers, civil engineers, urban and regional planners.

7.3.3 MAMCA Step 3: Definition of Criteria and Weight Elicitation

The experience from MAMCA applications so far indicates that there is no common recipe that can be used in all cases regarding the identification of stakeholders' objectives and their translation into criteria (Keseru et al., 2015). Munda (2004) argues that it is preferable for the formulation of the criteria to be performed by the analyst(s)/researcher(s) because technical issues such as overlapping or linguistic vagueness should be avoided. An initial list with possible criteria could be formed based on the relevant bibliography and the specific decision problem, and then stakeholders could be given the opportunity to express their opinion on these criteria through an interactive process (telephone interviews or workshops) to validate them, and/or suggest different/additional ones (Macharis et al., 2012).

The above process is rational when the transport policy being examined – the alternatives of which are to be evaluated – is familiar to the majority of stakeholders. Even when some of the alternatives are novel, from the beginning the stakeholders usually have a general idea about their attitude towards the policy. Therefore, when investigating VCF policies, the following issue arises: in cases where value capture is well established as a policy option for financing transportation infrastructure at national, regional and/or local levels, the approach can be adopted according to which the initial list of criteria is discussed with representatives from all the stakeholder groups. In countries/regions where one or more mechanism(s), belonging to the value capture family, have been or are being currently used for financing transportation infrastructure, obviously there will be many stakeholders who have already been involved in the implementation procedure and even more who, regardless of whether or not they have been directly involved, have been informed in detail about the VCF concept. Contrary to that, in countries/regions with no tradition in such transportation financing practices, Greece being one of them, it is normal and rather expected for even key actors to have limited (or no) familiarization with these financing techniques. Hence, in these cases, communicating with stakeholders to ask them to define their targets and, correspondingly, criteria would not offer much help to the researcher; it could even further complicate things. In light of this determination, it is desirable for the objectives/criteria in these cases to be suggested by the analyst/

researcher who, after having thoroughly studied the relevant literature, should have comprehensive knowledge on the topic, and be familiar with the international experience. Nevertheless, stakeholders should be given the freedom to express their views on the criteria forming their value tree because this notion is located at the heart of the MAMCA, that is, the substantial participation of stakeholders in all stages of the analysis.

It is thus suggested that this issue is addressed by incorporating a relevant question in a special part of the questionnaire, which would be located after the multi-criteria part used for the weight elicitation (described below). This way, all stakeholders will be informed about the value capture concept through the descriptive introductory part of the questionnaire, and some of them may meet the term for the first time. This approach provides yet another advantage; it gives the opportunity for each one of the stakeholders, with no exception, to express their opinion on the topic, which is not easily achievable if, for example, a workshop is organized. It is rather utopian to believe that it would be possible to gather all participants from the six groups that have been formed at the same place and time, as usually they are very busy persons with tight work schedules and thus extremely limited time. Moreover, physical presence is often impeded by geographical distance, for example, in the first group decision makers from the central and local policy-making levels co-exist. While being able to eliminate the distance using modern technologies (for example: Skype video calls), the difficulties identified above remain unsolved.

The different criteria that are selected for each stakeholder group comprise the overall decision value tree, which is illustrated in Figure 7.1.

The diagram reveals that Group A (Government/Local Authorities) is the one with the greatest number of identified assessment criteria (15). This is rational since Group A is the main decision-makers' group, including actors from all levels of authority, and hence their objectives are multiple as they are supposed to represent the interests of the society as a whole (see also Macharis and Nijkamp, 2011; Vermote et al., 2013).

The weight elicitation in this case is performed using the Analytic Hierarchy Process (AHP), introduced by Saaty (1977, 1986). It is a scaling method for deriving priorities (weights) for a set of activities according to their importance. The method uses a hierarchic or network structure to represent the problem in question and then the relations within this structure are built using pairwise comparisons (Saaty, 1990, 2005).

AHP is one of the most common MCDA methods used in the transportation research field. Vargas (1990) and Vaidya and Kumar (2006) collected many publications involving the use of AHP. The researchers underline that the USA appears to be the country where the majority of interdisciplinary AHP applications have taken place so far; nevertheless,

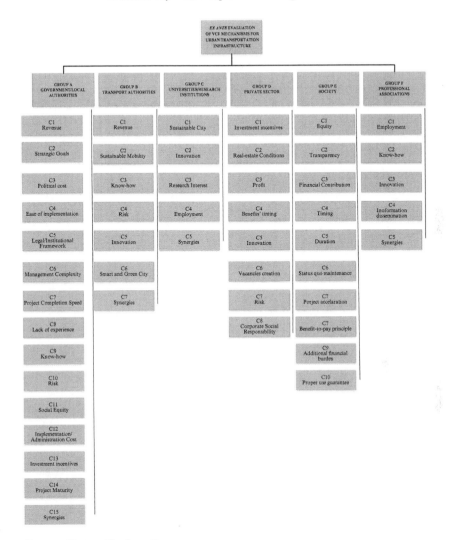

Source: Designed by the authors.

*Figure 7.1   Decision tree for the ex ante evaluation of VCF mechanisms
for urban transportation infrastructure*

there is a sound geographical coverage all over the world. A recent and
comprehensive bibliographical review regarding the use of MCDA methods on transportation-related projects between 1985 and 2012 was carried
out by Macharis and Bernardini (2015), who reviewed 276 publications.

According to the authors, the predominance of AHP is clear as it is employed in 33 percent of the cases examined.

Lepetu (2012) claims that AHP is clearly a smart choice for eliciting weights when dealing with a decision-making problem for the following reasons: it is a well-established procedure that can be repeated; it allows consistency checks to be performed; both quantitative and qualitative data can be used as input; and it is appropriate for group decision making; in addition, it is applied widely in the academic literature. Moreover, AHP tends to highlight slight differences between the alternatives which decision makers cannot always comfortably perceive (Mau-Crimmins et al., 2005).

A comprehensive questionnaire survey was designed for the purposes of the weight elicitation, based on pairwise comparisons of the criteria, using the nine-point Saaty's scale. The survey was conducted between October and December 2015, mainly through personal interviews. Overall, 70 stakeholders from all six groups participated in the survey.

After the collection of the 70 questionnaires, the stakeholders' answers were used to calculate the geometric means per group, and these were used as input to the MAMCA software web platform (see Chapter 3). The weights of the criteria per actors' group were then calculated. The results are presented in Tables 7.1–7.3.

The most important criterion among actors of Group A (Government/ Local Authorities) appears to be social equity. The stakeholders of this group also consider important to what degree the financing mechanism could be compatible with the project maturity. The implementation/ administration cost is another influential criterion for them. At the other end are located the ease of implementation and lack of experience criteria (which could act as an implementation barrier, and the stakeholders are keen to avoid that). Low importance was given by this group's actors to the political cost criterion, which is rather surprising as this category includes, amongst others, politicians. This might be explained by an implicit "marketing" strategy; they know that it does not sound very nice to put emphasis on political cost during an interview of any kind and they attempt to shed light on social equity instead. In any case, the motivation behind this result is worth further investigation. The estimated revenue does not concern the actors as much as, for instance, the achievement of strategic goals or the investment incentives (Table 7.1).

Stakeholders from Group B (Transportation Authorities) believe that the risk associated with each VCF financing mechanism should be a prevailing criterion in the assessment process, slightly more important than the estimated revenue for the authority. The promotion of sustainable mobility follows, whereas the development of synergies between different

Table 7.1   Criteria weights analysis for Group A and Group B

	Group A		Group B	
Code	Criterion	Weight (%)	Criterion	Weight (%)
C01	Revenue	5.08	Revenue	28.00
C02	Strategic Goals	7.5	Sustainable Mobility	14.60
C03	Political Cost	3.24	Know-how	7.30
C04	Ease of implementation	3.42	Risk	29.46
C05	Legal Institutional Framework	8.46	Innovation	7.60
C06	Management Complexity	5.89	Smart and Green City	8.43
C07	Project Completion Speed	5.85	Synergies	4.60
C08	Lack of experience	2.67		
C09	Know-how	4.35		
C10	Risk	6.72		
C11	Social equity	15.91		
C12	Implementation/ administration cost	9.39		
C13	Investment incentives	7.57		
C14	Project Maturity	9.84		
C15	Synergies	4.12		

Source: Designed by the authors based on the collected data.

disciplines and authorities is the least important criterion according to them (Table 7.1).

The most significant criterion for Group C (Universities/Research Institutions) is the promotion and enhancement of the sustainable city vision. Synergies are placed relatively high in their value tree as well, almost sharing second place with the employment creation criterion. The least critical criterion for them is innovation, but with a slight difference from the remaining one, namely, the research interest (Table 7.2).

For the actors of Group D (Private Sector), three criteria are predeterminant: the profit, the risk and the benefits' timing, while innovation and corporate social responsibility are weighted as the least important among their seven criteria (Table 7.2). Societal actors would like to be sure that the revenue from the VCF mechanisms will be used for the decided purpose only, and they want to avoid the phenomena of corruption and/or improper use of the collected revenue, making a guarantee of proper use

Table 7.2　Criteria weights analysis for Group C and Group D

Group C			Group D	
Code	Criterion	Weight (%)	Criterion	Weight (%)
C01	Sustainable City	34.25	Investment incentives	10.98
C02	Innovation	12.96	Real-estate Conditions	9.94
C03	Research interest	14.05	Profit	20.26
C04	Employment	19.19	Benefits' timing	21.05
C05	Synergies	19.55	Innovation	4.91
C06			Vacancies' creation	6.56
C07			Risk	21.38
C08			Corporate Social Responsibility	4.93

Source:　Designed by the authors based on the collected data.

their first choice among the criteria. This way of thinking is supported by the fact that the next important criterion according to them is transparency followed by equity and benefit-to-pay principle. The maintenance of their status quo (usually related to the Not In My Backyard Syndrome) is the least significant criterion for them (Table 7.3).

Stakeholders included in the Professional Associations group (Group F) argue that know-how acquisition is the most crucial criterion, followed by synergies' creation and then employment vacancies' creation. The dissemination of information is the least important criterion in their view, having only a slightly lower weight than innovation (Table 7.3).

7.3.4　MAMCA Step 4: Indicators and Measurement Methods

One of the MAMCA's strengths is that is can be performed, from the beginning to the end, without using a single quantitative criterion, only with the use of qualitative judgments. This approach might not be preferable when quantitative data is available, however, the possibility to draw conclusions even in cases where there is a lack of data, utilizing every kind of available information, is extremely important (Geudens et al., 2009). In the current analysis, the ratings of the majority of criteria cannot be expressed in quantitative or monetary terms, as VCF policies have a long-term impact and the criteria are of a heterogeneous nature; this was also the case in Dooms and Macharis (2003). Similar to the approach

Table 7.3   Criteria weights analysis for Group E and Group F

Group E			Group F	
Code	Criterion	Weight (%)	Criterion	Weight (%)
C01	Equity	12.60	Employment	18.86
C02	Transparency	19.63	Know-how	27.33
C03	Financial contribution	4.11	Innovation	16.78
C04	Timing	2.96	Information dissemination	15.00
C05	Duration	4.35	Synergies	22.03
C06	Status quo maintenance	2.46		
C07	Project acceleration	5.36		
C08	Benefit-to-pay principle	12.01		
C09	Additional financial burden	9.20		
C10	Proper use guarantee	27.32		

Source: Designed by the authors based on the collected data.

followed by Macharis and Crompvoets (2014), the measurement methods related to the indicators are all qualitative in nature as the alternatives considered are future situations that have not yet been studied.

7.3.5   MAMCA Step 5: Overall Analysis and Ranking

In this step every alternative (from Step 1) is evaluated with respect to the different criteria for each stakeholder group (Step 2).

In this case, the GDSS PROMETHEE (for more information see Brans and Mareschal, 2005; Macharis et al., 2004) method is used for the evaluation of different scenarios. This allows interesting comparisons with Roukouni et al. (2018) in which the authors applied AHP for this task, similar to the weight elicitation. The evaluation was based on the authors' experience of multi-year research on the topic, and was also supported by key experts' consultation combined with an in-depth literature study (this approach was also followed by Bergqvist et al., 2015; Macharis and Compvoets, 2014).

A main differentiation with AHP is that in the case of PROMETHEE, being a preference ranking method, the different scenarios are not evaluated through pairwise comparisons; each scenario is evaluated against each one of the established criteria (using a point scale ranging from "very negative" to "very positive") and then the synthesis of preferences takes place and the so-called preference flows are calculated.

7.3.6   MAMCA Step 6: Results

The global outcome of the MAMCA is illustrated in Figure 7.2 as the multi-actor view using PROMETHEE. The vertical axis corresponds to the evaluation score of each one of three alternative scenarios, while the six different stakeholder groups are displayed on the horizontal axis. The three lines represent Scenario 1 (Betterment tax), Scenario 2 (TIF) and Scenario 3 (Joint Development). Scenario 1 appears to have obtained high scores only in Group A (Government/Local Authorities), and its score is lower, but remains quite stable in the other five actors' groups. In contrast, Scenario 2 has the lowest evaluation score among the three alternatives in Group A and the highest in the Professional Associations (Group C). Scenario 3 obtains the highest score from the Private Sector (Group D).

Despite the fact that this multi-actor view allows a clear comparison between the preferences of the stakeholder categories, more important than the overall ranking is to gain insight into the strong and weak aspects of each alternative for the different stakeholder groups. This is achieved through the production of single-actor view diagrams (Bergqvist et al., 2015; Turcksin et al., 2011).

Using the PROMETHEE method, the net preference flows that are calculated can have a negative sign. This explains why some of the bars are below the x-axis in the bar charts.

Figure 7.3 presents the evaluation of the three different scenarios from the view of the Governmental/Local Authorities' actors (Group A). It is noteworthy that Scenario 1 gets a remarkably high score (net flow with positive sign) in many criteria that are related to implementation issues (for example, ease of implementation and the existence of a supportive legal/institutional framework), while in others, such as the political cost and the provision of investment incentives, the flow has a negative sign. The scores for revenue and risk criteria are also high with regard to Scenario 1. Group A appears to associate the introduction of the TIF mechanism more with potential political cost, and the lack of experience in this specific financing tool seems to worry this group more compared with the other two scenarios. Joint development is considered the financing option which is capable of accelerating the project construction more than the others, while stimulating investment in the area. This is not a surprise as investment incentives is inherently connected with the notion of joint

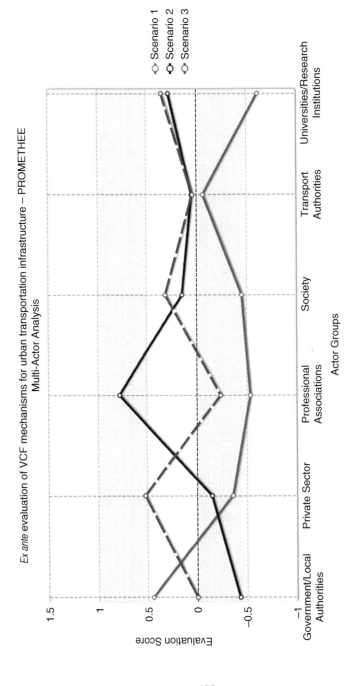

Source: Designed by the authors based on the collected data.

Figure 7.2   Multi-actor line chart

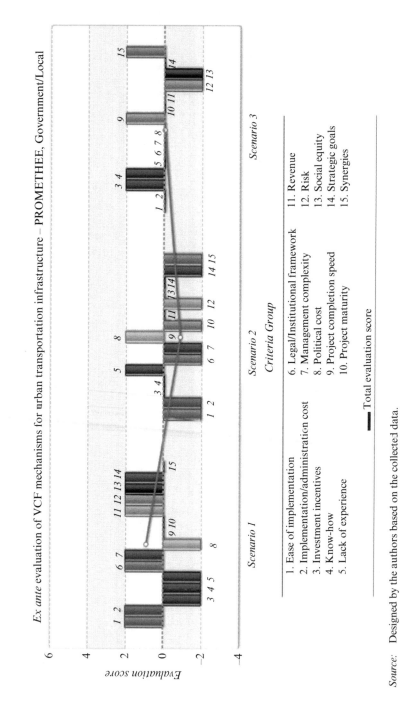

Source: Designed by the authors based on the collected data.

Figure 7.3 Criteria Group A evaluation linebar chart

development mechanisms. Furthermore, the actors of this group appear to prefer Scenario 3 in terms of synergies' promotion; however, in terms of social equity (which is a particularly important criterion for this group, as revealed by Step 3 of the analysis), this option gets last place and Scenario 1 gets indisputable precedence.

Actors belonging to the Transport Authorities' group (Group B) believe that the introduction of a betterment tax would bring more revenue to their treasury, but they do not consider this mechanism very innovative, as a TIF scheme could be. Apart from novelty, TIF policy gets a higher evaluation score on the know-how criterion as well, but it is also associated with the highest risk among the three alternatives. In terms of sustainable mobility, for Group B, joint development appears to be the VCF policy most likely to achieve it. This might be related to the beneficial role of joint development in supporting TOD, which was mentioned earlier in this chapter. In terms of synergies, Scenario 3 is in first place again, while Scenario 1 scores notably low on this criterion. The interesting aspect in this stakeholder group is that the overall aggregated line is quite flat, which means that no truly intense differentiation is observed among the three scenarios in Group B (Figure 7.4).

Actors from Universities/Research Institutions (Group C) are in favor of Scenario 2 in terms of research interest, innovation and synergies. Scenario 3 appears the most promising regarding potential job vacancies' creation, and does not have a very low score in any of the criteria (no negative flows). Sustainable city is the criterion with the highest score in Scenario 1, but this seems to be outbalanced by the low scores achieved for the other criteria (Figure 7.5).

Actors in the Private Sector (Group D), score Scenario 3 remarkably high in almost all the criteria, and seem to relate joint development policies with a low risk percentage. Scenario 2 presents a more balanced image (negative sign only in the flow of one criterion, benefits' timing), with investment incentives having the highest value in the evaluation. In contrast, Scenario 1 is considered rather risky and probably as a result, its score for all the remaining criteria is low (Figure 7.6).

Societal actors (Group E) appear rather indecisive, as revealed by their bar chart (Figure 7.7). There is large divergence among criteria scores regarding all three alternative scenarios. Scenario 1 gets a high score on the benefit-to-pay principle and equity criterion, with the reverse for Scenario 3, while Scenario 2 is considered much more transparent but not good for project acceleration.

Group F comprises actors from Professional Associations. Figure 7.8 reveals that this group tends to be in favor of Scenario 2, as it comes first in four out of five of the established criteria, with the creation of employment

Ex ante evaluation of VCF mechanisms for urban transportation infrastructure – PROMETHEE, Transport Authorities

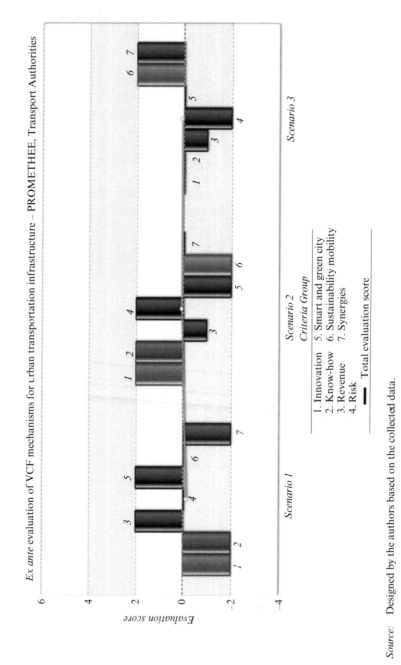

Source: Designed by the authors based on the collected data.

Figure 7.4   Criteria Group B evaluation line-bar chart

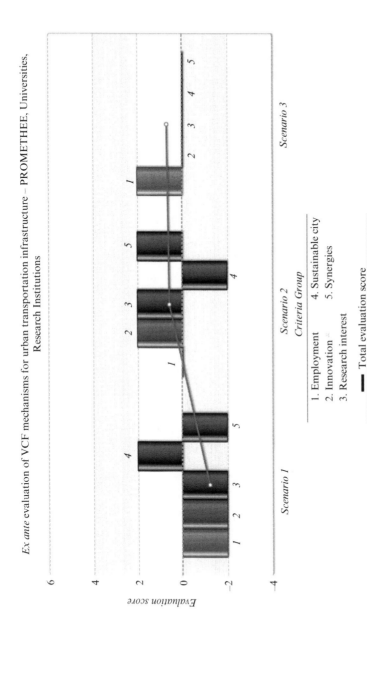

Source: Designed by the authors based on the collected data.

Figure 7.5 Criteria Group C evaluation line/bar chart

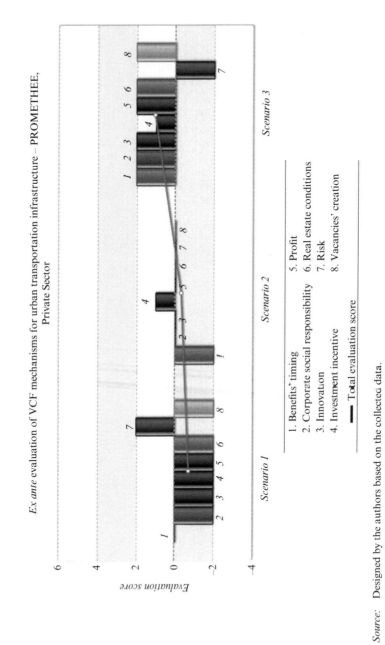

Ex ante evaluation of VCF mechanisms for urban transportation infrastructure – PROMETHEE, Private Sector

1. Benefits' timing
2. Corporate social responsibility
3. Innovation
4. Investment incentive
5. Profit
6. Real estate conditions
7. Risk
8. Vacancies' creation

━━ Total evaluation score

Source: Designed by the authors based on the collected data.

Figure 7.6   Criteria Group D evaluation line/bar chart

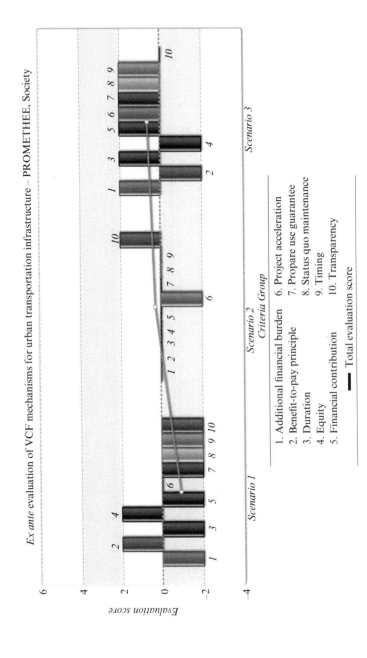

Ex ante evaluation of VCF mechanisms for urban transportation infrastructure – PROMETHEE, Society

Criteria Group

1. Additional financial burden
2. Benefit-to-pay principle
3. Duration
4. Equity
5. Financial contribution
6. Project acceleration
7. Propare use guarantee
8. Status quo maintenance
9. Timing
10. Transparency

— Total evaluation score

Source: Designed by the authors based on the collected data.

Figure 7.7 Criteria Group E evaluation line/bar chart

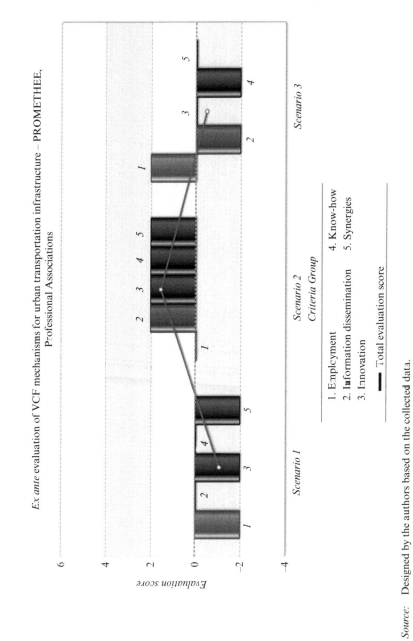

Ex ante evaluation of VCF mechanisms for urban transportation infrastructure – PROMETHEE, Professional Associations

1. Employment   4. Know-how
2. Information dissemination   5. Synergies
3. Innovation

— Total evaluation score

Source: Designed by the authors based on the collected data.

Figure 7.8   Criteria Group F evaluation line/bar chart

opportunities the only exception, but still having no flow with a negative sign.

A noteworthy observation is that no crucial differentiations between the results of the AHP application (in Roukouni et al., 2018) and the application of GDSS PROMETHEE herein are observed. This fact is an indication of the robustness and stability of the MAMCA process; it shows that its outcome can be consistent regardless of the methodology that is chosen for the evaluation of the alternative scenarios.

7.4 CONCLUSIONS AND PERSPECTIVES

This chapter introduces the MAMCA as an *ex ante* evaluation method for different VCF mechanisms for urban transportation infrastructure. The MAMCA emerges as a robust methodology for this assessment, as it is proved capable of dealing with the complexity of VCF and its multidisciplinary nature. Moreover, the use of the MAMCA software facilitated the analysis process and contributed to the better understanding and interpretation of the MAMCA output through the variety and high quality visualization of the results. The analysis and synthesis of the results obtained revealed very interesting observations concerning the degree of acceptability of innovative financing policies based on the value capture concept and highlighted the benefits as well as the limitations through the eyes of those who will have an impact on (or be affected by) potential future implementation of those policies. Interesting similarities as well as contradictions emerged among stakeholder groups, highlighted by the different criteria used for each group. Ideas for future research include testing the methodological framework developed using different case studies (for example, projects that are in the operational phase and not under construction, cities of different scale and therefore possibly with more stakeholders involved) to investigate its effectiveness and validate its applicability.

REFERENCES

Annema, J.A., Mouter, N. and Razaei, J. (2015) Cost-benefit analysis (CBA), or multi-criteria decision-making (MCDM) or both: politicians' perspective in transport policy appraisal. *Transportation Research Procedia* **10**:788–97.
Banister, D. and Thurstain-Goodwin, M. (2011) Quantification of the non-transport benefits resulting from rail investment. *Journal of Transport Geography* **19**:212–23.

Banville, C., Landry, M., Martel, J.M. and Boulaire, C. (1998) A stakeholder approach to MCDA. *Systems Research and Behavioral Science* **15**(1):15–32.

Berechman, J. (2009) *The Evaluation of Transportation Investment Projects.* Routledge Advances in Management and Business Studies. New York and London: Routledge.

Bergqvist, R., Macharis, C., Meers, D. and Woxenius, J. (2015) Making hinterland transport more sustainable: a multi actor multi criteria analysis. *Research in Transportation Business & Management* **14**:80–9.

Beria, P., Maltese, I. and Mariotti, I. (2012) Multicriteria versus Cost Benefit Analysis: a comparative perspective in the assessment of sustainable mobility. *European Transport Research Review* **4**(3):137–52.

Bowes, D.R. and Ihlanfeldt, K.R. (2001) Identifying the impacts of rail transit stations on property values. *Journal of Urban Economics* **50**:1–25.

Brans, J.P. and Mareschal, B. (2005), "Promethee Methods" in Multiple Criteria Decision Analysis: state of the art surveys", in Figueira, J., Greco, S. and Ehrgott, M. (eds), *International Series in Operations Research & Management Science*, New York: Springer, pp. 163–86.

Cascetta, E., Carteni, A., Pagliara, F. and Montanino, M. (2015) A new look at planning and designing transportation systems: a decision-making model based on cognitive rationality, stakeholder engagement and quantitative methods. *Transport Policy* **38**:27–39.

Cervero, R. and Duncan, M. (2002) Benefits of proximity to rail on housing markets: experiences in Santa Clara County. *Journal of Public Transportation* **5**(1):1–18.

Cervero, R. and Landis, J. (1993) Assessing the impacts of urban rail transit on local real estate markets using quasi-experimental comparisons. *Transportation Research Part A: Policy and Practice* **27**:13–22.

Cidell, J. and Prytherch, D. (eds) (2015) *Transport, Mobility and the Production of Urban Space.* Routledge Studies in Human Geography. New York and London: Taylor & Francis Group.

Coeck, C. and Haezendonck, E. (2007) Conclusion: evolution towards integrated project appraisal. In Haezendonck, E. (ed.), *Transport Project Evaluation: Extending the Social Cost-Benefit Approach.* Cheltenham, UK and Northampton, MA, USA: Edward Elgar, pp. 217–20.

Coyle, S. (2011) *Sustainable and Resilient Communities: A Comprehensive Action Plan for Towns, Cities and Regions.* Hoboken, NJ: Wiley.

De Brucker, K., Macharis, C. and Verbeke, A. (2013) Multi-criteria analysis and the resolution of sustainable development dilemmas: a stakeholder management approach. *European Journal of Operational Research* **224**:122–31.

Dooms, M. and Macharis, C. (2003) A framework for sustainable port planning in inland ports: a multistakeholder approach. In *Proceedings of the 43rd European Congress of the Regional Studies Association (ERSA)*, University of Jyväskylä, Finland, August 27–30, pp. 1–23.

Dooms, M., Verbeke, A. and Haezendonck, E. (2013) Stakeholder management and path dependence in large-scale transport infrastructure development: the port of Antwerp case (1960–2010). *Journal of Transport Geography* **27**:14–25.

Fogarty, N., Eaton, N., Belzer, D. and Ohland, G. (2008) *Capturing the Value of Transit, Reconnecting America's Center for Transit-oriented Development.* Report prepared for the United States Department of Transportation, Federal

Transit Administration. http://www.reconnectingamerica.org/assets/Uploads/ct odvalcapture110508v2.pdf (accessed December 2017).

Freeman, R.E. (1984) S*trategic Management: A Stakeholder Approach.* Boston, MA: Pitman.

Geudens, T., Macharis, C., Crompvoets, J. and Plastria, F. (2009) Assessing spatial data infrastructure policy strategies using the Multi Actor Multi Criteria Analysis. *International Journal of Spatial Data Infrastructures Research* 4:265–97.

Geurs, K.T. and Van Wee, B. (2004) Accessibility evaluation of land-use patterns and transport strategies: review and research directions. *Journal of Transport Geography* 12:127–40.

Gibbons, S. and Machin, S. (2004) Valuing rail access using transport innovations. Centre for Economic Performance, London School of Economics and Political Science. http://eprints.lse.ac.uk/19989/1/Valuing_Rail_Access_Using_Transport_Innovations.pdf (accessed December 2017).

GVA Grimley (2004) Developing a methodology to capture land value uplift around transport facilities. Study for Scottish Executive. http://www.scotland. gov.uk/Publications/2004/11/20385/48337 (accessed December 2017).

Hess, D.B. and Almeida, T.M. (2007) Impact of proximity to light rail rapid transit on station-area property values in Buffalo. *Urban Studies* 44(5–6):1041–68.

Iacono, M., Levinson, D., Zhirong, Z. and Lari, A. (2009) *Value Capture for Transportation Finance*. Report to the Minnesota Legislature. Center for Transportation Studies, University of Minnesota.

Iniestra, J.G. and Gutierrez, J.G. (2009) Multicriteria decisions on interdependent infrastructure transportation projects using an evolutionary-based framework. *Applied Soft Computing* 9:512–26.

Keseru, I., Bulckaen, J. and Macharis, C. (2015) Enhancing stakeholder participation in urban mobility planning: the NISTO evaluation framework. In Schrenk, M., Popovich, V., Zeile, P., Elisei, P. and Beyer, C. (eds), *Proceedings of REAL CORP Tagungsband*, Ghent, Belgium, May 5–7, pp. 1–10.

Lami, I.M. (2014) Evaluation tools to support decision-making process related to European corridors. In Lami, I.M. (ed.), *Analytical Decision-making Methods for Evaluating Sustainable Transport in European Corridors*. Cham: Springer International Publishing Switzerland, pp. 85–102.

Langley, J. (2013) Releasing new funding for infrastructure and urban renewal: capturing value. Consult Australia and Sinclair Knight Merz (SKM), 49th ISCORP Congress, Brisbane. http://www.globalskm.com/Site-Documents/Insigh ts/Publications/Value-Capture-Report/ValueCaptureReport_SKM.pdf (accessed December 2017).

Lepetu, J.P. (2012) The use of analytic hierarchy process (AHP) for stakeholder preference analysis: a case study from Kasane Forest Reserve, Botswana. *Journal of Soil Science and Environmental Management* 3(10):237–51.

Macharis, C. (2004) The optimal location of an intermodal bargeterminal. In Beuthe, M., Himanen, V., Reggiani, A. and Zamparini, L. (eds), *European Strategies in the Globalising Markets: Transport developments and Innovations in an Evolving World*. Berlin: Springer-Verlag, pp. 211–32.

Macharis, C. (2005) The importance of stakeholder analysis in freight transport. *European Transport/Transporti Europei* 25–26:114–26.

Macharis, C. and Bernardini, A. (2015) Reviewing the use of Multi-Criteria

Analysis for the evaluation of transport projects: time for a multi-actor approach. *Transport Policy* **37**:177–86.

Macharis, C. and Crompvoets, J. (2014) A stakeholder-based assessment framework applied to evaluate development scenarios for the spatial data infrastructure for Flanders. *Computers, Environment and Urban Systems* **46**:45–56.

Macharis, C. and Nijkamp, P. (2011) Possible bias in Multi Actor Multi Criteria transportation evaluation: issues and solutions. Research Memorandum 2011-13, Vrije Universiteit Amsterdam, Amsterdam. http://degree.ubvu.vu.nl/repec/vua/wpaper/pdf/20110031.pdf (accessed December 2017).

Macharis, C., Springael, J., De Brucker, K. and Verbeke, A. (2004) PROMETHEE and AHP: the design of operational synergies in multicriteria analysis: strengthening PROMETHEE with IDEAS of AHP. *European Journal of Operational Research* **153**(2):307–17.

Macharis, C., Turcksin, L. and Lebeau, K. (2012) Multi actor multi criteria analysis (MAMCA) as a tool to support sustainable decisions: state of use. *Decision Support Systems* **54**:610–20.

Marttunen, M., Mustajoki, J., Dufva, M. and Karjalainen, T.P. (2015) How to design and realize participation of stakeholders in MCDA processes? A framework for selecting an appropriate approach. *European Journal on Decision Processes* **1**(1–2):197–214

Mathur, S. (2014) *Innovation in Public Transport Finance: Property Value Capture.* Transport and Mobility Series. Farnham: Ashgate.

Mau-Crimmins, T., de Steiger, J.E. and Dennis, D. (2005) AHP as a means of improving public participation: a pre-post experiment with university students. *Forest Policy and Economics* **7**:501–14.

Medda, F.R. (2012) Land value capture finance for transport accessibility: a review. *Journal of Transport Geography* **25**:154–61.

Munda, G. (2004) Social multi-criteria evaluation: methodological foundations and operational consequences. *European Journal of Operational Research* **158**:662–77.

Riabacke, M., Danielson, M. and Ekenberg, L. (2012) State-of-the-art prescriptive criteria weight elicitation. *Advances in Decision Sciences* **2012**: 1–25.

Roukouni, A. (2016), Investigation of innovative financing schemes for transport projects. PhD Thesis, Aristotle University of Thessaloniki, Greece.

Roukouni, A. and Medda, F. (2012) Evaluation of Value Capture mechanisms as a funding source for urban transport: the case of London's Crossrail. *Procedia Social and Behavioral Sciences* **48**:2393–404.

Roukouni, A., Basbas, S., Stephanis, B. and Mintsis, G. (2015) Is VCF a relevant alternative for financing transport infrastructure? *Scientific Cooperations Journal of Civil Engineering and Architecture* **1**(1):18–24.

Roukouni, A., Macharis, C., Basbas, S., Stephanis, B. and Mintsis, G. (2018) Financing urban transportation infrastructure in a multi-actors environment: the role of value capture. *European Transport Research Review* **10**(14):1–19.

Rybeck, R. (2004) Using value capture to finance infrastructure and encourage compact development. *Public Works Management & Policy* **8**(4):249–60.

Saaty, T.L. (1977) A scaling method for priorities in hierarchical structures. *Journal of Mathematical Psychology* **15**:234–81.

Saaty, T.L. (1986) Axiomatic foundations of the Analytic Hierarchy Process. *Management Science* **32**(7):841–55.

Saaty, T.L. (1990) How to make a decision: the Analytic Hierarchy Process. *European Journal of Operational Research* **48**:9–26.

Saaty, T.L. (2005) The Analytic Hierarchy and Analytic Network Process for the measurement of intangible criteria and for decision making. In Figuera, J., Greco, S. and Ehrgott, M. (eds), *Multiple Criteria Decision Analysis: State of the Art Surveys*. International Series in Operations Research Management Science, New York: Springer, pp. 345–407.

Salon, D. (2014) Location value capture opportunities for urban public transport finance: a White Paper prepared for the Transit Leadership Summit, London, Regional Plan Association (RPA) and Volvo Research & Educational Foundations. http://library.rpa.org/pdf/TLS-2014-Research-Paper-Value-Capt ure.pdf (accessed December 2017).

Sclar, E.D. Lönnroth, M. and Wolmar, C. (eds) (2014) *Urban Access for the 21st Century: Finance and Governance Models for Transport Infrastructure*. New York and London: Routledge, Taylor & Francis Group.

Smith, J., Gihring, T. and Litman, T. (2015) Financing transit systems through value capture – an annotated bibliography. Victoria Transport Policy Institute. http://www.vtpi.org/smith.pdf (accessed December 2017).

Stough, R.R. and Rietveld, P. (1997) Institutional issues in transport systems. *Journal of Transport Geography* **5**(3):207–14.

Taschner, S. and Fiedler, M. (2009) D2.1 *Stakeholder Involvement Handbook. WP2 – Identification of User Needs and Good Practice Collection*. AENEAS Project. http://www.eltis.org/sites/eltis/files/tool/aeneas_stakeholderinvolvementhandboo k_0.pdf (accessed December 2017).

Thomopoulos, N., Grant-Muller, S. and Tight, M.R. (2009) Incorporating equity considerations in transport infrastructure evaluation: current practice and a proposed methodology. *Evaluation and Program Planning* **32**:351–9.

Tsamboulas, D. (2007) A tool for prioritizing multinational transport infrastructure investments. *Transport Policy* **14**:11–26.

Tsamboulas, D., Yiotis, G.S. and Panou, K.D. (1999) Use of multicriteria methods for assessment of transport projects. *Journal of Transportation Engineering* **125**(5):407–14.

Turcksin, L., Macharis, C., Lebeau, K. et al. (2011) A Multi Actor Multi Criteria framework to assess the stakeholder support for different biofuel options: the case of Belgium. *Energy Policy* **39**:200–14.

UN-HABITAT (2013) *The Economics and Financing of Urban Mobility in Planning and Design for Sustainable Urban Mobility, Global Report On Human Settlements*. New York: United Nations Human Settlement Program.

Vaidya, O.S. and Kumar, S. (2006) Analytic hierarchy process: an overview of applications. *European Journal of Operational Research* **169**:1–29.

Vargas, L.G. (1990) An overview of the analytic hierarchy process and its applications. *European Journal of Operational Research* **48**(1):2–8.

Van Wee, B. (2012) How suitable is CBA for the ex-ante evaluation of transport projects and policies? A discussion from the perspective of ethics. *Transport Policy* **19**:1–7.

Vermote, L., Macharis, C. and Putman, K. (2013) A road network for freight transport in Flanders: Multi Actor Multi Criteria Assessment of alternative ring ways. *Sustainability* **5**:4222–46.

Wefering, F., Rupprecht, S., Bührmann, S. and Böhler-Baedeker, S. (2013) Guidelines: Developing and Implementing a Sustainable Urban Mobility Plan.

European Commission, Directorate-General for Mobility and Transport. http://www.eltis.org/sites/eltis/files/guidelines-developing-and-implementing-a-sump_final_web_jan2014b.pdf (accessed December 2017).

Worsley, T. and Mackie, P. (2015) Transport policy, appraisal and decision-making. Royal Automobile Club Foundation for Motoring Ltd. http://www.racfoundation.org/assets/rac_foundation/content/downloadables/Transport_policy_appraisal_decision_making_worsley_mackie_May_2015_final_report.pdf (accessed December 2017).

Zhao, Z.J., Das, K.V. and Larson, K. (2012) Joint development as a value capture strategy for public transit finance. *Journal of Transport and Land Use* **5**(1):5–17.

8. Evaluating innovative solutions for sustainable city logistics: an enhanced understanding of stakeholder perceptions

Tom van Lier, Dries Meers, Heleen Buldeo Rai and Cathy Macharis

8.1 INTRODUCTION

Mechelen, a medium-sized Belgian city of 83,000 inhabitants, pursues an efficient and sustainable urban freight transport system by facilitating innovative pilots. Urban freight transport poses complex challenges to cities like Mechelen, whose medieval city structure is not fully complementary with large-scale logistics operations. In fact, a difficult balance exists between the increasing pedestrianization of the city center – aimed at providing a pleasant shopping environment – and the in-time supply of shops located in this same city center. It is for this reason that the city of Mechelen – further referred to as Mechelen – wants to implement innovative and sustainable solutions to get goods efficiently in and out of the city.

In this chapter, the Multi Actor Multi Criteria Analysis (MAMCA) methodology is applied to evaluate different possible measures to increase the sustainability of urban freight transport in Mechelen. Mechelen wants to analyse the support for these potential measures, and test the most suitable one(s) in a pilot. The analysis follows the MAMCA framework: (1) selection of six potential urban freight measures to improve sustainability; (2) identification of the relevant stakeholder groups; (3) identification of stakeholders' objectives and evaluation criteria; (4) weighting of the criteria by the stakeholders; (5) evaluation of the scenarios; (6) discussion of the results; and (7) processing the results and implementation of a pilot.

The MAMCA approach was chosen due to its ability to assess the perceptions of the stakeholders about different potential pilot projects, to look for support and to potentially find participants for the pilots. An important decision in setting up the MAMCA was to allow stakeholders to evaluate the scenarios. Parallel, similar scenarios implanted elsewhere were reviewed to evaluate the scenarios based on scientific literature and reports. Comparing both results allowed checking whether the impacts expected by the stakeholders correspond to the actual or estimated impact of similar pilots in other cities.

Finally, the chapter discusses how the results of the MAMCA are used in practice in Mechelen to set up real-life pilots.

8.2 LITERATURE

Research interest in urban freight transport problems and solutions has increased during recent decades with an intensification of research output and a conference dedicated to the topic since 1999. With the concept of city logistics, Taniguchi et al. (2001) point to the practice of optimizing logistics activities in cities by considering effects on traffic, safety, energy and environment. The interest for sustainable urban freight operations by policy makers coincides with the increasing (public) concern about environmental problems and safety and security issues. Both market initiatives and policy measures can help in tackling these issues. The policy measures can be subdivided into pricing initiatives, licensing and regulation initiatives and parking and unloading initiatives (Quak, 2008). Companies can also take initiatives, irrespective of such (stringent) policies or with the explicit support of local authorities. Russo and Comi (2010) classify measures that can be taken by public authorities, private companies or public-private partnerships into measures related to: material infrastructure (for example, setup of an urban consolidation center), immaterial infrastructure (for example, use of intelligent transportation systems (ITS) for smart routing), equipment (for example, using other vehicles types, a modal shift) and governance. It is, however, challenging for cities to select the most appropriate measures, given their limited resources and their potential effect on different stakeholders. Strikingly, Macharis and Kin (2017) argue that the implementation of such policy measures often fail due to the lack of stakeholder involvement. A second reason for the unsuccessful implementation of policy measures is the lack of insight in the effects of the measure, not only impacting different subsystems but also different people (Macharis and Milan, 2015). To complicate matters, reliable data on freight transport performance, let alone the potential effects of new policy measures, is often incomplete or lacking (Leonardi et al., 2009). For these reasons, Buldeo Rai et al. (2017) developed a toolbox, consisting of four evaluation methodologies, relevant for the evaluation of urban freight transport policy measures: the Cost-Effectiveness Analysis (CEA), the Social Cost-Benefit

Analysis (SCBA), the Multi Criteria Analysis (MCA) and the MAMCA as well as an extensive indicator framework. The context-based needs of a specific case study require the selection of the most appropriate method or combination of methods. For the case study elaborated in this chapter, the MAMCA seemed most appropriate.

Multiple arguments can be given for applying the MAMCA in this case study. First, it allowed us to compare rather different scenarios in a straightforward manner. Second, the MAMCA was set up in a stakeholder workshop, allowing direct interaction with all relevant stakeholder groups involved. We expected that the evaluated policy measures would have multiple effects on the city and the stakeholder groups. This approach not only allows insight to be gained into the preferences of the stakeholders, but also on their perception of the proposed measures. *Ex ante*, this approach also allows the attitude of stakeholders to be influenced, to adapt the scenarios towards stakeholders' needs and for the local authorities to interact with the relevant stakeholder groups. Following Dablanc et al. (2011), this should enhance the acceptability of the implemented urban freight transport measure. Macharis et al. (2014) argue that unconsidered stakeholder interests are often the basis for unsuccessful implementations. A third argument for applying the MAMCA was the limited availability of both time and money to conduct deeper impact analyses based on extensive data collections, since the MAMCA allows the use of qualitative evaluations.

The MAMCA has already been successfully applied in the context of urban freight transport. Verlinde and Macharis (2016) compare different scenarios about off-hour deliveries to supermarkets in Brussels. Their analysis showed that a shift towards such deliveries should receive overall support. Verlinde et al. (2014) apply the MAMCA to research when a mobile depot for last-mile deliveries and first-mile pick-ups could become profitable and how stakeholders would be impacted. Milan et al. (2015) discuss the case of pick-ups at Oxfam donation banks in the UK. Lebeau et al. (2017) use the MAMCA methodology to assess the support of stakeholder groups for the electrification of city logistics. The ultimate assessment method, however, does not exist (yet) and Lagorio et al. (2016) state that there is not yet a shared perspective on how to involve stakeholders in urban freight transport decision-making, but given these earlier references and the specific challenges that Mechelen faces in this case study (consideration of multiple alternatives, demand for active stakeholder involvement and awareness), the authors are confident that the MAMCA is an appropriate methodology to analyse the problem and contribute to a solution.

8.3   MAMCA APPLICATION

Mechelen developed a strong interest in its urban freight transport system and for that reason launched a study involving freight trip data collection (Technum, 2015). The study identified the most pressing issues related to urban freight transport, which were the current time window policy, issues with (un)loading locations, poor traffic flows and parking problems. Mechelen has the ambition to become 'climate neutral', it participates in the European Covenant of Mayors initiative and aims to actively support the local retailers. Important measures currently in place are the so-called 'circulation plan', a weight limit for vehicles entering the city, and a limited traffic zone with time windows for delivery and pick-up in the inner city. Mechelen is nevertheless looking for additional measures to improve the sustainability of its urban freight transport system. The following sections describe the stepwise application of the MAMCA.

8.4   SELECTION OF POLICY MEASURES TO IMPROVE SUSTAINABILITY

A consortium consisting of civil servants from Mechelen, VIL (a logistics industry organization) and the authors of this chapter was established to delineate the potential policy measures to be evaluated in the MAMCA. The composition of the consortium ensured the combination of local logistics knowledge, easy access to a stakeholder pool, academic knowledge on city logistics (pilots) and experience with setting up local pilots.

As numerous actions to improve the sustainability of city logistics operations have been researched and tested (Lagorio et al., 2016), we started from a long list of potential pilots. The consortium finally selected a shortlist of six potential measures. The selection criteria were the following: diversity of measures, feasibility, suitability, cost and non-exclusiveness of participants. The six final policy measures (or scenarios in the MAMCA terminology) are the following (Buldeo Rai et al., 2017):

1. *Neutral party assesses retailers' shared transport options.* A neutral party collects anonymized data on transportation assignments that occur on a regular and planned basis, based on which consolidation possibilities are identified. Local retailers are enabled to adjust their deliveries in accordance with their logistics service provider. In this way, deliveries of different retailers can be consolidated.

2. *Bundling of flows using a web platform (online auction).* An online web platform for ad hoc transport assignments from and to Mechelen is

set up, in which logistics service providers (LSPs), local retailers and carriers are able to input their assignments. Based on this input, other carriers can offer to take up deliveries in their routing and consolidate them.

3. *Mandatory registration for use of (un)loading zones.* Carriers can reserve a loading and unloading spot online, via a mobile application. Online registration is required to use these zones, which are only available within certain time windows. Traffic wardens find out online whether a zone is reserved and occupied. Extra surveillance is executed to check if reservations were not made.

4. *Time windows based on sustainability criteria.* Deliveries using cleaner vehicles are stimulated by applying broader time windows for emission-free vehicles and narrower time windows for less clean vehicles. Surveillance is executed through the use of existing cameras when entering the city. A phased implementation gives carriers time to adjust their vehicle fleet.

5. *Urban consolidation centers.* Mechelen stimulates and supports the use of current and planned consolidation centers with awareness campaigns. Private partners manage the consolidation center and offer additional services for retailers: warehousing with on-demand delivery, labeling, packaging, returns and pick-ups.

6. *Network of lockers.* Open-brand – which means that all LSPs can use them – lockers are placed at strategic locations. The lockers are used for consolidating deliveries to retailers that receive multiple, small deliveries, but also for small deliveries, e-commerce and return deliveries to retailers, carriers and consumers. The lockers are available 24/7 and notifications are made when goods are delivered.

8.5   SELECTION OF RELEVANT STAKEHOLDER GROUPS

Different authors identify the relevant stakeholder groups in city logistics settings. Behrends (2011) classifies the relevant stakeholders in city logistics problems into shippers and receivers, authorities and transport operators. Taniguchi (2014) identifies the same main stakeholder groups, except for the receivers and adds the residents. The stakeholders that should be included in the evaluation of a certain case study can be selected from this range of actors, and divisions into subgroups can be made when required to address (expected) heterogeneity within stakeholder groups. Based on the literature reviewed and in consultation with the consortium, representatives of five stakeholder groups were invited to the workshop.

Representatives of the following groups agreed to participate in the workshop: logistics service providers, residents, local retailers, public services (including IT services as well as representation from the cultural center) and city council members (local government). The public services were added as a separate group of receivers (besides the retailers), as they have different needs and requirements, and because the local authorities believe that city services can play an active role in city logistics, leading by example. In total, 36 invited participants contributed to the MAMCA workshop.

8.6   STAKEHOLDERS' ASSESSMENT CRITERIA AND WEIGHTS

At the workshop, the stakeholders could not change the proposed scenarios but were asked instead to validate a series of criteria and if important ones were missing, to provide additional ones. These criteria were defined by the stakeholder groups as prime concerns regarding urban freight transport. The proposed criteria were based on a set of indicators provided in a policy assessment framework (Buldeo Rai et al., 2017) and complemented with criteria formulated from the different stakeholder groups' perspectives. The analysis of Van den broeck (2016) confirms that the criteria proposed by the authors correspond to a large extent to those mentioned in similar studies. The stakeholders could adjust the criteria during the workshop to obtain a validated set of criteria for each group. As criteria are in general not valued equally by the stakeholder groups, they allocated weights by using Analytic Hierarchy Process (AHP) pairwise comparisons using the MAMCA software. Both the decision on the final set of criteria and the criteria weights were based on consensus in the stakeholder groups. Working with such a consensus-based approach can influence the outcome of the analysis, especially when strong heterogeneity occurs within a stakeholder group. A major advantage is the fact that stakeholders within a group are required to discuss the importance and potential impacts with each other, which enables more informed decision-making. A drawback could be when dominant characters have greater influence on the final 'consensuses'. In the MAMCA workshop, a high number of LSPs participated, requiring them to be split up into two separate groups. Their criteria weights and evaluations were aggregated, but their results could also be discussed separately. The first group contained mainly smaller, 'younger' companies that do not operate in an international setting, while the second group mainly contained larger and older players. The comparison between the results of both groups allows some insight to be gained into the heterogeneity within the LSP sample. The criteria of all stakeholder groups and the corresponding weights are displayed in Table 8.1.

Next, we can ascertain whether the weights from the stakeholders are in line with those attributed in similar MAMCA evaluations (Lebeau et al., 2017; Milan et al., 2015; Verlinde and Macharis, 2016; Verlinde et al., 2014). In general, the weights of the stakeholders seem to be very much in line with those from earlier workshops, at least for the stakeholder groups that were already questioned before. Differences can be attributed to – among other reasons – different problem contexts, criteria definitions and the number of criteria included. Slightly surprising, however, was that the LSPs in our workshop gave a relative low weight to profit, especially when compared to employee satisfaction. The retailers who participated in the workshop seem to pay more attention to the quality of the delivery compared to the price paid. The results for the residents were not surprising, although the low importance attributed to accessibility is remarkable, but in line with the weights derived in Lebeau et al. (2017). The weights derived from the local authorities were also slightly different when compared to previous research: with greater importance attached to implementation cost and lower weight for air quality and noise nuisance.

8.7   EVALUATION OF THE SCENARIOS

In the second part of the MAMCA workshop, stakeholder groups assessed the policy measures by indicating for each criterion if a measure scored better, neutral or worse compared to the actual situation, which we named the 'business as usual' (BAU) scenario. The scenarios were compared to the BAU scenario using a qualitative scale of PROMETHEE: 'positive', 'slightly positive', 'neutral', 'slightly negative' or 'negative' on all stakeholder groups' criteria. The evaluation of the BAU scenario was fixed, scoring 'neutral' on all criteria. This allowed an easier interpretation of the results in the analysis. All stakeholder groups received the same basic explanation of the different scenarios that needed evaluation. The evaluation itself was thus based on this explanation and the stakeholder groups' assessments, based on experience, expertise and estimation. This approach allowed insights to be gained on stakeholders' perception in a relatively easy, fast and cost-effective manner. In the discussion section, the outcomes of the evaluations are compared to examples of results of similar solutions in other cities, to assess whether stakeholders' perceptions are grounded.

Table 8.1   Stakeholder criteria and weight derived from the workshop

Stakeholder	Criterion	Criterion definition	Weight (%)
Logistics service providers	Maximal profit	Maximal positive difference between revenues and costs for logistics services	10
	Service quality	Satisfied shippers and retailers	30
	Return on investments	Positive expected return on investments	24
	Employee satisfaction	Employees are satisfied with work and working environment	23
	Attention to environment and noise	Positive attitude with regards to environmental impact	13
Local retailers	Minimal cost	Minimal cost for receiving goods	24
	Qualitative deliveries	Deliveries that do not disturb retailers' operations: timely, fast and without damage	63
	Attractive shopping environment	Attractive shopping environment for customers	10
	Attention to environment and noise	Positive attitude with regards to environmental impact	3
Residents	Good air quality	Reduction in air polluting emissions	37
	Minimal noise nuisance	Minimal noise nuisance	12
	Attractive shopping environment	Attractive shopping environment for consumers	6
	Good accessibility	Minimal congestion	4
	High traffic safety	Less traffic victims and improved safety, particularly with regards to vulnerable road users	41
City council	Positive business environment	Positive business environment for retailers	17
	Good air quality	Reduction in air polluting emissions	11
	Feasible enforcement	Measures that are easy to enforce	2
	Minimal cost of policy measure	Minimal costs for measure and enforcement	17
	Good accessibility	Minimal congestion	13
	Broad support	Support of inhabitants for measures	10

Table 8.1   (continued)

Stakeholder	Criterion	Criterion definition	Weight (%)
	Minimal noise nuisance	Minimal noise nuisance	3
	High traffic safety	Less traffic victims and improved safety, particularly with regards to vulnerable road users	26
City council services	Minimal cost	Minimal cost for receiving goods	5
	Qualitative deliveries	Deliveries that do not disturb retailers' operations: timely, fast and without damage	44
	Attractive shopping environment	Attractive shopping environment for customers	41
	Attention to environment and noise	Positive attitude with regards to environmental impact	10

8.8   DISCUSSION OF THE RESULTS

The multi-stakeholder view (Figure 8.1) shows a very dispersed image. All scenarios are compared to the BAU scenario, which was evaluated the same by all stakeholder groups. This means that all scenarios with a positive score are considered better that the BAU and all scenarios with a negative score worse. The figure illustrates that some actor groups, such as the citizens and the local authorities, are open to most pilots while the retailers seem to oppose all pilots. Other groups, such as the LSPs and the city services, are open to a few pilots, but more reluctant to others. None of the proposed pilot solutions are supported unanimously by all the stakeholders involved.

Half of the measures are judged worse than the BAU scenario by three stakeholder groups and therefore seem challenging to implement. This concerns scenarios 1, 2 and 3. The two bundling scenarios are evaluated negatively by the LSPs, retailers and city services. Only the actor groups not directly involved in the physical logistics process (citizens and local authorities) seem positive. The mandatory registration for (un)loading zones is, however, supported by LSPs and considered acceptable by retailers, but not by the citizens, city services and local authorities.

More stakeholder groups seem to support solutions 4, 5 and 6. The network of lockers seems interesting for LSPs, citizens and local authorities.

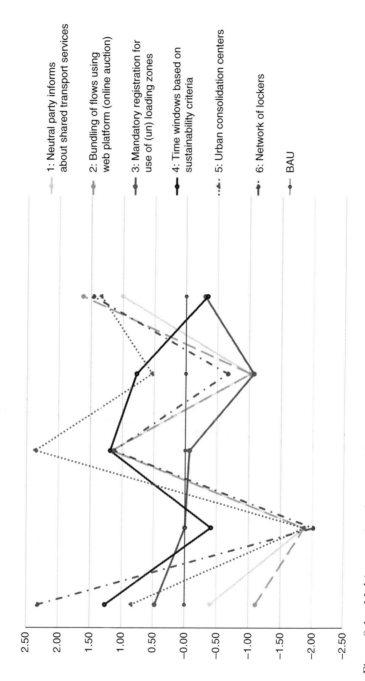

1: Neutral party informs
about shared transport services

2: Bundling of flows using
web platform (online auction)

3: Mandatory registration for
use of (un) loading zones

4: Time windows based on
sustainability criteria

5: Urban consolidation centers

6: Network of lockers

BAU

2.50
2.00
1.50
1.00
0.50
-0.00
-0.50
-1.00
-1.50
-2.00
-2.50

Figure 8.1   Multi-actor view (own setup)

City services are slightly opposed, but the retailers are the strongest opponents. Most stakeholders support the stimulation of urban consolidation centers, again apart from the retailers who strongly oppose. In addition, the scenario with time windows based on sustainability criteria could be an alternative to further investigate, as only retailers and local authorities slightly oppose. For the local authorities, however, it is still the least preferred alternative.

Looking solely at the multi-stakeholder view, it seems challenging to select an appropriate alternative. A deeper analysis might, however, show opportunities.

First, the local retailers object to all changes. They estimate that all alternatives, apart from the mandatory registration, will have very negative effects on their prime criteria, which are qualitative deliveries and minimal costs. As the local authorities also attach a great deal of importance to the criterion of creating a positive business environment, this issue deserves particular attention. The MAMCA analysis indeed shows that the local retailers perceive that most alternatives oppose their objectives, but it does not show on what this negative perception is based.

Second, the citizens seem to welcome most of the alternatives. This stakeholder group evaluates all measures as equally good or better than the current situation. This might indicate that room for improvement exists in Mechelen and that citizens are welcoming new initiatives.

Third, LSPs show interest in most alternatives, apart from those focusing on the consolidation of flows that are currently handled by different LSPs. A deeper analysis of the results obtained in the workshop, however, shows that not all LSPs object to this idea of consolidation. The first group, containing mainly smaller and younger companies, seemed to attach greater importance to environmental criteria and service quality, while the second group, containing mainly larger and older players, gave greater importance to profit and the return on investment. In addition, the evaluation of the alternatives differed. The results show that the first group was open to all alternatives, scoring alternatives 1, 2 and 3 as neutral or slightly positive, while the other three were considered very positive. The second group of LSPs also showed a strong interest in the lockers solution and a moderate interest in alternatives 3 and 4. The two bundling scenarios were considered very negative and this LSP group also opposed the urban consolidation center solution.

Finally, the local authorities seem open to four policy measures, while two others are estimated to be worse than the BAU. The mandatory registration for (un)loading and the time windows require a top-down regulation, while the measures that are preferred are much more market-driven.

We are aware that perception can play a role in the stakeholders' evaluation of the alternatives. Looking at the evaluation of similar solutions in a similar context can shed some light on the positive or negative perceptions expressed in the workshop, which do not match the outcomes of city logistics pilots elsewhere. After the discussion of the pilot implementation, stakeholder perceptions are compared to literature findings for the selected pilots. The final choice of a pilot by the local authorities is thus challenging, given the non-agreement among stakeholders on acceptable solutions and possibly unjustified (negative) perceptions of certain aspects of the alternatives considered. This required increased insight into both the potential impact of measures and the grounds for the negative perceptions of stakeholder groups. Such insight could help in identifying proper abatement measures, potentially satisfying disadvantaged stakeholder groups.

8.9   IMPLEMENTATION OF A PILOT

The final elaboration and implementation of the pilot(s) was up to the local authorities.[1] Even though no alternative was accepted by all stakeholder groups, the MAMCA still gave useful input for the further elaboration of the pilot(s) and for the reevaluation of current policies impacting city logistics. In hindsight, the local authorities stated that the MAMCA workshop was a good approach in seeking support for potential pilots and in identifying stakeholder-related bottlenecks in their implementation (Recour, 2017).

The choice of pilot projects was based on the MAMCA evaluation. Two of the scenarios that were supported by most groups were chosen for implementation: the open-brand lockers and the urban consolidation center scenario. In all cases, the retailers had to be convinced of all possible pilots in any case. Special attention was paid to this group, given their reluctance to the proposed pilots. First, the local authorities administered a survey to gain better insight behind the reasoning and reluctance of the retailers, but limited participation led to unusable results. Second, different retailers were questioned individually about their reluctance regarding price and service quality and on their potential interest in the two selected pilots. Third, a major precondition for the pilots was put forward, being that the use of the pilot services would not come at an additional (transport) cost for the retailers. In case additional costs would be incurred as a result of the pilot, the city arranged that these had to be borne by the LSP(s) involved. Despite these additional efforts, the practical elaboration

---

[1]   The pilots have not started yet, so no results can be compared to the evaluations of the stakeholders.

of the pilots followed the original description. The urban consolidation center scenario was, however, slightly elaborated, given that the last-mile delivery is to be executed by the cargo bikes of a specific LSP.

8.10   PERCEPTIONS IN SCENARIO EVALUATIONS

As explained previously, wrong perceptions on the outcome of pilots can influence the results of the presented MAMCA. Given that the pilots are yet to be implemented, we compare the evaluations of the stakeholders to some experiences with similar pilots in other cities.

A first example relates to the urban consolidation center pilot. Different researchers recognize the potential of urban consolidation centers to reduce the number of trips and the distance covered (Dablanc et al., 2011) and to reduce operational transport costs (Macharis and Kin, 2017; MDS Transmodal, 2012). The implementation should also result in more reliable deliveries and increased revenues for LSPs exploiting the center (Browne et al., 2005). Nevertheless, challenges still exist for setting up profitable distribution centers. The above findings are not in accordance with some of the stakeholders' expectations. In particular, the local retailers expect increased transport costs and a worse service level.

An often-cited example of automated pick-up locker boxes is Packstation. Dablanc et al. (2011) claim that this system enables the bundling of deliveries, a higher rate of successful deliveries and a decrease in operational costs for the LSPs. Residents can benefit from less air pollution and more efficient energy usage. Torrentellé et al. (2012) also stress the reduced delivery costs, which can also benefit the consumer using the lockers if transport prices are accordingly decreased. However, additional effort needs to be performed to pick up the delivery, which takes extra time. Also, the evaluation of the service quality aspect is dubious, as indeed the deliveries have to be picked up by the receiver, but this pick-up can be performed during off-hours and combined with other possible deliveries, avoiding missed deliveries at the same time (Augereau and Dablanc, 2008).

These two examples show that participation in the pilots could be beneficial for the retailers in Mechelen, especially when they have the guarantee that transport prices will not increase compared to their earlier deliveries. This analysis thus indicates that the pilots can also potentially bring advantages to the stakeholder groups that had rather negative perceptions during the MAMCA workshop.

8.11   CONCLUSION

In this chapter, we described the application of the MAMCA in a city logistics case study. As the local authorities in Mechelen want to set up pilot projects to increase the sustainability of deliveries to retailers, a workshop was set up to assess the objectives of the relevant stakeholder groups and to evaluate the proposed pilot projects.

The results show a very diverse image. All scenarios are compared to the BAU scenario, and not one pilot is preferred to the BAU by all stakeholder groups. Strikingly, the retailers reckon that none of the proposed pilots can improve the current situation, based on their concern for delivery costs and service quality. Examples from similar practices in other cities, however, show that these fears might be groundless. This finding therefore played an important role in the final selection and further elaboration of the implemented pilots.

The local authorities decided to implement the two alternatives that were supported by most stakeholder groups and tried to mitigate the retailers' price-related concern. Specifically, for this case study, further research could investigate to what extent the different stakeholders' perceptions about the implemented pilots corresponded to reality.

REFERENCES

Augereau, V., Dablanc, L., 2008. An evaluation of recent pick-up point experiments in European cities: the rise of two competing models? In: Taniguchi, E., Thompson, R.G. (eds), *Innovations in City Logistics* (pp. 303–20). New York: Nova Science.

Behrends, S., 2011. Urban freight transport sustainability – the interaction of urban freight and intermodal transport. Chalmers University of Technology, Gothenburg.

Browne, M., Sweet, M., Woodburn, A., Allen, J., 2005. *Urban Freight Consolidation Centres: Final Report.* London: University of Westminster.

Buldeo Rai, H., van Lier, T., Meers, D., Macharis, C., 2017. Improving urban freight transport sustainability: policy assessment framework & case study. *Research in Transportation Economics* **64**, 26–35.

Dablanc, L., Diziain, D., Levifve, H., 2011. Urban freight consultations in the Paris region. *European Transport Research Review* **3**, 47–57. doi:10.1007/s12544-011-0049-2.

Lagorio, A., Pinto, R., Golini, R., 2016. Research in urban logistics: a systematic literature review. *International Journal of Physical Distribution & Logistics Management* **46**, 908–31. doi:10.1108/IJPDLM-01-2016-0008.

Lebeau, P., Macharis, C., Van Mierlo, J., Janjevic, M., 2017. Implementing an urban consolidation centre: involving stakeholders in a bottom-up approach. *Transportation Research Part A: Policy and Practice.* Under review.

Leonardi, J., Browne, M., Allen, J. et al. 2009. *Green Logistics WM3: Data Management and Data Collection Techniques for Sustainable Distribution.* Data needs and data review for Green Logistics research report, London.

Macharis, C., Kin, B., 2017. The 4 A's of sustainable city distribution: innovative solutions and challenges ahead. *International Journal of Sustainable Transportation* **11**, 59–71. doi:10.1080/15568318.2016.1196404.

Macharis, C., Milan, L., 2015. Transition through dialogue: a stakeholder based decision process for cities: the case of city distribution. *Habitat International* **45**, 82–91. doi:10.1016/j.habitatint.2014.06.026.

Macharis, C., Milan, L., Verlinde, S., 2014. A stakeholder-based multicriteria evaluation framework for city distribution. *Research in Transportation Business & Management* **11**, 75–84. doi:10.1016/j.rtbm.2014.06.004.

MDS Transmodal, 2012. *DG MOVE European Commission: Study on Urban Freight Transport.* Chester.

Milan, L., Kin, B., Verlinde, S., Macharis, C., 2015. Multi Actor Multi Criteria analysis for sustainable city distribution: a new assessment framework. *International Journal of Multicriteria Decision Making* **5**, 334–54. doi:10.1504/IJMCDM.2015.074088.

Quak, H.J., 2008. *Sustainability of Urban Freight Transport: Retail Distribution and Local Regulations in Cities.* Erasmus University Rotterdam.

Recour, A., 2017. Interview by D. Meers, March 27, 2017.

Russo, F., Comi, A., 2010. A classification of city logistics measures and connected impacts. *Procedia – Social and Behavioral Sciences* **2**, 6355–65. doi:10.1016/j.sbspro.2010.04.044.

Taniguchi, E., 2014. Concepts of city logistics for sustainable and liveable cities. *Procedia – Social and Behavioral Sciences*, 8th International Conference on City Logistics **151**, 310–17. doi:10.1016/j.sbspro.2014.10.029.

Taniguchi, E., Thompson, R.G., Yamada, T., van Duin, R., 2001. *City Logistics: Network Modelling and Intelligent Transport Systems.* Oxford: Pergamon.

Technum, 2015. Haalbaarheid stedelijk distrbitutie centrum Mechelen.

Torrentellé M., Tsamboulas D., Moraiti P., 2012. Elicitation of the good practices on UFT, CE Liege Deliverable D2.1, Available at http:// www.cliege.eu (accessed January 20, 2015).

Van den broeck, B., 2016. Duurzame Stadsdistributie: een gevalsstudie van Mechelen. Vrije Universiteit Brussel.

Verlinde, S., Macharis, C., 2016. Who is in favor of off-hour deliveries to Brussels supermarkets? Applying Multi Actor Multi Criteria Analysis (MAMCA) to measure stakeholder support. *Transportation Research Procedia* **12**, 522–32. doi:10.1016/j.trpro.2016.02.008.

Verlinde, S., Macharis, C., Milan, L., Kin, B., 2014. Does a mobile depot make urban deliveries faster, more sustainable and more economically viable: results of a pilot test in Brussels. *Transportation Research Procedia* **4**, 361–73. doi:10.1016/j.trpro.2014.11.027.

9. Multi Actor Multi Criteria Analysis for educational purposes and practical-oriented research: examples from the Amsterdam University of Applied Sciences

Susanne Balm

9.1 INTRODUCTION

9.1.1 Context

The Amsterdam University of Applied Sciences (AUAS) is located in the Netherlands and has around 46,000 students, 3,900 employees, about 80 bachelor and masters' programmes within seven faculties and six broad research programmes that are carried out together with academics and professionals. One of the research programmes is Urban Technology, which is embedded in the Faculty of Technology (Figure 9.1). The Faculty of Technology educates engineers with bachelor programmes in Aviation, Built and Environment, Engineering, Forensic Science, Logistics, Maritime Studies and Mathematical Engineering. Considering the fast changing world and rapid development of technology, the "engineer of the future" needs to be inventive, entrepreneurial, flexible and able to learn continuously (Faculteitsplan Techniek, 2015–20).

AUAS aims to inspire students to develop creative solutions and sustainable innovations for current problems and for the future: to connect today with tomorrow (AUAS, 2017). Students work together with a variety of professionals on solutions in particular for the region of Amsterdam. *Creating Tomorrow*, the slogan of AUAS, represents the active societal role that AUAS fulfils. Practical-oriented research is an important component of the educational programmes offered by AUAS. By combining education and research, AUAS aims to contribute to the development of professional practice and society in and around Amsterdam.

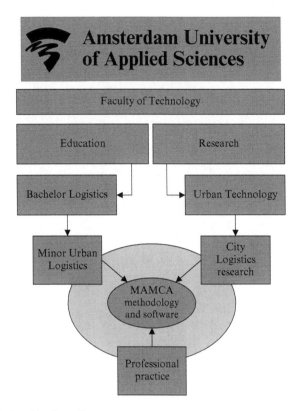

Source: Designed by the author.

Figure 9.1   Practical-oriented research in AUAS

AUAS carries out practical-oriented research to achieve the following societal goals (Vereniging van Hogescholen, 2016): (1) make education up-to-date (responsive to changes); (2) improve the quality of graduates; and (3) innovate professional practice. Practical-oriented research is driven by questions from professional practice and education. The research contributes directly to the professional development of students. This leads to a unique interaction between education, research and practice (Figure 9.2).

The research programme Urban Technology develops and tests technical solutions for complex and intractable problems that arise in cities. The multi-disciplinary projects address challenges relating to urban design, logistics and mobility, smart energy systems and circular economy. This includes questions like:

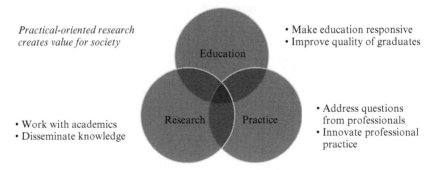

Practical-oriented research
creates value for society

• Make education responsive
• Improve quality of graduates

• Work with academics
• Disseminate knowledge

• Address questions
  from professionals
• Innovate professional
  practice

Source: Designed by the author.

Figure 9.2   Relationship between education, research and practice

- How do we ensure that the city remains accessible when public space is getting scarcer?
- How do we prepare cities for the effects of climate change, such as extreme rainfall and heat waves?
- How do we develop smart technologies to reduce the need for fossil fuels?

By developing practical-oriented knowledge, in close cooperation with academics and professionals from the particular disciplines, the Urban Technology programme aims to contribute to a sustainable, livable and connected city. A mix of lecturers, teachers, researchers, PhD students and AUAS students work together within projects. The collaboration with the educational programmes within and beyond the faculty is intensified continuously. We further elaborate on this by taking a closer look at research on city logistics.

9.1.2   City Logistics and Multi Actor Multi Criteria Analysis (MAMCA)

City logistics is very diverse. It includes supply of shops, offices, the hospitality industry, construction sites, field service work, home delivery and collection of waste. Cities face increasing pressure of freight and service deliveries, which are often carried out with commercial delivery vans and large trucks. It leads to congestion, poor air quality, problems with noise and safety, and nuisance for the environment. Freight vehicles need to share the space with other road users such as cyclists, pedestrians, personal cars and a growing number of cargo bikes. Politicians, entrepreneurs and citizens want an attractive environment, without a lot of space being allocated for freight vehicles and with clean air. Therefore, various cities, including Amsterdam, have imposed rules that restrict access by polluting and/or large vehicles at certain times and locations (for example, environmental zones) (Ploos van Amstel, 2015).

The City Logistics research group[1] at AUAS is closely connected to, and provides input for, policy development and implementation in Amsterdam. The research group works closely with logistics service providers, vehicles suppliers, shippers, logistics clients, other knowledge institutions and teachers and students. Cooperation with students and teachers from AUAS takes place by providing content (material and persons) for courses, defining assignments for internships and research/graduation projects (act as principle/client for students) and exchanging networks. The MAMCA workshop is an example of how the City Logistics research group provides content for the educational programmes at AUAS, specifically for the minor Urban Logistics (Figure 9.1).

The minor[2] Urban Logistics at AUAS addresses the increase of freight and mobility in cities and according challenges: How to deliver to shops and consumers smartly and efficiently? Which clean vehicle and ICT technologies can be used? How do people behave when they move through cities? How to prevent congestion? The minor offers a combination of theory, practical assignments, company visits and personal development.

The MAMCA is a valuable method to develop and evaluate solutions for urban logistics problems. For this reason, the MAMCA has been incorporated in the minor since 2015. The students learn about MAMCA theory, attend a MAMCA workshop and are encouraged to apply the MAMCA in their research assignment. It contributes to the goals of the "Educational board" which states that students from a University of Applied Sciences need to acquire research competences (Onderwijsraad, 2014). The following sections present examples of how the MAMCA has been used and their outcomes.

---

[1] Dr Walther Ploos van Amstel, professor City Logistics, started the research group City Logistics at AUAS, as part of the research programme Urban Technology of the Faculty of Technology, in 2014.

[2] A minor is a 20-week programme that students from different disciplines can choose and for which they obtain 30 ECTS (European Credit Transfer and Accumulation System).

9.2 CASE 1: MAMCA WORKSHOP CONSTRUCTION LOGISTICS[3]

The MAMCA workshop for students of the minor Urban Logistics was first developed in 2015. At that time, AUAS was developing a new campus building. In 2016 it was decided to cancel the construction plans. The case is the situation as it was presented to the students in 2015.

9.2.1 Application Case Description

AUAS is developing a new campus building in the inner city of Amsterdam, called the Conradhuis. Sustainability is important for AUAS and, in line with that, the organization aims to build the most sustainable campus of the Netherlands. However, the construction project is complex for several reasons. First, the location of the construction site, which is near the Amstel River, is next to a very busy intersection (Marnixstraat/ Wibautstraat) and there is barely any space for inventory on site. Second, the site is surrounded by campus buildings and student apartments that are already in use. This means that there are many citizens, cyclists and pedestrians around the site. Recently, the University of Amsterdam, a close partner of AUAS, has experienced several disputes with local citizens during construction works, which led to delays and negative publication. Therefore, AUAS recognizes the importance of a multi-actor multi-criteria approach when deciding on construction and transport alternatives (time windows, modalities, road access and so on) and mitigating measures (compensation for nuisance, sound block fences and so on).

9.2.2 Elicitation of the Alternatives

Based on an analysis of the local situation, stakeholder consultation and literature (Quak et al., 2011; STRAIGHTSOL, 2012; Landqvist and Rowland, 2014), three possible alternatives were identified and presented to the students. First, the business as usual (BAU) represents the situation in which no action is taken, meaning that freight vehicles arrive and depart irregularly during the day, leading to fragmented deliveries. The three potential logistics solutions are:

1. *Night deliveries*: goods are delivered with trucks at night (before morning peak hours).

---

[3] Text for this case has been used in a paper for the Transportation Research Board (Macharis et al., 2016).

2. *Urban consolidation centre (UCC) and electric vehicles (EV)*: impos-
    ing a central delivery address at the city border, after which goods
    are consolidated and delivered with electric freight vehicles to the
    construction site.
3. *Urban consolidation centre (UCC) and waterway transport*: imposing a
    central delivery address at the city border, after which goods are consol-
    idated and delivered by waterway transport near the construction site.

These solutions were chosen as they are sufficiently distinctive and compre-
hensible for students that have just started to learn about city logistics, even
without detailed information. It was decided to leave the interpretation of
the alternatives to a large extent to the students.

9.2.3   Stakeholder Groups and Criteria

Five stakeholder groups as well as their objectives are identified as being
involved in the project. The objectives are based on the local situation
as well as a literature review focusing on city (construction) logistics
(STRAIGHTSOL, 2014). The five stakeholder groups are: logistics service
provider, supplier (construction wholesale), building contractor, (receiver)
citizen and municipality. The students were assigned to these groups and
asked to project themselves into the stakeholder's position and objectives.
They were informed about the various possible criteria of each stakeholder
group during an introductory presentation. For example, citizens desire a
certain maximum noise level, public space (for example, to park the car
or for children to play) and traffic safety. Suppliers and builders want to
deliver/receive a high level of service with low transport costs. Logistic
service providers aim for profitable operations and satisfied employees.
The municipality wants to have an attractive environment for citizens and
companies, with little enforcement. An overview of all the criteria per
stakeholder group is presented in Table 9.1.

  The students, alias specific stakeholders, were first asked to give weights
to their criteria by using a pairwise comparison method, namely, the 1 to
9 Saaty scale (Analytical Hierarchy Process, AHP). Each group contained
four students who discussed the attribution of the weights of the criteria
and were asked to come to a joint decision (they were free to decide how
they aggregated individual opinions). Per stakeholder group the sum
of the weights is 1. Table 9.1 below shows the weights of the respective
criteria. The weights give a first insight into the preferences of the different
stakeholders with regard to their criteria.

  The LSP attributes almost equal importance to four of its criteria
except employee satisfaction. For the supplier, the quality of the service

Table 9.1   Stakeholder groups with their weighted criteria (case I)

Actor	Criterion	Criterion definition	Weight
Logistics service provider (LSP)	High level service	Receiver and supplier satisfaction	0.21
	Employee satisfaction	Employees are satisfied with their work and working environment	0.04
	Profitable operations	Making profit by providing logistics services	0.26
	Viability of investment	A positive return on investment	0.29
	Green concerns	Positive attitude towards environmental impact	0.20
Suppliers	High level service	Receiver satisfaction	0.31
	Quality of pick-ups	Punctual and secure pick-ups with no damage	0.52
	Transportation costs	Low costs for transportation	0.05
	Green concerns	Positive attitude towards environmental impact	0.12
Building contractor (receiver)	Convenient high level deliveries	Deliveries that do not compromise the receiver operations	0.42
	Transportation costs	Low costs to receive goods	0.08
	Security	Security of goods, less thefts	0.40
	Green concerns	Positive attitude towards environmental impact	0.10
Munici-pality	Quality of life	Attractive environment for citizens	0.43
	Positive business climate	Attractive environment for companies	0.32
	Infrastructure	Optimal use of existing infrastructure	0.06
	Cost measures	Low costs to implement measures	0.14
	Enforcement	Ease of compliance	0.04
Citizens	Traffic safety	Positive impact on traffic safety	0.34
	Air quality	Reduce emissions of NOx (nitrogen oxides) and PM (particulate matter)	0.04
	Public space	Attractive environment	0.27
	Accessibility	Reduce freight transport, less congestion	0.20
	Noise nuisance	Reduce noise nuisance	0.15

Source: Macharis et al. (2016).

and quality of the pick-ups are by far more important than its other two criteria, green concerns and transportation costs. Especially with regard to the latter, this is remarkable. In line with this, the building contractor attaches more importance to convenient deliveries and security than to the costs of transportation and green concerns. The municipality values the quality of life of its citizens and an attractive business climate, respectively, as most important, whereas the weights attached to the other three criteria are relatively low. Finally, the citizens living in Amsterdam find traffic safety the most important, followed by a pleasant public space, accessibility, noise nuisance and air quality. This may be explained by the fact that air pollution is difficult to observe and interpret. The consequences of dangerous traffic situations or unpleasant public spaces are clearer.

9.2.4   Evaluation of Alternatives

The evaluation of the alternatives was carried out by the students, within their stakeholder group. It should be kept in mind that the evaluation of the alternatives is based on their perception of the situation and not based on objective research. For the evaluation the PROMETHEE method is used, with a 5-point scale ranging from very negative to very positive. For each alternative every stakeholder group evaluated to what extent BAU and the three alternatives contributed to each criterion. The MAMCA analysis in Figure 9.3 leads to a multi-actor view on the three alternatives and BAU. On the x-axis the different stakeholder groups are displayed. The y-axis, ranging from –1.8 to 1.8, shows the evaluation scale. This represents the (qualitative) evaluation scale as used for the evaluation of the different alternatives with regard to the criteria. The coloured lines in the figure represent the alternatives.

The first observation that can be made from this figure is that the current situation (BAU) contributes the least to their criteria for almost all stakeholders. Only for the supplier does the alternative with the bundling hub and the water contribute slightly less to its criteria. From this first observation a tentative conclusion can be drawn that every way of delivering the construction site is an improvement vis-à-vis the business as usual situation with fragmented deliveries by freight vehicles.

During the workshop each stakeholder group explained why they attributed the weights in the way they did and clarified the evaluation of the alternatives. At the end of the workshop, the students were asked to further elaborate on the results by taking the position of the client, the real estate department of AUAS: which solution would be most favourable and why? This led to different suggestions. Some groups argued that *Bundling hub + EV* would be most favourable, as this is most in line with the preferences

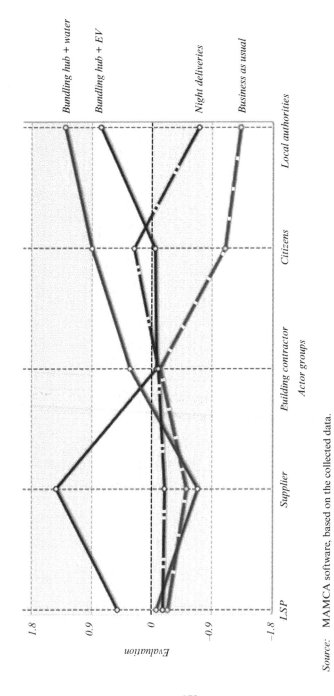

Source: MAMCA software, based on the collected data.

Figure 9.3   Multi-actor evaluation of alternatives

of the groups that should carry out the work: LSP, suppliers and building contractor. Another group stated that the preference of citizens (*Bundling hub + water*) should be most determinant as this group is, unlike commercial parties, not exchangeable.

9.3   CASE 2: MAMCA WORKSHOP CITY LOGISTICS IN A DENSE NEIGHBOURHOOD

The research programme City Logistics carries out research in De Oude Pijp in Amsterdam, a neighbourhood in the South district. AUAS cooperates with the local government. In 2016, a MAMCA workshop was organized for students of the Urban Logistics and for municipal officials of Amsterdam District South. The latter included two persons: a project leader responsible for city logistics and a communication manager responsible for communication with stakeholders in the neighbourhood. Furthermore, a project leader from De Gezonde Stad participated (De Gezonde Stad sets up bottom-up city initiatives with local stakeholders) and two academics from the research programme.

9.3.1   Case Description

The Oude Pijp is home to 15,000 citizens and has the second highest density of restaurants, cafes and shops in Amsterdam. Making deliveries to the shops, hotels, restaurants, cafes, businesses and construction sites is important for the vitality of the quarter. Unfortunately, the down-side is that residents, entrepreneurs and visitors are bothered by it. The quality of life and road safety are at risk. Traffic flows obstruct each other, and noise pollution and other emissions abound. The area will get busier over the coming years due to the realization of the "Rode Loper" (Red Carpet) project to improve public areas and accessibility, and the new North/South metro line. Public space must be used in different ways, which means organizing deliveries to premises in a smart and clean manner (Figure 9.4).[4]

---

[4] "Picturing City Logistics: delivery of goods in the 'Oude Pijp' district of Amsterdam: characteristics and opportunities", Amsterdam University of Applied Sciences, 2016. Retrieved from https://www.researchgate.net/publication/314279842_City_logistics_in_ Amsterdam's_Oude_Pijp (accessed 17 July 2017).

Source: Photo by Susanne Balm.

Figure 9.4   Neighbourhood Oude Pijp in Amsterdam

9.3.2   Elicitation of the Alternatives

Four alternative solutions were identified and presented at the MAMCA workshop:

1. *Smart parking*: sensors and IT systems in vehicles are used to register and monitor parking behaviour. Freight vehicles can reserve a place for loading/unloading and illegal behaviour can be fined more easily.
2. *Local pick-up point*: a building in the neighbourhood will be assigned as the reception point for freight deliveries. Suppliers and logistics transport operators drop off the goods at this point. Businesses and residents pick up their goods from here.
3. *UCC + waterway*: goods are delivered at a consolidation centre at the edge of the city. From here, goods are further transported by barge to the Oude Pijp. Light electric vehicles are used to transport the goods from the quay to the individual addresses.
4. *Concession for freight transport*: the municipality selects five transport operators which are allowed to deliver in the Oude Pijp. The neighbourhood is closed for other freight traffic.

9.3.3 Stakeholder Groups and Criteria

In total eight stakeholder groups (actors) were defined. Each group consisted of four or five persons being a mix of students, academics and professionals (Figure 9.5). Students were grouped based on already existing team compositions. The professionals were allowed to choose their group. For example, the municipal official that works at the Communication Department preferred to join the citizens group, as this is the stakeholder group that she mainly needs to communicate with. Unlike case 1, where a general stakeholder definition was given, the groups received a specific description of the actor that they represented, such as:

- Resident: "you have bought a house near the Albert Cuyp market seven year ago, and you have two kids".
- Retailer: "you are franchise owner of the HEMA at the Ferdinand Bolstraat and you are responsible for procurement and delivery".
- Transport operator: "you work as account manager for Peter Appel and represent the needs of client Sligro, a food wholesaler".
- Business: "you work at an Automobile Repair shop and are responsible for the procurement and inventory of materials".

Source: Photo by Jan Henk Tigelaar from De Gezonde Stad.

Figure 9.5   Workshop with students, academics and professionals

The groups were asked to project themselves onto the actor's position. For each group, four criteria were given. The criteria were based on the previous case, but with a few adjustments to make them more concrete and suitable for the situation in the Oude Pijp. For example, the criterion "quality of life" (municipality) was replaced by "improvement of air quality". For the logistics service provider, "profitable operations" and "viability of investment" were grouped into "low transportation costs". Unlike the previous case, we now have three commercial receivers (shopkeeper, restaurant and business) for which the criterion "accessibility of neighbourhood" was defined, as this is an issue in the Oude Pijp.

The groups weighted their criteria by using the pairwise comparison method (1 to 9 scale, AHP). This led to lively discussions between the students and professionals. They were free to decide how to aggregate the individual opinions. One of the groups noted that they would have preferred a 5-point scale as this would have made the pairwise comparison easier.

An overview of the groups, criteria and allocated weights are shown in Table 9.2. Per stakeholder group the sum of the weights is one. The table shows the importance of the different criteria. For residents, noise nuisance is most important. Proving or receiving service during delivery is important for the restaurant, shopkeeper, food wholesaler, logistics service provider and carrier. For the business (the Automobile Repair shop) an accessible neighbourhood is considered as most important.

9.3.4   Evaluation of Alternatives

Each stakeholder group evaluated how the alternatives would contribute to each criterion. For the evaluation the PROMETHEE method is used, with a 7-point scale (see Chapter 3), ranging from very negative to very positive. The multi-actor outcome is shown in Figure 9.6., with the actor groups on the horizontal axis and the evaluation score on the vertical axis. The coloured lines represent the four different alternatives. It becomes clear that stricter enforcement and smart parking are most favourable for the majority of actors. Residents favour the local pick-up point most, but this alternative receives a negative score from all other actors, especially for shops. This is in line with reality. During the research of AUAS in the Oude Pijp,[5] 86 shops were asked whether they would favour a local distribution

---

[5]   "Picturing city logistics", Amsterdam University of Applied Sciences, EVO, LeanCargo Consultancy, City of Amsterdam and Amsterdam District South, 2016. Commissioned by Connekt/Topsector Logistiek. Retrieved from http://www.hva.nl/kc-techniek/gedeelde-con tent/publicaties/publicaties-algemeen/stadslogistiek-in-beeld.html (accessed 17 July 2017).

Table 9.2   Stakeholder groups with their weighted criteria (case II)

Actor	Criterion	Criterion definition	Weight
Resident	Public (parking) space	Available parking spaces	0.21
	Improvement of air quality	Reduce emissions of NOx (nitrogen oxides) and PM (particulate matter)	0.24
	Accessibility of neighbourhood	Reduce freight transport, less congestion	0.22
	Noise reduction	Lower noise nuisance	0.33
Shopkeeper	Accessibility of neighbourhood	Reduce freight transport, less congestion	0.24
	Service level of delivery	Punctual and complete deliveries and customer intimacy	0.28
	Sustainability	Positive attitude towards societal and environmental impact	0.22
	Delivery costs	Low costs for delivery	0.26
Restaurant	Accessibility of neighbourhood	Reduce freight transport, less congestion	0.25
	Service level of delivery	Punctual and complete deliveries and customer intimacy	0.30
	Sustainability	Positive attitude towards societal and environmental impact	0.21
	Delivery costs	Low costs for delivery	0.24
Business	Accessibility of neighbourhood	Reduce freight transport, less congestion	0.30
	Service level of delivery	Punctual and complete deliveries and customer intimacy	0.21
	Sustainability	Positive attitude towards environmental impact	0.26
	Delivery costs	Low costs for delivery	0.23
Food wholesaler	Sustainability	Positive attitude towards societal and environmental impact	0.12
	Service at delivery	Receiver satisfaction	0.54
	Transport costs	Low costs for transportation	0.27
	Flexibility	No restrictions for transport planning	0.06
Logistics service provider (LSP)	Service level	Client satisfaction	0.31
	Transport costs	Low costs for transportation	0.27
	Job satisfaction of drivers	Employees are satisfied with their work	0.22
	Sustainability	Positive attitude towards societal and environmental impact	0.21

Table 9.2   (continued)

Actor	Criterion	Criterion definition	Weight
Municipality	Positive business climate	Attractive environment for companies	0.31
	Improvement of air quality	Reduce emissions of NOx (nitrogen oxides) and PM (particulate matter)	0.26
	Implementation costs	Low costs to implement measures	0.21
	Less traffic congestion	Reduce hindrance from freight transport	0.22
Carrier	Transport costs	Low costs for transportation	0.20
	Service level	Client satisfaction	0.33
	Sustainability	Positive attitude towards societal and environmental impact	0.32
	Job satisfaction of drivers	Employees are satisfied with their work	0.15

Source: Designed by the author based on the collected data.

centre for the delivery of parcels and 80 per cent reacted negatively. Shops noted that they prefer direct delivery at the door, they do not have personnel to pick up goods or that the goods are too heavy.

The evaluation of an UCC and a freight concession really differ per actor group. For example, the group that represented the logistics service provider assumed that they would win the concession and therefore gave a positive score to this alternative, as it would make their business more cost-efficient. The group that represented the carrier, on the other hand, expected that the concession would lead to a loss of their inner city business activities and therefore ranked this alternative negatively. The municipality gave a negative score for the implementation costs and business climate of a concession, but a positive score for the impact on air quality and congestion.

The workshop setting with mixed teams of students, academics and professionals enabled fruitful discussions. It helps students to develop the ability to reflect critically and to use the knowledge of others when making a judgement. At the same time, it also helps the professionals to step away from daily practice and to reflect on their work from another perspective.

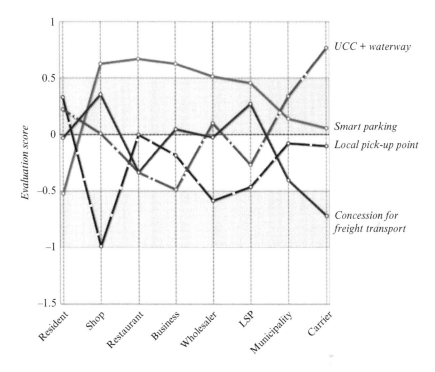

Source: MAMCA software, based on the collected data.

Figure 9.6   Multi-actor evaluation of alternatives (case II)

9.4   LIMITS OF THE APPROACH

After the workshop, the students were asked to provide feedback on the MAMCA workshop, software and the use of the MAMCA for practical purposes. Students mentioned that the criteria should be better defined to avoid ambiguity. General criteria lead to unnecessary discussions within the stakeholder groups (for example, what do we mean by "accessibility" or "sustainability"?). Also, the pros and cons and effects of alternatives should be described in more detail to support the actors in their evaluation. In the current set-up, it was difficult to discuss and interpret the effects for the different criteria. An improvement would be to have more time for preparation, both for workshop coordinators and for the participants. The students and other participants could be asked to carry out literature research prior to the MAMCA workshop on the effects of the criteria and assessment options. This also helps to keep education up-to-date by providing new literature on the issue at hand. Another option would be to provide more insights into the effects during the workshop itself. This could be done hypothetically, based on literature or based on practice. For example, it is desirable to quantitatively describe the degree to which the alternatives reduce freight movements and air pollution. Next, it should be known whether an actor invests or pays for the alternative. Will residents pay for solutions through a tax increase? And who pays for smart IT solutions? This information is essential for the evaluation in practice.

One of the groups advised that the municipality should not participate in the MAMCA as an actor, but should make clear which options are realistic to consider from a political perspective, that is, whether there would be political support. It was also proposed that stakeholders should participate actively in the identification of alternatives.

One group mentioned that eight actor groups is too many, while another group stated the opposite. They mentioned that a restaurant cannot represent the entire hospitality industry as a cafeteria or hotel may have different criteria. This representativeness issue is not harmful when the MAMCA is applied for educational purposes, but should be carefully taken into account when the MAMCA is applied in practice. Overall, the MAMCA is perceived as a valuable tool to learn about the complex environment in which city logistics problems occur and to (re) define solutions.

9.5   CONCLUSION: MAMCA BENEFITS PRACTICAL-ORIENTED RESEARCH

The use of the MAMCA in education and research is in line with the three goals for practical-oriented research.

First, it helps to *keep education up-to-date* by providing new theories (on stakeholder involvement, mathematics, evaluation and assessment), and it makes education responsive as the presented cases within the MAMCA can be changed easily from semester to semester.

Second, it helps to *improve the quality of graduates* as it teaches students to reflect on different perspectives and to make well-considered judgements. The MAMCA requires students to put themselves in the position of the different stakeholders of the logistics supply chain, for example, they enter into the role of a municipal official or a client. Being able to take the perspective of another will help them when they start as a logistics professional in a multi-disciplinary or multi-stakeholder work environment.

Next, when professionals also join the workshop (case II), students can meet and discuss with them in mixed groups. This supports their ability to use knowledge from others and helps them to get a better understanding of daily professional practice.

Third, it helps to *innovative professional practice* in two ways. First, when professionals join the MAMCA workshop, they contribute to the discussion on stakeholders' criteria and alternative solutions. These discussions can increase understanding about another's perspective, which in turn can lead to more consensus in real-life decisions. Second, professionals can learn how to use the MAMCA themselves. For example, as an instrument in stakeholder or expert sessions, which are guided by an independent facilitator or in public-private partnerships.

Furthermore, the development of the MAMCA workshop for students of the minor Urban Logistics has helped to enhance the cooperation between the logistics research group and logistics bachelor programme at the Facility of Technology. It provides opportunities for the research group to intensify cooperation with a scientific university abroad and to publish our work.

REFERENCES

AUAS (Amsterdam University of Applied Sciences) 2017, Visie. Retrieved from http://www.hva.nl/over-de-hva/visie (accessed 29 March 2017).

Landqvist, M. and Rowland, A., 2014. Stakeholder requirements affecting urban freight transportation to and from construction sites in the city, Master's thesis, Chalmers University of Technology. Retrieved from http://publications.lib.chalmers.se/records/fulltext/205741/205741.pdf (accessed 17 July 2017).

Ploos van Amstel, W., 2015. Citylogistiek: op weg naar een duurzame stadslogistiek voor aantrekkelijke steden. Lectorale rede, Amsterdam University of Applied Sciences.

Macharis, C., Kin, B., Balm, S. and Ploos van Amstel, W., 2016, Multi-actor participatory decision-making in urban construction logistics, *Transportation Research Record: Journal of the Transportation Research Board*, No. 2547, 16-2337, Transportation Research Board 95th Annual Meeting, Washington, DC, 10 January.

Onderwijsraad, 2014. Meer innovatieve professionals, Den Haag, No. 20140262/1069, November. https://www.onderwijsraad.nl/upload/documents/publicaties/volledig/Meer-innovatieve-professionals-1.7.pdf (accessed 17 July 2017).

Quak, H., Klerks, S., Aa van der, S., Ree de, D., Ploos van Amstel, W., Merrienboer van, S., 2011. Bouwlogistieke oplossingen voor binnenstedelijk bouwen. TNO rapport TNO-060-DRM-2011-02965. Retrieved from http://publications.tno.nl/publication/105251/lEGk1r/TNO-060-DTM-2011-02965.pdf (accessed 17 July 2017).STRAIGHTSOL, 2012. Deliverable 3.2. Report on stakeholders, criteria and weights. Retrieved from http://www.straightsol.eu/deliverables.htm

(accessed 17 July 2017).Vereniging van Hogescholen, 2016. Onderzoek met impact: Strategische Onderzoeksagenda 2016-2020. Retrieved from http://www. vereniginghogescholen.nl/system/knowledge_base/attachments/files/000/000/601/ original/Onderzoek_met_Impact_%28website%29.pdf?1471955342 (accessed 17 July 2017).

10. Assessing the stakeholder support for different biofuel options in France by 2030 using the range-based Multi Actor Multi Criteria Analysis framework

Gino Baudry and Thomas Vallée

10.1 INTRODUCTION

The transition from a fossil fuel to a low carbon-based energy system is one of the most important challenges of the coming decades (Braconier et al., 2014), particularly in the transport sector, which is almost completely dependent on petroleum-based fuels (Demirbas, 2007). According to the European Parliament (EP, 2009), if the transport sector had achieved the same reductions as other sectors, greenhouse gas (GHG) emissions from 1990 to 2005 would have fallen by 14 percent instead of nearly 8 percent. Consequently, the support for and the development of energy alternatives plays critical roles worldwide, but politics is no less important than technology. A first Renewable Energy Directive (RED) was adopted in 2003 to set a target share of 5.75 percent renewable energy in the transport sector by 2010 (European Parliament, 2003).

Until recently, biofuels were considered the most suited option to replace fossil fuels (Gnansounou, 2011; Turcksin et al., 2011). The European demand for land has risen considerably, as have concerns for land-use competition that call into question the large-scale deployment of conventional biofuels (Ahlgren and Di Lucia, 2014; Bracco, 2015; Gawel and Ludwig, 2011; Mueller et al., 2011). Consequently, the European Parliament passed a new Directive in 2008 that included sustainability criteria to consider additional values at stake for promoting advanced biofuels, for example, to limit food security impact. Given the difficulties of deploying a harmonized certification regarding sustainability criteria (Bracco, 2015; Markevičius et al., 2010; Scarlat and Dallemand, 2011), the relative and relevant contribution of conventional and advanced biofuels to meet the European Directive requirements is still highly debated among the different stakeholders (Buchholz et al., 2009; Gallego Carrera and Mack, 2010; Turcksin et al., 2011).

In recent years, many articles have focused on European biofuel implementation and its associated issues (Bracco, 2015; De Lucia and Bartlett, 2014; Sandoval and Popartan, 2014). The importance of the socio-economic context at the national level was highlighted by Bomb et al. (2007), who focused on the markets of the United Kingdom and Germany. Di Lucia and Nilsson (2007) noted the lack of consensus on the prioritization of competing policy objectives and suggested allowing member states more flexibility relative to their national specificities. Based on Bomb et al. (2007), Di Lucia and Nilsson (2007) and Turcksin et al. (2011), common vision and strategy between the different sectors are indispensable factors for a successful market uptake of biofuels. According to the European farmer associations, the conventional biofuel support scheme can have a severe impact on the development of the advanced biofuels given that stakeholders and investors are in most part common to both technologies.

Relying on a strong agro-food industry, France began supporting biofuel development in 1992 to create new market opportunities and improve its feed self-sufficiency. Biofuel development is a highly strategic issue for France, which is the largest European bioethanol producer and second-largest European biodiesel producer. To meet the European target for biofuel incorporation, French sub-targets were also set starting from 1.2 percent in 2005 to 7 percent in 2010. Despite many national actions to promote biofuel diffusion, such as specific tax systems and nearly 2 billion euros in industrial investments, the target was not reached. In 2015, France set an ambitious target of a mix of 15 percent of renewable energy in the transport sector by 2030, mostly based on the contribution of the first generation biofuels, including national and imported production (ADEME, 2014).

In this complex context, the range-based Multi Actor Multi Criteria Analysis (MAMCA) has been deployed to evaluate the French stakeholders' support for different biofuel options by 2030. The chapter presents the range-based MAMCA application step by step.

10.2   THE STAKEHOLDER ANALYSIS

Based on a literature review, seven stakeholder groups, 20 biofuel alternatives and nearly 40 criteria were identified as relevant regarding the French biofuel context by 2030. The stakeholder analysis has led us to discuss, validate or invalidate the relevance of these biofuel options, criteria list and stakeholder groups while suggesting others (Baudry et al., 2017). The present section presents different steps of the stakeholder analysis. It is worth reminding that the different steps are partly overlapping and that the procedure is iterative.

10.2.1 Identification of the Biofuel Option Set

Each involved stakeholder was asked to respond to a questionnaire through face-to-face meetings or call conferences, followed by an unstructured discussion concerning the scope of the problem. The first part of the questionnaire focused on the identification of the set of biofuels we should consider in the study (Table 10.1).

For each of the options, stakeholders were asked to give their viewpoints with regards to their expected contribution in meeting the French objectives for the transport sector by 2030. Stakeholders could add their suggestions, which led us to consider additional biofuel options. Based on their perspectives, we chose to consider all the options which exceeded a consensus degree of 50 percent concerning at least a low-scale contribution. The biofuel options are then sorted into alternatives and sub-alternatives based on their characteristics (Table 10.2).

The contribution of each sub-alternative to each alternative is also based on the stakeholder perspective, particularly on the ADEME (French Environment and Energy Management Agency) inputs (ADEME, 2014).

10.2.2 Identification of the Stakeholder Groups

The second part of the questionnaire focused on the identification of the stakeholder groups (Table 10.3). Stakeholders were asked about the relevance of involving the other stakeholder groups. They were also allowed to add their suggestions.

We kept all the groups that reached more than a 50 percent degree of consensus as outlined below.

The feedstock producer group was represented by the agricultural sector and the biomass-based industry through syndicates, producers and traders. The biofuel producer group includes agro-industry, biotechnology companies and producers. The refiner group was represented by two of the three French refinery companies. The fuel distributor group includes both petroleum industry and large-scale retail, which share the French fuel distribution market. The end-user group was represented by the French car users' association. The car manufacturer group was represented by a syndicate and car manufacturers. The government group includes specialized energy and environmental institutions and the French agricultural,

Table 10.1   Biofuel set identification results

First generation biofuels		Stakeholders' viewpoints – expected contribution				
Food crop biofuels	*Feedstocks*	*NA* (%)*	*None (%)*	*R&D stage (%)*	*Low-scale (%)*	*Large-scale (%)*
FAME-biodiesel	Rapeseed oil	0	0	0	8	92
FAME-biodiesel	Soybean oil	0	3	0	9	88
FAME-biodiesel	Palm oil	0	3	0	15	82
HVO-biodiesel**	Rapeseed oil	0	0	0	54	46
HVO-biodiesel	Palm oil	0	3	0	51	46
Ethanol & ETBEa	Sugar-beet	0	0	0	8	92
Ethanol & ETBEa	Wheat	0	0	0	8	92
Ethanol & ETBEa	Corn	0	0	0	8	92
Ethanol & ETBEa	Sugar-cane	0	5	0	14	81
Waste-based biofuels	*Feedstocks*	*NA**	*None*	*R&D stage*	*Low-scale*	*Large-scale*
FAME-biodiesel	UCO, animal fat	0	0	0	80	20
HVO-biodiesel**	UCO, animal fat	0	0	0	69	31
Cellulosic biofuels	*Feedstocks*	*NA**	*None*	*R&D stage*	*Low-scale*	*Large-scale*
BtL-biodiesel	Agro-residues	3	2	0	61	37
BtL-biodiesel	Forestry residues	3	0	0	53	47
BtL-biodiesel	Energy crops	3	13	0	43	44
Cellulosic-ethanol	Agro-residues	3	0	3	75	22
Cellulosic-ethanol	Forestry residues	3	2	3	63	32
Cellulosic-ethanol	Energy crops	3	11	3	56	30
Microalgae biofuels	*Feedstocks*	*NA**	*None*	*R&D stage*	*Low-scale*	*Large-scale*
FAME-biodiesel	Microalgae	33	0	44	43	13
HVO-biodiesel**	Microalgae	33	9	45	33	13
Ethanol	Microalgae	33	32	36	19	13

Notes:
*   No answers; ** suggested by stakeholders.
a.   Ethyl Tertiary Butyl Ether.

Source: Based on Baudry et al. (2017).

Table 10.2   The set of alternatives

#	Alternative	Process	Feedstock	Mix (%)
1	Ethanol 1G	Fermentation	Sugar-beet	50
		Fermentation	Wheat	38
		Fermentation	Corn	10
		Fermentation	Sugar-cane	2
2	Biodiesel 1G	Transesterification	Rapeseed oil	100
3	Waste-based biofuels	Transesterification	Animal fats	14
		Transesterification	UCO	56
		Hydrotreatment	UCO	30
4	Ethanol 2G	Biochemical	Agricultural residues	78
		Biochemical	Energy crops	22
5	Biodiesel 2G	Thermochemical-BtL	Agricultural residues	25
		Thermochemical-BtL	Forestry residues	75
6	Biodiesel 3G (RW)	Transesterification	Microalgae	100
7	Biodiesel 3G (PBR)	Transesterification	Microalgae	100
8	Imported feedstock	Transesterification	Soybean oil	35
		Transesterification	Palm oil	35
		Hydrotreatment	Palm oil	15
		Hydrotreatment	Rapeseed oil	15
9	Imported biofuels	Transesterification	Palm oil	50
		Transesterification	Soybean oil	50

Note: RW – RaceWay; PBR – photobioreactor.

Source: Designed by the authors.

energy, ecological and finance ministers. Finally, the non-governmental organization (NGO) group was represented by associations that focus on North-South economics, energy or socio-environmental issues.

In this range-based MAMCA application, stakeholder groups are considered of equal importance. At the overall level, nearly 50 stakeholders were involved in the study, including the ones who were interviewed but finally considered irrelevant by the other stakeholders such as the aircraft manufacturers. The academics and research and development (R&D) group was represented by researchers from public institutions, private companies and by consultants. This group is not considered a stakeholder group in the range-based MAMCA, it is considered the expert group

Table 10.3   Stakeholder group identification

Stakeholder group	Proposed by	Degree of consensus (%)	Group	Expert	Irrelevant
Investment banks	Authors	21			x
Academics and R&D	Authors	98		x	
Feedstock producers	Authors	100	x		
Biofuel producers	Authors	100	x		
Refining industry	Stakeholders	94	x		
Fuel distributors	Authors	94	x		
Car manufacturers	Authors	100	x		
Aircraft manufacturers	Stakeholders	6			x
End-users	Authors	95	x		
Government	Authors	100	x		
NGOs & associations	Authors	98	x		

Source: Based on Baudry et al. (2017).

which evaluates and/or validates the EBDLs (expert-based distribution laws, see Chapter 5).

10.2.3   Criteria Identification and Weight Elicitation

Based on a literature review (Gnansounou, 2011; Markevičius et al., 2010; Turcksin et al., 2011), a list of criteria was proposed and discussed with each stakeholder group to build the criteria trees (Figure 10.1). The critical part of criteria identification is to fit the stakeholders' points of view while anticipating the biofuel performance measurement step (including the identification of the uncertainty factors). In the present case, the Analytic Hierarchy Process (AHP) method was used to express the stakeholders' priorities (see Chapter 3, Appendix 3A.1).

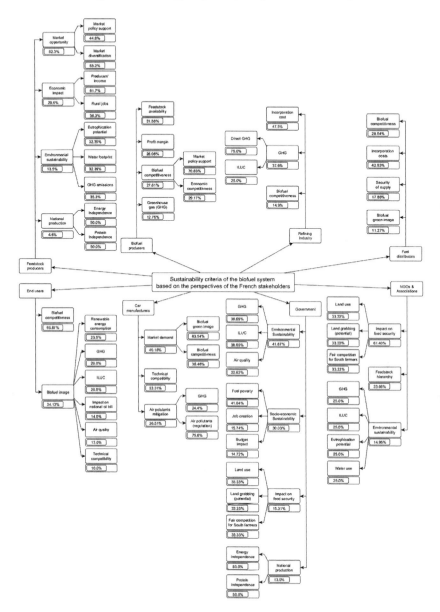

Source: Designed by the authors based on the stakeholders' inputs.

Figure 10.1   Criteria trees

10.3   THE BIOFUELS PERFORMANCE ASSESSMENT

Based on the stakeholders' inputs, the performances of the biofuels were assessed by constructing the EBDLs (see Chapter 5) – based on a broad literature review and/or biofuel-expert consultations.

10.3.1   EBDLs and Data Collection

For each criterion and each biofuel option, data has to be collected to enable the construction of the EBDLs based on the stakeholders' inputs, as illustrated in Table 10.4.

The biofuel competitiveness criterion was common between almost all the stakeholders. The performance of the different biofuels by 2030 relies on different uncertainty factors either specific (feedstock price, including the yield of the process) or shared between several options (processing costs/oil price).

10.3.2   Monte Carlo Simulation and Multi-criteria Method

EBDLs capture the uncertainty concerning each criterion. The Monte-Carlo simulation then consists of randomly picking a set of biofuel performance values from all the EBDLs to generate a scenario. Monte-Carlo Simulation consists of repeating this process many times to capture the many scenario possibilities. For each iteration, a multi-criteria analysis is performed to compare the biofuel alternatives (see Chapter 5). In the present case, the weighted sum method (see Wang et al., 2009) was used as the decision-method because of its understandability and transparency regarding the stakeholders.

10.4   RESULTS

The aggregation of the different groups' perspectives can be considered as a starting base for discussion (Figure 10.2). Nevertheless, the aggregation does not necessarily lead to a Pareto optimal ranking given the heterogeneity of the stakeholder groups.

The X-axis presents the different biofuel options. The Y-axis represents the options' score regarding their capacity to fulfill stakeholders' criteria. The higher the score, the higher the stakeholder's support for the biofuel option. Considering the different uncertainty factors, the range of the possible biofuel scores is represented by a boxplot. In other words, this range of values represents the extent of how the uncertainty factors may affect

Table 10.4 Example of data collection: biofuel competitiveness criterion

Biofuel competitiveness (€/l)		Feedstock		Process		Coproducts		Biofuel
Food crop biofuels	*Feedstocks*	*Min*	*Max*	*Min*	*Max*	*Min*	*Max*	*Prob.*
FAME-biodiesel	Rapeseed	0.66	1.10	0.18	0.30	0.14	0.28	1.04
FAME-biodiesel	Soybean	1.83	2.23	0.18	0.30	1.18	1.48	1.19
FAME-biodiesel	Soybean*	0.76	0.92	0.18	0.30	0.007	0.054	1.06
FAME-biodiesel	Palm oil*	0.55	1.19	0.18	0.30	0.009	0.068	1.28
HVO-biodiesel	Rapeseed	0.75	1.25	0.18	0.30	0.003	0.012	1.2
HVO-biodiesel	Palm oil	0.62	1.32	0.18	0.30	0.020	0.067	1.01
Ethanol	Sugar-beet	0.25	0.30	0.11	0.27	0.020	0.067	0.74
Ethanol	Wheat	0.33	0.40	0.12	0.26	0.10	0.12	0.89
Ethanol	Corn	0.27	0.33	0.12	0.26	0.10	0.12	0.79
Ethanol	Sugar-cane**	0.22	0.37	0.11	0.27	0.29	0.47	0.78
Waste-based biofuels	*Feedstocks*	*Min*	*Max*	*Min*	*Max*	*Min*	*Max*	*Prob.*
FAME-biodiesel	UCO	0.38	0.64	0.36	0.60	0.009	0.072	1.08
FAME-biodiesel	Animal fat	0.13	0.30	0.36	0.60	0.009	0.072	0.82
HVO-biodiesel	UCO	0.40	0.67	0.36	0.54	0.020	0.067	0.99
HVO-biodiesel	Animal fat	0.12	0.28	0.22	0.54	0.020	0.067	0.97

Table 10.4 (continued)

Biofuel competitiveness (€/l)		Feedstock		Process		Coproducts		Biofuel
Cellulosic biofuels	*Feedstocks*	*Min*	*Max*	*Min*	*Max*	*Min*	*Max*	*Prob.*
BtL-biodiesel	Agro-residues	0.24	0.36	0.67	0.81	0.11	0.36	1.01
BtL-biodiesel	Ft-residues	0.33	0.42	0.67	0.81	0.11	0.36	1.08
BtL-biodiesel	Energy crops	0.28	0.62	0.67	0.81	0.11	0.36	1.16
Cellulosic-ethanol	Agro-residues	0.2	0.3	0.41	0.5	0.01	0.2	1.04
Cellulosic-ethanol	Agro-residues	0.28	0.36	0.41	0.5	0.01	0.2	1.15
Cellulosic-ethanol	Ft-residues	0.24	0.51	0.41	0.5	0.01	0.2	1.25
Microalgae biofuels	*Feedstocks*	*Min*	*Max*	*Min*	*Max*	*Min*	*Max*	*Prob.*
FAME-biodiesel (RW)	Microalgae	2.15	2.63	0.18	0.30	0.77	1.32	1.82
FAME-biodiesel (PBR)	Microalgae	3.57	4.36	0.18	0.30	0.77	1.32	3.60
Units		€/l	€/l	€/l	€/l	€/l	€/l	€/loea

Notes:
*   Imported oil; ** imported biofuel.
a. loe – liter oil equivalent: liter diesel equivalent for biodiesel and liter gasoline equivalent for ethanol.

Source: Baudry et al. (2017).

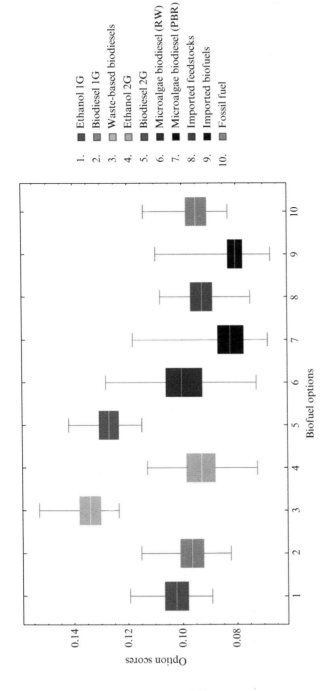

1. ■ Ethanol 1G
2. ■ Biodiesel 1G
3. ■ Waste-based biodiesels
4. ■ Ethanol 2G
5. ■ Biodiesel 2G
6. ■ Microalgae biodiesel (RW)
7. ■ Microalgae biodiesel (PBR)
8. ■ Imported feedstocks
9. ■ Imported biofuels
10. ■ Fossil fuel

Source: Designed by the authors.

Figure 10.2   Overall aggregation of the biofuel scores

Table 10.5   Probability that the microalgae biodiesel outperforms the other options

Biofuel options	Microalgae biodiesel (RW) (%)
Ethanol 1G	43.5
Biodiesel 1G	59.1
Waste-based biodiesel	0.0
Ethanol 2G	72.1
Biodiesel 2G	0.3
Microalgae biodiesel (RW)	–
Microalgae biodiesel (PBR)	86.5
Imported feedstock	72.5
Imported biofuels	94.4
Fossil fuel reference	64.7

Source: Designed by the authors.

the option desirability for the stakeholders. The boxplot medians, upper and lower boundaries represent the most probable, most optimistic and most pessimistic scores, respectively.

Table 10.5 presents the probability that microalgae biodiesel RW (RaceWay) outperforms the other options at the overall aggregation level. Despite a lack of economic competitiveness, RW may outperform the imported feedstock and biofuels, thanks to its socio-environmental benefits, with a probability of 72.5 and 94.4 percent, respectively.

The most supported option at the overall level is the waste-based biofuels, followed by biodiesel 2G. In other words, these advanced biodiesels are most suited regarding the stakeholders' criteria. Nevertheless, such a result cannot lead to any absolute conclusion without identifying and analysing the weaknesses and strengths of each option at the stakeholder level.

10.4.1   Feedstock Producers

Feedstock producers' concerns are the market opportunities (52 percent), socio-economic impacts (29.6 percent), environmental sustainability (13 percent) and the national production of protein and energy (5 percent) (Figure 10.3).

Microalgae biodiesels and food crop-based biodiesels (biodiesel 1G) are the most suited regarding the feedstock producers' criteria with a probability of 74 percent and 26 percent, respectively. Microalgae biodiesel yields 20–50 tons of biomass per hectare compared with 4.1–4.6 tons

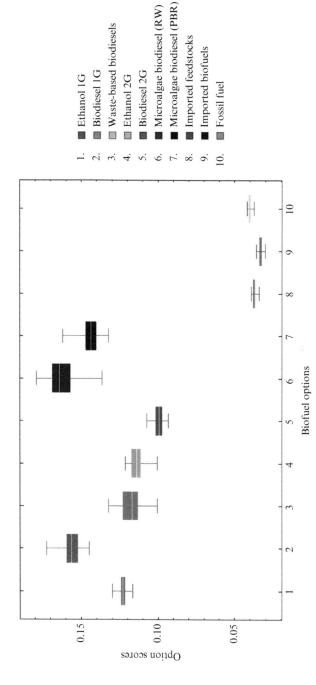

1. ■ Ethanol 1G
2. ■ Biodiesel 1G
3. ■ Waste-based biodiesels
4. ■ Ethanol 2G
5. ■ Biodiesel 2G
6. ■ Microalgae biodiesel (RW)
7. ■ Microalgae biodiesel (PBR)
8. ■ Imported feedstocks
9. ■ Imported biofuels
10. ■ Fossil fuel

Source: Designed by the authors.

Figure 10.3   *Feedstock producers' outputs*

for biodiesel 1G (Bobban and Subhadra, 2011; Bonnet and Lorne, 2009; Delrue et al., 2012; IAE and OCDE, 2011). Microalgae biomass offers a wider range of market opportunities such as energy, medicine, plastic, cosmetic, feed and food coproducts (Bobban and Subhadra, 2011; IEA and IRENA, 2013). In terms of environmental sustainability, microalgae biodiesel always outperforms biodiesel 1G because of a lower water footprint (Gerbens-Leenes et al., 2009, 2014) and a limited eutrophication impact (Hugues, 2015).

When focusing on the socio-economic impacts, biodiesel 1G always outperforms microalgae biodiesel as it creates 5.5 rural jobs per kton of biomass (Raes et al., 2013), which is five times more than microalgae biodiesel (Baudry et al., 2017). In terms of incomes, microalgae biomass can generate high incomes or losses depending on the byproduct markets. Microalgae biomass generates high value products but they are limited to niche markets. Relying on these markets while scaling up the microalgae biomass production may generate market gluts and economic bottlenecks for producers (Bobban and Subhadra, 2011). Regardless of the byproducts, the biodiesel retailing price is expected to be in the range of 980 to 1170 euros per ton by 2030 (IEA and IRENA, 2013). Microalgae oil is assumed to cost between 2100 and 4500 euros per ton (Delrue et al., 2012). Additional support schemes could be developed to partly drive microalgae biomass towards biofuel markets while considering the byproduct markets constraint.

10.4.2 Biofuel Producers

For biofuel producers, concerns mainly focus on economic aspects: feedstock availability (31 percent), profit margin (28 percent) and biofuel competitiveness (28 percent). GHG mitigation is their only environmental criterion (13 percent).

For biofuel producers (Figure 10.4), imported feedstock is the most interesting option with a probability of 50 percent, followed by waste-based biodiesel (31 percent) and ethanol 1G (16 percent). Uncertainty about these options mainly lies in the profit margin which is linked to feedstock prices. The biofuel producers ranking is characterized by a high uncertainty as most of the boxplots are overlapping. In other words, the uncertainty factors may widely affect the biofuel producers' support of the different biofuel options, mainly through the economic concerns.

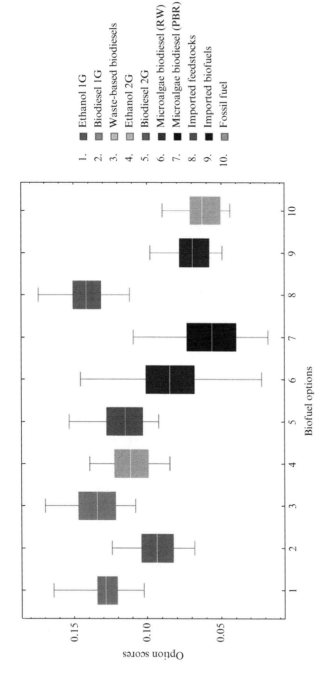

1. Ethanol 1G
2. Biodiesel 1G
3. Waste-based biodiesels
4. Ethanol 2G
5. Biodiesel 2G
6. Microalgae biodiesel (RW)
7. Microalgae biodiesel (PBR)
8. Imported feedstocks
9. Imported biofuels
10. Fossil fuel

Source: Designed by the authors.

Figure 10.4 Biofuel producers' outputs

197

10.4.3   Refining Industry

For the refining industry, the incorporation cost is the most important concern (47 percent), followed by the GHG emissions (38 percent) and the biofuel competitiveness (15 percent).

In France, the fuel consumption is currently – and expected to be by 2030 – imbalanced and dominated by diesel (74 percent). Nevertheless, the oil refining process only enables the production of 20 to 40 percent of diesel per barrel compared to 50 percent for gasoline (UFIP, 2012). Refiners therefore have to import a large amount of diesel and export gasoline surplus in the European and Asian fuel markets. Additional costs are thus induced which are strengthened by a significant lack of competitiveness of the French refining industry due to its aging facilities and higher legal constraints. When incorporating ethanol, a larger amount of gasoline must be exported which further exacerbates the problem (Baudry et al., 2017). On the contrary, incorporating biodiesel helps to rebalance the fuel consumption. Consequently, biodiesel options outperform ethanol ones from the refiners' perspective (Figure 10.5).

Rising concerns about land-use issues may lead to the inclusion of indirect land-use changes (ILUC) in the biofuel support scheme, which may have severe impacts on the refining industry. It may lower the GHG mitigation accounting of biofuels which will eventually and mechanically increase the incorporation rates to achieve GHG mitigation objectives in the transport sector. Such a scenario may imply important additional costs for the refiners. Consequently, they prefer the biofuel options characterized by a high GHG mitigation performance, including the consideration for ILUC. For refiners, waste-based biodiesel is the most suitable option with a probability of 59 percent, followed by the biodiesel 2G (41 percent).

10.4.4   Fuel Distributors

Fuel distributors' concerns are shared between the incorporation cost (43 percent), the security of supply (18 percent) and the end-users' demand that includes the sustainability image of biofuels (11 percent) and their competitiveness (28 percent).

When focusing on the fuel distributors' preferences, the reference is the most suited option, which underlines the need to strengthen the policy support for this group. Nevertheless, given the uncertainty factors, the suitability of the different options may vary widely. As shown by Figure 10.6, the reference is the preferred option with a probability of 27 percent, followed by imported feedstock (26 percent) and waste-based biodiesel (21 percent).

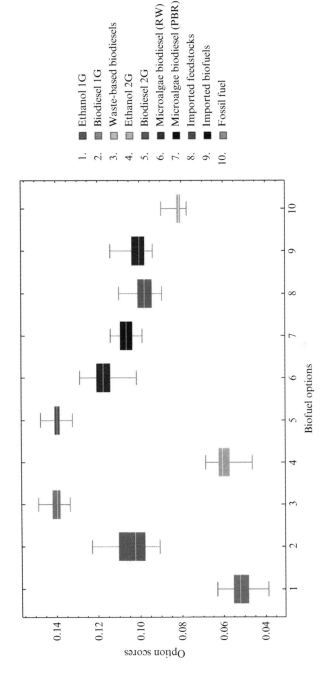

1. ▨ Ethanol 1G
2. ▨ Biodiesel 1G
3. ▨ Waste-based biodiesels
4. ▨ Ethanol 2G
5. ▨ Biodiesel 2G
6. ■ Microalgae biodiesel (RW)
7. ■ Microalgae biodiesel (PBR)
8. ▨ Imported feedstocks
9. ■ Imported biofuels
10. ▨ Fossil fuel

Source: Designed by the authors.

Figure 10.5   Refiners' outputs

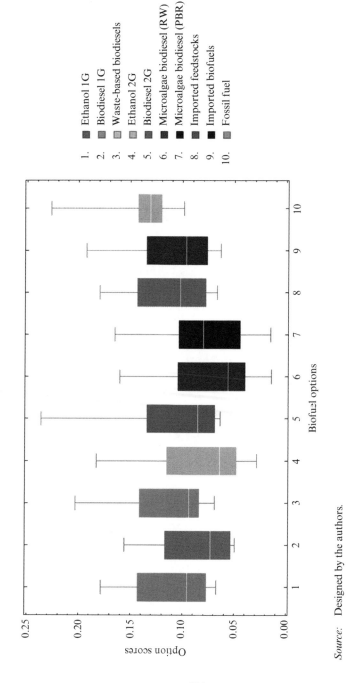

1. ■ Ethanol 1G
2. ■ Biodiesel 1G
3. □ Waste-based biodiesels
4. ■ Ethanol 2G
5. ■ Biodiesel 2G
6. ■ Microalgae biodiesel (RW)
7. ■ Microalgae biodiesel (PBR)
8. ■ Imported feedstocks
9. ■ Imported biofuels
10. ■ Fossil fuel

Source: Designed by the authors.

Figure 10.6   Fuel distributors' outputs

Uncertainty factors mainly affect the biofuel incorporation cost for distributors through the logistics costs and the requirement for a legislation harmonization concerning the blending rates. Currently, the blending limit for biodiesel differs between European and French legislation, being 7 percent and 8 percent, respectively. Some car manufacturers have announced that exceeding the 7 percent threshold – the European standard – would void the manufacturer warranties. It may thus be required for distributors to develop a wider range of fuels and/or adapt the existing infrastructure. The conversion cost of a tank ranges between 5–30 k\$. Adding a new tank and pump may cost from 50–200 k\$ depending on the fuel type (Moriarty et al., 2009). Consequently, drop-in biofuels are well suited because they do not need a specific tank or pump (HVO and BtL biodiesel).

A competitive retailing price is mandatory for ensuring the end-users' demand, which is why imported biofuels as well as biofuels produced from imported feedstock fit the distributors' concerns. Distributors state that they are torn between their need to be competitive and their "moral duty" to offer market opportunities to the French biofuel industry. To cope with distributors' concerns, multiple counting mechanism may be helpful to facilitate the implementation of the most sustainable biofuel options.

10.4.5   End-users

End-users' criteria are shared between economic considerations (66 percent) and socio-environmental issues (34 percent).

Even if they are not the cheaper options, biodiesel 2G and waste-based biodiesel are the preferred options for end-users (Figure 10.7). Because of the French tax system, the price gap between the different biofuels "at the pump" is greatly lowered (Baudry et al., 2017), leading to relatively strengthen their concerns for sustainability. In other words, biodiesel 2G and waste-based biodiesel offer a better balance between economic and socio-environmental issues regarding the end-users' concerns. The fossil fuels reference remains attractive for end-users, also because of the tax scheme for fuels which is based on volumes rather than energy content. Given the lower energy content of most of the biofuels compared to fossil fuels (ADEME, 2010; Gehrer et al., 2014), they are mechanically more taxed per liter, which is highly criticized by most of the stakeholders.

10.4.6   Car Industry

The car industry's concerns are shared between the market demand (40 percent), the technical compatibility (33 percent) and the air pollutants mitigation (27 percent).

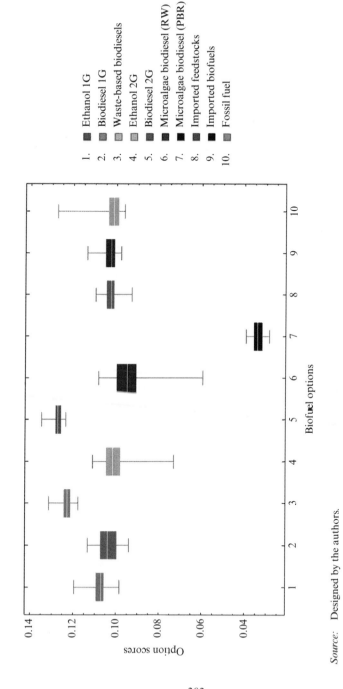

Source: Designed by the authors.

Figure 10.7 End-users' outputs

The final rankings are not widely affected by the uncertainty (Figure 10.8). Biodiesel 2G is the most suited option with a probability of 100, followed by the oil reference. The car manufacturers highlight a lack of support for the implementation of biofuel in the car industry. The GHG mitigation objective is accounted for from *tank to wheel* while biofuels' GHG mitigation are accounted for from *field to tank*. In other words, the GHG objective can only be reached by improving the engine efficiency. For these reasons, drop-in biofuels are preferred by the car industry because they do not require car engine adaptation. The failure of the biofuel policy for car manufacturers may be illustrated by the fact that the flex-fuel technology has been available and economically viable for many years (50–100 euros per car[1]), but has not deployed because of a lack both demand and policy support.

10.4.7   Government

The government has the widest set of criteria, including GHG, ILUC, air quality, fuel poverty, job creation, budget impact, land-use, land grabbing, fair competition, energy and protein independency.

From the government's perspective, advanced biofuels are the most suited options (Figure 10.9) given their high concerns for sustainability and land-use issues. Microalgae biodiesel remains the exception, particularly because of its higher cost that may affect the budget or fuel poverty. Despite the economic impact in terms of agricultural sector support and job creation, biodiesel 1G is outperformed by the oil-based reference. Even if is also produced from food crops, there is a high probability that ethanol 1G is preferred compared with the fossil fuel options because it has better yields, which lowers many drawbacks related to land-use issues.

10.4.8   NGOs

NGOs' criteria include the food security (61 percent), the hierarchy of feedstock use (24 percent) and environmental impacts (15 percent).

Given the NGOs' concerns, there is no uncertainty about the final rankings (Figure 10.10). Waste-based biodiesel is the most suited option, followed by microalgae biodiesels. The other options cannot outperform the reference because of the NGOs' concerns for land use and food security. Although cellulosic biofuels offer environmental benefits, they are also subject to the risk of land grabbing, which consists of the large-scale

---

[1]   Flex-fuel technology enables high blending of ethanol in gasoline engines (up to 85 percent) – estimation by the PSA group.

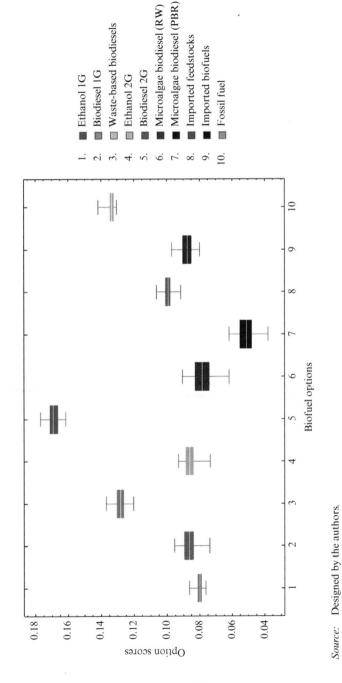

1.	Ethanol 1G
2.	Biodiesel 1G
3.	Waste-based biodiesels
4.	Ethanol 2G
5.	Biodiesel 2G
6.	Microalgae biodiesel (RW)
7.	Microalgae biodiesel (PBR)
8.	Imported feedstocks
9.	Imported biofuels
10.	Fossil fuel

Source: Designed by the authors.

Figure 10.8 Car industry's outputs

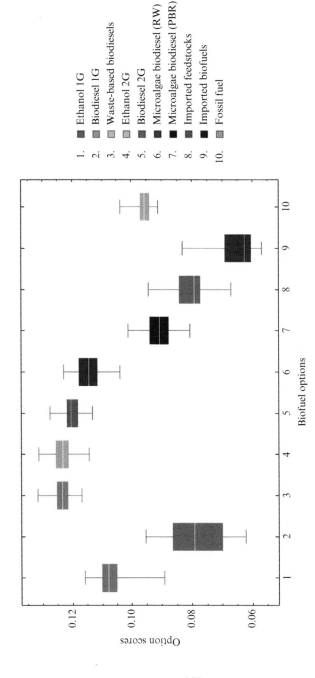

Legend:
1. ■ Ethanol 1G
2. ■ Biodiesel 1G
3. ■ Waste-based biodiesels
4. ■ Ethanol 2G
5. ■ Biodiesel 2G
6. ■ Microalgae biodiesel (RW)
7. ■ Microalgae biodiesel (PBR)
8. ■ Imported feedstocks
9. ■ Imported biofuels
10. ■ Fossil fuel

Source: Designed by the authors.

Figure 10.9 Government's outputs

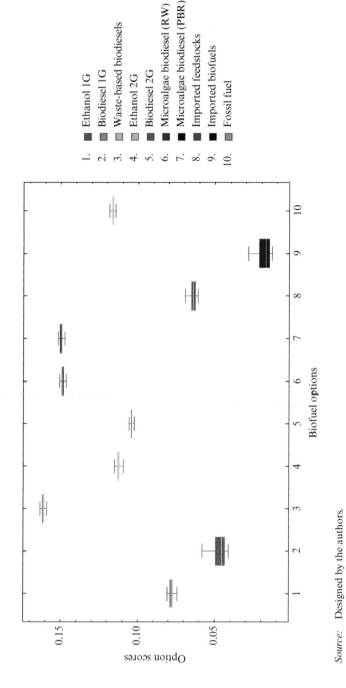

Legend:

1. ▨ Ethanol 1G
2. ▨ Biodiesel 1G
3. ▨ Waste-based biodiesels
4. ▨ Ethanol 2G
5. ▨ Biodiesel 2G
6. ■ Microalgae biodiesel (RW)
7. ■ Microalgae biodiesel (PBR)
8. ■ Imported feedstocks
9. ■ Imported biofuels
10. ▨ Fossil fuel

Source: Designed by the authors.

Figure 10.10 NGOs' outputs

acquisition of foreign lands by countries in order to fulfill their own needs for agricultural feedstock (Bracco, 2015). For the NGOs, a hierarchy should ensure the efficiency of the feedstock life cycle – to make it as long as possible – as does the waste hierarchy which is promoted by the European Commission.

10.5　CONCLUSION

In this chapter, a range-based MAMCA methodology (Baudry et al., 2014) has been elaborated to assess French stakeholder support for different biofuel options by 2030. Throughout the overlapping and iterative procedures, the range-based MAMCA allowed stakeholders to have better insights and understanding about the consequences of any decision taken about the biofuel deployment (Salo and Hämäläinen, 2010), including the risk of making mistaken or at least not-optimal decisions because of the uncertainty (Van Der Kleij et al., 2003).

Overall, the range-based MAMCA showed that most probably (80 percent of the scenarios), BtL-biodiesel is the most suited option to stakeholders' preferences. More importantly, this methodology allows a deeper analysis of the points of views of each stakeholder group. For example, fossil fuel will still be the preferred option for fuel distributors and car manufacturers. European legislation might partly consider GHG saving from biofuel consumption for car manufacturers to encourage higher biofuel blending car deployment. Food crop-based biofuels are most suited to feedstock and biofuel producers' preferences whereas they are clearly the least preferred option for NGOs. Indeed, whatever the uncertainty about food crop-based biofuels, fossil fuel is most suited to the preferences of NGOs because of land-use and food security issues. Consequently, support for biofuels might require higher sustainability standards, especially for land-use issues. For several groups, unbalanced consumption between gasoline and diesel imply a higher preference for biodiesel options. Differentiated policy for ethanol and biodiesel incorporation might be required with regards to gasoline and diesel consumption balance.

In April 2015, the European Parliament set a 7 percent limit on food crop biofuels while setting a non-binding 0.5 percent target for advanced biofuels by 2020. Based on the present study, without additional policy measures, such a policy mainly suits feedstock and biofuel producers' preferences but potentially conflicts with other stakeholders' points of view such as NGOs. Additional policy measures have to be deployed to ensure biofuel competitiveness while avoiding any kind of dumping to avoid downstream drawbacks. In the present case, developing more incentives and ambitious objectives for advanced biofuels would provide a long-term signal to all stakeholder groups and a more stable policy framework.

REFERENCES

ADEME, 2010. Analyses de Cycle de Vie appliquées aux biocarburants de première génération consommés en France. ADEME.

ADEME, 2014. Vision 2030–2050, L'exercice de prospective de l'ADEME. ADEME.

Ahlgren, S., Di Lucia, L., 2014. Indirect land use changes of biofuel production – a review of modelling efforts and policy developments in the European Union. *Biotechnology for Biofuels* **7**, 35. https://doi.org/10.1186/1754-6834-7-35 (accessed June 4, 2018).

Baudry, G., Macharis, C., Vallée, T., 2014. A range based Multi-Actor Multicriteria Analysis to incorporate uncertainty in stakeholder based evaluation processes. Working Paper LEMNA 2014-16, University of Nantes.

Baudry, G., Delrue, F., Legrand, J., Pruvost, J., Vallée, T., 2017. The challenge of measuring biofuel sustainability: a stakeholder-driven approach applied to the French case. *Renewable & Sustainable Energy Reviews* **69**, 933–47. https://doi.org/10.1016/j.rser.2016.11.022 (accessed June 4, 2018).

Bobban, G. and Subhadra, M.E., 2011. Coproduct market analysis and water footprint of simulated commercial algal biorefineries. *Applied Energy* **88**, 3515–23. https://doi.org/10.1016/j.apenergy.2010.12.051 (accessed June 4, 2018).

Bomb, C., McCormick, K., Deurwaarder, E., Kåberger, T., 2007. Biofuels for transport in Europe: lessons from Germany and the UK. *Energy Policy* **35**, 2256–67. https://doi.org/10.1016/j.enpol.2006.07.008 (accessed June 4, 2018).

Bonnet, J.F., Lorne, D., 2009. Eau et biocarburants, impacts sur l'eau du développement des biocarburants en France à l'horizon 2030. IDDRI, Paris.

Bracco, S., 2015. Effectiveness of EU biofuels sustainability criteria in the context of land acquisitions in Africa. *Renewable & Sustainable Energy Reviews* **50**, 130–43. https://doi.org/10.1016/j.rser.2015.05.006 (accessed June 4, 2018).

Braconier, H., Nicoletti, G., Westmore, B., 2014. *Policy Challenges for the Next 50 Years* (OECD Economic Policy Papers). Paris: Organisation for Economic Co-operation and Development.

Buchholz, T., Luzadis, V.A., Volk, T.A., 2009. Sustainability criteria for bioenergy systems: results from an expert survey. *Journal of Cleaner Production, International Trade in Biofuels* **17** (Suppl. 1), S86–S98. https://doi.org/10.1016/j.jclepro.2009.04.015 (accessed June 4, 2018).

De Lucia, C., Bartlett, M., 2014. Implementing a biofuel economy in the EU: lessons from the SUSTOIL project and future perspectives for next generation biofuels. *Renewable & Sustainable Energy Reviews* **29**, 22–30. https://doi.org/10.1016/j.rser.2013.08.058 (accessed June 4, 2018).

Delrue, F., Setier, P.-A., Sahut, C. et al., 2012. An economic, sustainability, and energetic model of biodiesel production from microalgae. *Bioresource Technology* **111**, 191–200. https://doi.org/10.1016/j.biortech.2012.02.020 (accessed June 4, 2018).

Demirbas, A., 2007. Importance of biodiesel as transportation fuel. *Energy Policy* **35**, 4661–70. https://doi.org/10.1016/j.enpol.2007.04.003 (accessed June 4, 2018).

Di Lucia, L., Nilsson, L.J., 2007. Transport biofuels in the European Union: the state of play. *Transport Policy* 14, 533–43.

European Parliament, 2003. Directive EC/30/2003.

Gallego Carrera, D., Mack, A., 2010. Sustainability assessment of energy technologies via social indicators: results of a survey among European energy experts. *Energy Policy* 38, 1030–9.

Gawel, E., Ludwig, G., 2011. The iLUC dilemma: how to deal with indirect land use changes when governing energy crops? *Land Use Policy* 28, 846–56. https://doi.org/10.1016/j.landusepol.2011.03.003 (accessed June 4, 2018).

Gehrer, M., Seyfried, H., Staudacher, S., 2014. Life cycle assessment of BtL as compared to HVO paths in alternative aviation fuel production. Paper presented at the Deutscher Luft- und Raumfahrtkongress 2014.

Gerbens-Leenes, W., Hoekstra, A.Y., Meer, van der, T.H., 2009. The water footprint of bioenergy. *Proceedings of the National Academy of Science USA* 106, 10219–23. https://doi.org/10.1073/pnas.0812619106 (accessed June 4, 2018).

Gerbens-Leenes, P.W., Xu, L., de Vries, G.J., Hoekstra, A.Y., 2014. The blue water footprint and land use of biofuels from algae. *Water Resources Research* 50, 8549–63.

Gnansounou, E., 2011. Assessing the sustainability of biofuels: a logic-based model. *Energy* 36, 2089–96. https://doi.org/10.1016/j.energy.2010.04.027 (accessed June 4, 2018).

Hugues, P., 2015. Stratégies technologique et réglementaire de déploiement des filières bioénergies françaises. Ecole nationale supérieure des Mines de Paris, Sophia Antipolis.

IAE, OCDE, 2011. Technology roadmap biofuels for transport. Paris.

IEA, IRENA, 2013. Production of liquid biofuels, technology brief. IEA-ESTAP, IRENA. https://www.irena.org/DocumentDownloads/Publications/IRENA-ET SAP%20Tech%20Brief%20P10%20Production_of_Liquid%20Biofuels.pdf (accessed June 4, 2018).

Markevičius, A., Katinas, V., Perednis, E., Tamašauskienė, M., 2010. Trends and sustainability criteria of the production and use of liquid biofuels. *Renewable & Sustainable Energy Reviews* 14, 3226–31. https://doi.org/10.1016/j.rser.2010.07.015 (accessed June 4, 2018).

Moriarty, K., Johnson, C., Sears, T., Bergeron, P., 2009. E85 Dispenser Study (No. NREL/TP-7A2-47172). National Renewable Energy Laboratory, Golden, CO.

Mueller, S.A., Anderson, J.E., Wallington, T.J., 2011. Impact of biofuel production and other supply and demand factors on food price increases in 2008. *Biomass Bioenergy* 35, 1623–32. https://doi.org/10.1016/j.biombioe.2011.01.030 (accessed June 4, 2018).

Raes, T., Spiegel, I., Lubek, J., 2013. Évaluation du poids socio-économique et environnemental de la filière biodiesel en France. *Oilseeds and fats, Crops and Lipids* 20. https://doi.org/: 10.1051/ocl/2013028 (accessed June 4, 2018).

Salo, A., Hämäläinen, R.P., 2010. Multicriteria Decision Analysis in group decision processes, in D.M. Kilgour and C. Eden (eds), *Handbook of Group Decision and Negotiation* (Advances in Group Decision and Negotiation). Amsterdam: Springer Netherlands, pp. 269–83.

Sandoval, I.S., Popartan, L., 2014. The implementation of the EU biofuels policy in Spain and the UK: a case of contested Europeanization. *Biofuels* 5, 129–40. https://doi.org/10.4155/bfs.13.73 (accessed June 4, 2018).

Scarlat, N., Dallemand, J.-F., 2011. Recent developments of biofuels/bioenergy sustainability certification: a global overview. *Energy Policy* **39**, 1630–46. https://doi.org/10.1016/j.enpol.2010.12.039 (accessed June 4, 2018).

Turcksin, L., Macharis, C., Lebeau, K. et al., 2011. A multi-actor multi-criteria framework to assess the stakeholder support for different biofuel options: the case of Belgium. *Energy Policy* **39**, 200–14. https://doi.org/10.1016/j.enpol.2010.09.033 (accessed June 4, 2018).

UFIP (U.F. des I.P.), 2012. Les biocarburants en France. Union Française des Industries Pétrolières (UFIP).

Van Der Kleij, C., Hulscher, S., Louters, T., 2003. Comparing uncertain alternatives for a possible airport island location in the North Sea. *Ocean & Coastal Management* **46**, 1031–47.

Wang, J.-J., Jing, Y.-Y., Zhang, C.-F., Zhao, J.-H., 2009. Review on multi-criteria decision analysis aid in sustainable energy decision-making. *Renewable & Sustainable Energy Reviews* **13**, 2263–78. https://doi.org/10.1016/j.rser.2009.06.021 (accessed June 4, 2018).

11. Ranking charities using Multi Actor Multi Criteria Analysis methodology: the case of Public Benefit Organizations in Poland

Ewa Chojnacka and Dorota Górecka

11.1 INTRODUCTION

Charities are important institutions not only in Poland but all over the world. Charities or voluntary organizations are also called non-profit organizations (NPOs) and non-governmental organizations (NGOs). In the economy, they are part of the third sector and they are established for serving the public interest in different areas such as, for example, education, research, health, social services, environment and religion.

The number of NGOs in different countries depends on law regulations as well as on the methodology of the official statistics and registers. According to the available data, the largest non-governmental sector is in the US (it has almost 1 million entities) whereas in Europe the biggest number of NGOs is in Germany (616,254 entities).[1] In Poland, intensive development of third sector entities has been observed since 1989, after the collapse of communism. The number of charities in Poland is increasingly growing. Statistics indicate that there were about 27,400 registered NPOs in 1997, about 67,500 in 2005 and about 100,700 in 2014 (Central Statistical Office, 2009, 2016). In 2003 Polish legislators introduced a special type of NPO known as the Public Benefit Organization (PBO). As we can see from Figure 11.1, the number of PBOs is also increasing. In 2004 there were 2,200 registered PBOs compared to 9,000 in 2015.

According to Polish law, a PBO is a non-governmental organization, understood as a corporate and non-corporate entity, which does not form part of the public finance sector and which does not operate for

---

[1] Liczba NGO na świecie, Zespół badawczy Stowarzyszenia Klon/Jawor, http://fakty.ngo. pl/wiadomosc/2069932.html (accessed 8 June 2017).

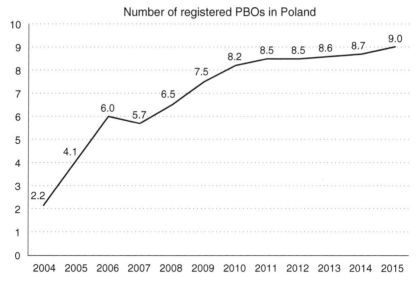

Source: Central Statistical Office (2017).

Figure 11.1   *Number of registered Public Benefit Organizations in Poland (in thousands)*

profit and is entitled to perform an activity for the benefit of society in the area of public tasks, called a public benefit activity. The legislation indicates 37 areas of public activity (Act of law, 2003). PBOs are registered in the National Court Register. They must engage exclusively in public benefit activities (they may run commercial activities, but only in addition to public benefit activities).

The number of NGOs indicates their importance for the economy. Moreover, NGOs' role in the economy is also represented by their volume of funds. Based on a survey on charities and PBOs in Poland, 99 per cent of all registered PBOs reported a total income of 7.4 billion PLN (Polish Zloty). The average income per charity equalled 863,300 PLN while the average turnover of small and medium-sized enterprises (SMEs) in Poland in 2014 was only about 36 per cent higher and equalled 1.18 million PLN (Central Statistical Office, 2016).

PBOs in Poland are recognized as the top charity organizations and they are granted many benefits. For example, Polish taxpayers may donate 1 per cent of the value of personal income tax (PIT) paid to support PBOs (Piechota, 2015). This benefit is considered a very important way of supporting PBOs. In 2005, PBOs received 42 million PLN from 1 per cent of PIT paid. In 2009 it increased to 380 million PLN. In 2016, the amount from 1 per cent of PIT equalled 618 million PLN (which is almost 15 times that in 2005) (Central Statistical Office, 2017).

Taking into consideration the significant role of the third sector organizations in the economy, we developed a new framework for evaluating these entities, which is based on the Multi Actor Multi Criteria Analysis (MAMCA) approach (Macharis, 2000, 2004, 2005; Macharis et al., 2012). Firstly, such a new assessment method is needed since charities' characteristic features, such as for example non-profit orientation, mean that tools designated for corporate finance are not appropriate. Secondly, a new assessment method should include both financial and non-financial information. Thirdly, there are more and more charities, which start to compete for funds with one another. Thus, these organizations should also be interested in measuring their activities so they will be able to demonstrate their efficiency and obtain funding.

11.2   METHODOLOGY

Our case study is based on the assessment of PBOs from one of the Polish provinces operating in the field of 'Children and youth recreation'. The recommended approach is based on the MAMCA methodology (Macharis, 2000, 2004, 2005; Macharis et al., 2012) and it uses methods belonging to the PROMETHEE family, namely:

- PROMETHEE II (Brans and Vincke, 1985; Brans et al., 1986)
- PROMETHEE IIv (Górecka, 2013, 2014; Górecka and Muszyńska, 2011; Górecka and Pietrzak, 2012)
- EXPROM IIv (Górecka, 2014, 2015; Górecka and Szałucka, 2013; see also Diakoulaki and Koumoutsos, 1991).

Considering the advantages and disadvantages of various Multi Criteria Decision Aid (MCDA) techniques (see Górecka, 2010, 2011, 2013) we decided to employ the above-mentioned methods because they are considered to be user-friendly ones, that is, simple and easily understood – all steps can be quite easily explained to the decision-maker(s) since they are neither very complex nor mathematically challenging. Furthermore, thanks to the introduction of the veto threshold the PROMETHEE IIv and EXPROM IIv methods are partially compensatory (a really bad score on one criterion cannot be compensated with a good score on another). Besides, all these techniques allow us to obtain a complete pre-order of the alternatives to which the points are assigned in the final solution. This form of the final solution is recognized as being convincing for the potential users of MCDA methods. Finally, when weighing up all three methods, the PROMETHEE II and PROMETHEE IIv result in an ordinal scale of measurement, while the EXPROM IIv enables the decision-maker to rank alternatives on a cardinal scale. This is due to the notion of ideal and anti-ideal on which the EXPROM IIv method is based. It is worth emphasizing that cardinal scale is desirable from the perspective of comparing the alternatives considered.

The decision to apply the MAMCA was taken since it aims at providing insight into what is significant for each stakeholder, not just summing up different points of view and coming to a final conclusion. The MAMCA approach allows for thoughtful and thorough stakeholders' engagement in the decision-making process and leads to a more complete understanding of the different points of view as well as to a result that might be more advantageous for the majority of stakeholders (compared to, for example, an approach based on stochastic dominance rules) (see Górecka and Szałucka, 2016).

11.3   CASE STUDY

Three potential donors (decision-makers (DM) denoted as follows: EW-DM1, J-DM2, EM-DM3) were asked to participate in this case study. They would like to give their money to charitable organizations. They, together, want to help children, so they decided to support a charity which organizes recreation for children and teenagers. The potential donors are familiar with finance and accounting. Two of them are studying for their master's degrees. The third one has already graduated and is experienced in running charity accounting. Assuming that equal importance is attached to the point of view of each DM, it is necessary to point out the organization that would suit all of them.

The proposed procedure for evaluating PBOs comprises five steps:

1. The first step involves identification of the participants of the decision-making process.
2. The second step consists of identifying the performance evaluation criteria and their associated indicators.
3. The third step involves collecting data about organizations being considered. Based on the data collected, a table of assessments (evaluation matrix) is built.
4. In the fourth step, weights are elicited to express the stakeholders' preferences between their criteria. These may be determined arbitrarily or by using, for instance, one of the following techniques: the revised

Simos's procedure (Figueira and Roy, 2002) or the Hinkle's method (Hinkle, 1965; Rogers and Bruen, 1998).
5. The last step includes application of the MCDA methods and the MAMCA approach, building rankings of charities and taking a final decision about the donation.

Following the procedure, we first chose ten PBO alternatives that operate in the field of 'Children and youth recreation' based on the database of PBO reports.[2]

Table 11.1 contains brief characteristics of the charities analysed. Although they operate in the same field, there are some differences in their activities.

The second step in the procedure concerns the selection of the criteria and indicators. Most of these have been tracked through a literature review and four have been developed by the authors of this chapter based on research papers, independent evaluators' websites, PBOs' performance reports and financial statements as well as on the authors' own experience and expertise.

All criteria can be divided into two main groups that refer to financial ratings and information and reputation ratings. Taking into consideration the former studies, we can indicate that financial ratings reflect PBOs' efficiency and financial stability. Efficiency measures indicate how well charities carry out the organization's mission. Financial stability measures indicate the charities' ability to continue operations in a situation of decreasing resources (Parsons, 2003, cited in Trussel and Parsons, 2008).

The second group of criteria concerns information and reputation. Donors often cannot directly assess a charity's output and make a judgement about its quality (Gordon and Khumawala, 1999, cited in Trussel and Parsons, 2008). In such situations, donors very often rely on organizational reputation and assess output taking into consideration the charity's name (Trussel and Parsons, 2008). In some cases, an organization's reputation is even more important than a good financial situation or the low cost of an activity.

The criteria that a responsible donor should consider when selecting PBOs to support, as well as the indicators, are presented in Tables 11.2 and 11.3. It should be emphasised that the presented set of criteria is not regarded as the optimal one. Researchers may add new criteria in order to better assess NPOs.

Data was collected from the PBOs' web pages and from the database of

---

[2]   Public benefit organizations are obliged to publish the accepted reports (financial and performance reports) on the website of the National Institute in Public Information Bulletin. See: http://sprawozdaniaopp.mpips.gov.pl/Search.

Table 11.1   Information on PBOs considered for support

	Name of PBO	Goals of PBO
A	Stowarzyszenie Lokalne Salezjańskiej Organizacji Sportowej Rzeczpospolitej Polskiej w Bydgoszczy	Implements activities aimed at the broadly understood education of children and teenagers with emphasis on children and young people with material and social disadvantages. It focuses on sport, recreation and tourism.
B	Stowarzyszenie 'Bezpieczeństwo Dziecka'	Aims at preventing and combating alcoholism, drug abuse, violence, crime and so on in teenagers. It conducts and supports actions for the safety of children, adolescents and adults.
C	Brodnickie Stowarzyszenie Oświatowe	Aims at (among others) organizing various forms of pedagogical activity, such as recreation for children and adolescents, including for children from the poorest families. It runs a community day care centre for children and non-public kindergarten.
D	Gminny Klub Sportowy 'Spójnia'	A sport club that aims to develop various sports disciplines and organizes mass recreational and tourist events.
E	Wojewódzki Związek Rolników, Kółek i Organizacji Rolniczych w Bydgoszczy	Aims at (among others) supporting the economic development of rural areas, including entrepreneurship, and organization of leisure activities for children and teenagers.
F	Chorągiew Kujawsko-Pomorska Związku Harcerstwa Polskiego	A scouting organization. Its main aims are (among others) the creation of conditions for comprehensive, intellectual, social, spiritual, emotional and physical development and the creation of conditions for the establishment and maintenance of strong interpersonal relationships.
G	Caritas Diecezji Bydgoskiej	A church organization that aims at (among others) conducting charitable and caring activities, undertaking actions for the needy, the protection and promotion of health, and organizing leisure activities for children and teenagers.
H	'Fundacja Wspierania Rozwoju Impuls'	Conducts workshops for people with disabilities and classes for children with disabilities that are focused on rehabilitation, education and integration.
I	Stowarzyszenie Edukacyjne 'Nasza Szkoła' w Gorzycach	Aims to develop and support educational and cultural activities for children and the local community. It runs a non-public primary school.
J	Towarzystwo Przyjaciół Dzieci Oddział Miejski	Aims to improve the quality of children's life, looking after their comprehensive development, health, and safety. Runs two educational centres, offering educational, sport and therapeutic classes as well as different forms of holiday leisure for children and youths.

Source: Own elaboration.

Table 11.2   PBOs' performance assessment criteria: financial ratings

No.	Criterion (min/max/value of); (earlier studies)	Measure – calculation formula
f_{F1}	Average amount of aid per beneficiary (max)	cost of unpaid and paid statutory activities/number of beneficiaries
f_{F2}	Average revenue generated by people involved in organization's activities (max)	total revenue/number of people involved in PBO's activities (employees, volunteers, members)
f_{F3}	Change in revenue (max); (a)	(total revenue in current year – total revenue in previous year)/total revenue in previous year
f_{F4}	Change in expenses of statutory activities (max)	(total cost of unpaid and paid statutory activities in current year – total cost of unpaid and paid statutory activities in previous year)/total cost of unpaid and paid statutory activities in previous year
f_{F5}	Private revenue concentration ratio (% of private financing) (max); (b), (c)	(1% of personal income tax (PIT) + incomes from private sources including individual and institutional donations)/total revenue
f_{F6}	Labour cost in relation to total revenue (min)	gross salaries/total revenue
f_{F7}	Alternative labour costs (max); (b), (c)	(number of volunteers*gross salaries)/number of employees
f_{F8}	Administrative costs ratio (% of administrative costs) (value of 6.5%); (a), (b), (c), (d), (e)	administrative cost/total cost
f_{F9}	Financial stability ratio (value of 73); (b), (c)	cash and other short-term investments (in previous year)*365/total cost (in current year)
f_{F10}	Debt level (< 30%; min); (f)	total current debt/total income
f_{F11}	Fiscal deficits (scale 1;0;–1); (f)	net profit or loss within 2 years

Note: (a) Charity Navigator; (b) Dyczkowski (2015a); (c) Dyczkowski (2015b); (d) Frumkin and Kim (2001); (e) Trussel and Parsons (2008); (f) Penley (2012).

Source: Own elaboration.

Table 11.3   PBOs' performance assessment criteria: information and reputation ratings

No.	Criterion (min/max/value of); (earlier studies)	Measure – calculation formula
f_{R1}	Activity scope (value of 36); (b), (c)	number of beneficiaries/number of people involved in organization's activities
f_{R2}	Organization's age (max); (e)	the number of days an organization has PBO status
f_{R3}	Statutory goals and activities or projects (max); (c)	do annual statements of an organization or its promotional materials define precisely statutory goals and activities or projects undertaken to achieve those objectives? (appraisal of the DM on scale 0–3)
f_{R4}	Effects of activities (max); (c)	do annual statements of an organization or its promotional materials disclose accurately effects of activities undertaken by the organization in the recent period? (appraisal of the DM using scale 0–3)
f_{R5}	Beneficiaries of activities (max); (c)	do annual statements of an organization or its promotional materials characterize thoroughly the beneficiaries of activities conducted by the organization in the recent period? (appraisal of the DM using scale 0–3)
f_{R6}	Organization's image (max); (c)	does the website of the organization help to produce a positive image of the PBO? (appraisal of the DM on scale 0–3)

Note: (b) Dyczkowski (2015a); (c) Dyczkowski (2015b); (e) Trussel and Parsons (2008).

Source: Own elaboration.

PBOs' performance reports and financial statements. Data used for evaluation was based both on financial and non-financial information. One of the most important sources for the assessment of PBOs is the information presented in annual reports. Since PBOs are granted many benefits, they also have higher reporting standards compared to charities without this status. All together, we analysed 17 criteria, 11 are assigned as financial ratings and six as information and reputation ratings.

The first financial ratio (fF1) indicates the effect of PBO's activities obtained by beneficiaries. In order to calculate this ratio, we take into consideration the cost of paid and unpaid activity in the PBO. The Polish law requires PBOs to allocate their expenses into three categories:

- unpaid work – for which no remunerations is charged
- paid work – for which remuneration is charged, but this payment is lower or equal to the cost of such activities
- business activities – when the remuneration for an activity of a given public task exceeds the costs of such activity.

Any income generated in paid public benefit work shall be used only to perform public tasks (Act of law, 2003).

The next three ratios (fF2–fF4) specify growth in charities. An increasing amount of revenue enables the entity to not only sustain its programmes year to year but also to extend its activities. The growth in revenue should be followed by a growth in expenses of statutory activities. Organizations that show consistent annual growth in both primary revenue and programme expenses are able to perform their programmes year to year. We may expect that these organizations shall supply givers with greater confidence by maintaining broad public support for their programmes (Charity Navigator).

The ratio number 5 (fF5) is private revenue concentration ratio (per cent of private financing). This ratio indicates the structure of revenue. It's worth mentioning that private financing is more closely connected with a good relationship with donors and represents a more stable source of income. Public financing is more determined by the organizational skills of the entity (Dyczkowski, 2015a, 2015b).

The next three ratings (fF6–fF8) analyse the level of given costs, such as labour costs and administrative costs. The first criterion, labour costs in relation to total revenue, should be minimized. On the one hand, charities need talented managers, who want to be well paid, but, on the other hand, a good manager should be able to obtain higher revenue. In these types of entities, employees are often replaced by volunteers. Consequently, we also analyse alternative labour costs, which indicate the value of volunteer work as a cost-saving measure (Dyczkowski, 2015a, 2015b). Finally, there is an administrative costs ratio, which shows the share of the administrative cost in the total cost. In the literature (Trussel and Parsons, 2008), this ratio is used both as an efficiency and a financial stability ratio. A low share of administrative costs may indicate a charity's efficiency. It is also a stability ratio because in the situation of revenue reductions, an organization with larger administrative costs has the option to cut those costs instead of reducing the overall level of programme services offered (Trussel and Parsons, 2008). In our case study, we assumed a specific benchmark equal to 6.5 per cent, which is the median for Polish PBOs according to Dyczkowski (2015a).

The ninth ratio (fF9), financial stability ratio, is a kind of liquidity ratio as it indicates for how long cash and cash equivalents owned by the entity at the end of the previous year are sufficient to cover costs in the current year (Dyczkowski, 2015a, 2015b). We assume that most costs entail an outflow of cash. In the financial analysis of companies' liquidity a cash ratio is used. It is the relationship of cash and cash equivalents to current liabilities and the reference for it is 0.2. This means that cash and cash equivalents are sufficient to cover 20 per cent of current liabilities (Świderska and Więcław, 2009). We used this approach and the benchmark for our ratio is 0.2 of the 365 days, which is 73 days.

The last two financial ratings (fF10, fF11) are related to debt level and fiscal deficit. The aim of the debt level ratio is to verify whether obtained income is used on charities' activities and not on interest payment or debt repayment. We accepted Penley's proposition of a benchmark indicating that debt level should be less than 30 per cent. This level is partially based on industry standards for a healthy debt-to-income ratio for businesses (Penley, 2012). Organizations that generate profits are recognized as having financial resources for future actions. Charities are not for profit organizations, but they are not for deficit as well. Their budget should be balanced, which means that expenses ought to be at the same level as revenues. We evaluated PBOs using a grading scale from –1 to 1, and considered three situations: two years analysed ended with deficit (grade –1); one year ended in deficit, the other in profit (grade 0); two years analysed ended in profit (grade 1).

The first criterion on information and reputation ratings (fR1) serves to determine a charity's scale of impact. We compare the number of PBO beneficiaries with the number of people involved in the organization's activities. This ratio may also indicate the number of people that had contact with an organization as a kind of reputation measure (Dyczkowski, 2015a, 2015b). Since this value should neither be too low nor too high, in our case study we assumed a specific benchmark equal to 36, which is the median for Polish PBOs according to the research carried out by Dyczkowski (2015a).

The next ratio (fR2), the number of years with PBO status, is also a kind of reputation rating. Older organizations have had more time to establish themselves with donors and achieve name recognition (Bennett and DiLorenzo, 1994, cited in Trussel and Parsons, 2008).

The last four criteria (fR3–fR6) are related to information ratings. Taking into consideration an organization's annual statements, its promotional materials and website, individual donors may assess the quality of information. The information concerns statutory goals, effects of activities, beneficiaries and the organization's general image. We used a scale from 0 to 3.

After determining the performance evaluation criteria and the measures for them an analysis was carried out based on the official and publicly available annual reports of the organizations considered (from 2015) as well as information from their websites. Information and reputation ratings (fR3–fR6) were assessed individually by our DMs. They also determined independently (in an arbitrary way) the weighting coefficients for all evaluation criteria as well as their indifference (qk), preference (pk) and veto (vk) thresholds.

11.4 RESULTS

The model of preferences for the decision-making problem and measurement data are presented in Table 11A.1 in the Appendix. Tables 11.4–11.6 and Figures 11.2–11.4 provide the results obtained using the MAMCA approach with the PROMETHEE II, PROMETHEE IIv and EXPROM IIv methodology. Overall value scores situated on the right side of Tables 11.4–11.6 were established on the basis of the PROMETHEE GDSS procedure using the so-called '0-option', in which the global net flow for the whole group is calculated as the weighted sum of the individual net flows (Macharis et al., 1998).

Table 11.4   Results of the MAMCA approach with PROMETHEE II

PBO	EW-DM1	J-DM2	EM-DM3	Overall
A	0.4548	0.4272	0.4389	0.4403
B	0.6321	0.5923	0.5874	0.6039
C	0.4564	0.4887	0.4594	0.4682
D	0.4770	0.5419	0.5223	0.5137
E	0.4256	0.4176	0.4720	0.4384
F	0.6210	0.5683	0.5515	0.5803
G	0.4271	0.4403	0.4726	0.4466
H	0.6109	0.6531	0.5654	0.6098
I	0.5140	0.5328	0.5206	0.5225
J	0.3813	0.3381	0.4102	0.3765

Source: Own elaboration.

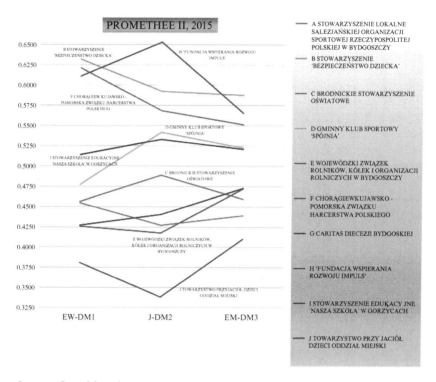

Source: Own elaboration.

Figure 11.2   Results of the MAMCA approach with PROMETHEE II

Table 11.4 and Figure 11.2 show the results obtained using the MAMCA model with the PROMETHEE II method. Values in the respective columns of the table present the final scores for each PBO obtained for each DM (EW-DM1, J-DM2, EM-DM3), taking into account their individual preferences. The higher the value, the better the performance of the charity from the point of view of a given DM. Shading used in the table aims to aid analysis of the results: the brighter the cell, the better the assessment of the PBO according to the criteria used; the darker the cell, the worse the position of the PBO from the point of view of a particular DM. Thus, as we can see, the most suited to the EW-DM1 preferences is PBO B, the second most suited is PBO F, and the third most suited is PBO H. In turn, the worst suited to the EW-DM1 preferences is PBO J, whereas the second worst suited one is PBO E, and the third worst suited is PBO G. The results obtained are also shown in the figure using the multi-actor line chart to represent particular organizations. In general, the higher the line is, the more preferred the entity is by a given DM; the less preferred the organization is, the lower the line is drawn. Hence, as can be seen, the most suited to the J-DM2 preferences is PBO H, the second most suited is PBO B, and the third most suited is PBO F. In turn, the worst suited to the J-DM2 preferences is PBO J, whereas the second worst suited one is PBO E, and the third worst suited is PBO A.

In trying to find a satisfying solution from the point of view of all DMs using the MAMCA model with the PROMETHEE II method, we have come to the conclusion that the best entity for donation is PBO B (it takes first place in the rankings of DM1 and DM3, and second place in the ranking of DM2), although its overall performance is a little bit lower than the overall performance of PBO H (which, in turn, wins third, first and second place in the rankings of DM1, DM2 and DM3, respectively). The third organization that can be considered for support is PBO F (it takes second place in the ranking of DM1 and third place in the rankings of DM2 and DM3). On the other hand, the results obtained indicate that our donors should not be interested in helping PBO J, which occupies the last spot in the ranking of each DM.

Table 11.5 and Figure 11.3 present the results obtained using the MAMCA model with the PROMETHEE IIv method. Values in the respective columns of the table show the final scores of each PBO gained for each DM (EW-DM1, J-DM2, EM-DM3), allowing for their individual preferences. Table 11.5 is constructed according to the same rules as Table 11.4. Consequently, the most suited to the EW-DM1 preferences is PBO H, the second most suited is PBO F, and the third most suited is PBO B. In turn, the worst suited to the EW-DM1 preferences is PBO A, whereas the

Table 11.5   Results of the MAMCA approach with PROMETHEE IIv

PBO	EW-DM1	J-DM2	EM-DM3	Overall
A	0.4137	0.4368	0.4738	0.4414
B	0.5283	0.5287	0.5262	0.5277
C	0.4771	0.5000	0.5000	0.4924
D	0.5255	0.5000	0.5000	0.5085
E	0.5000	0.5000	0.5000	0.5000
F	0.5376	0.5303	0.5121	0.5266
G	0.5055	0.5000	0.5000	0.5018
H	0.5770	0.5345	0.5000	0.5372
I	0.4895	0.5000	0.5000	0.4965
J	0.4461	0.4698	0.4880	0.4679

Source: Own elaboration.

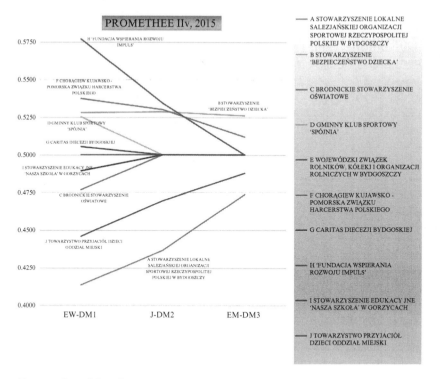

Source: Own elaboration.

Figure 11.3   Results of the MAMCA approach with PROMETHEE IIv

second worst suited one is PBO J, and the third worst suited is PBO C. The results obtained are also shown in the figure using the lines representing particular organizations. The rules of presentation are identical to those set out for Figure 11.2: the higher the line is, the more preferred the entity is by a given DM; the lower the line is, the less preferred the entity is. Hence, for instance, the most suited to the EM-DM3 preferences is PBO B and the second most suited is PBO F. The worst suited to the EM-DM3 preferences is PBO A, while the second worst suited is PBO J.

An attempt to determine a compromise solution for all DMs in the case of the MAMCA approach with the PROMETHEE IIv method has led us to conclude that there would be two widely accepted organizations, namely, PBO B and PBO F, although the latter seems more appropriate for donation since it is the second strongest in all rankings yielded. It is slightly incompatible with the overall performances obtained with the help of the PROMETHEE GDSS procedure, according to which our DMs should

Table 11.6   Results of the MAMCA approach with EXPROM IIv

PBO	EW-DM1	J-DM2	EM-DM3	Overall
A	0.4006	0.4267	0.4699	0.4324
B	0.5319	0.5324	0.5302	0.5315
C	0.4771	0.5000	0.5000	0.4924
D	0.5283	0.5000	0.5000	0.5094
E	0.5000	0.5000	0.5000	0.5000
F	0.5453	0.5415	0.5121	0.5329
G	0.5055	0.5000	0.5000	0.5018
H	0.5971	0.5410	0.5000	0.5460
I	0.4895	0.5000	0.5000	0.4965
J	0.4249	0.4585	0.4880	0.4571

Source: Own elaboration.

give their money to PBO H (which is followed by PBO B and PBO F in second and third place, respectively). The least preferred organization for donation is PBO A and the second least preferred one is PBO J.

Table 11.6 and Figure 11.4 demonstrate the results obtained using the MAMCA model with the EXPROM IIv method. Values in the respective columns of the table show the final scores for each PBO obtained in the case of each DM (EW-DM1, J-DM2, EM-DM3), taking into account their individual preferences. Table 11.6 is built using the same principles as described above for Tables 11.4 and 11.5. Thus, the most suited to the EW-DM1 preferences is PBO H, the second most suited is PBO F, and the third most suited is PBO B. In turn, the worst suited to the EW-DM1 preferences is PBO A, the second worst suited is PBO J, and the third worst suited is PBO C. To facilitate the analysis, the results are also shown in the figure using the lines to represent particular organizations. The most suited to the J-DM2 preferences is PBO F, the second most suited is PBO H, and the third most suited is PBO B. In turn, the worst suited to the J-DM2 preferences is PBO A, and the second worst suited one is PBO J.

The analysis of the results obtained using the MAMCA approach with the EXPROM IIv method reveals a fairly similar situation to the one described previously for the MAMCA model and the PROMETHEE IIv method: DMs could agree to donate to PBO B or PBO F. However, the latter seems more appropriate for support from the point of view of all three DMs as it is ranked second, first and second in the case of DM1, DM2 and DM3, respectively (while PBO B takes third place in the rankings of DM1 and DM2, and first place in the ranking of DM3). According to the overall value scores, the best entity for donation is once again PBO

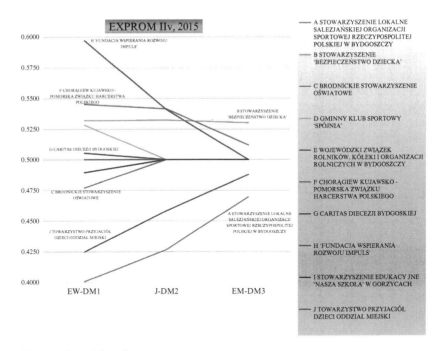

Source: Own elaboration.

Figure 11.4   Results of the MAMCA approach with EXPROM IIv

H, whereas PBO F comes second before PBO B. In turn, our DMs would not be willing to support PBO A or PBO J.

11.5   CONCLUSION

In view of all the results obtained and the whole analysis conducted, the most suited entity for donation for our DMs turned out to be PBO F – a scouting organization called Chorągiew Kujawsko-Pomorska Związku Harcerstwa Polskiego. It is one of the top three organizations according to the MAMCA with PROMETHEE II, and it is the most preferred one according to the MAMCA with PROMETHEE IIv and EXPROM IIv. It is worth emphasizing that the latter two methods – PROMETHEE IIv and EXPROM IIv – due to veto thresholds are slightly more reliable for our DMs than the PROMETHEE II technique.

Taking the increasing role of PBOs into consideration we have developed a reliable framework for assessing their performance. It is based on the MAMCA methodology and utilizes methods belonging to the PROMETHEE family, namely, PROMETHEE II, PROMETHEE IIv and EXPROM IIv. The MAMCA approach allows us to analyse, confront and incorporate diverse points of view in decision-making processes involving various stakeholders with different preferences and aspirations regarding decisions that are to be taken. In this chapter we have shown the way this methodology can be used to support donors in making trustworthy and confident decisions. Thanks to the approach proposed, money may be given to charities preferred by decision-makers – the ones most suited for them. Thus, the donations provided by the charitable givers may be more efficiently used and recipient organizations can develop faster and operate more effectively. The proposed framework may be applied by authorities (local and national) in the process of selecting entities which are to be delegated certain tasks financed with public funds. It may also help NPOs to perform self-monitoring and self-reporting more effectively and to validate their own attractiveness as fundraisers.

The framework presented can be used in the case of public service organizations all over the world. The research demonstrated in this chapter may serve as a guide. Nevertheless, we must not forget that the activity of such organizations may be evaluated differently across countries, taking into account the tradition of the third sector in the economy as well as the level of development of social capital and the model of voluntary service (for instance, engagement in voluntary service in Poland is very low compared to Western European countries). Additionally, it has to be taken into consideration that reports of PBOs are not harmonized even in the European Union (for example, in Poland it is mandatory to present administrative costs but there is no such position in English reports), not to mention other countries. Hence, indicators considered in the analysis should certainly be tailored to each state's specific conditions. However, bearing in mind the trend to promote accountability, openness and transparency in third sector organizations, these difficulties may be diminished in the future.

REFERENCES

Act of law of April 24th 2003 on Public Benefit and Volunteer Work, Ustawa z dnia 24 kwietnia 2003 r. o działalności pożytku publicznego i o wolontariacie, Dz. U. 2003 nr 96, poz. 873 z późn. zm.

Brans J.P., Vincke P. (1985) A preference ranking organization method: the PROMETHEE method for multiple criteria decision-making, *Management Science*, **31**, 647–56.

Brans J.P., Vincke P., Mareschal B. (1986) How to select and how to rank projects:

the PROMETHEE method, *European Journal of Operational Research*, **24**, 228–38.

Central Statistical Office (2009) Sektor non-profit w Polsce. Wybrane wyniki badań statystycznych zrealizowanych przez GUS na formularzach SOF, Warszawa.

Central Statistical Office (2016) Sektor non-profit w 2014 r., Studia i analizy statystyczne, Warszawa.

Central Statistical Office (2017) Organizacje pożytku publicznego i 1%. Notatka informacyjna, http://stat.gov.pl/obszary-tematyczne/gospodarka-spoleczna-wol ontariat/gospodarka-spoleczna-trzeci-sektor/organizacje-pozytku-publicznego-i-1,4,2.html (accessed 30 March 2017).

Charity Navigator – Your Guide to Intelligent Giving, http://www.charitynaviga tor.org/index.cfm?bay=content.view&cpid=2181 (accessed 10 October 2016).

Diakoulaki D., Koumoutsos N. (1991) Cardinal ranking of alternative actions: extension of the PROMETHEE method, *European Journal of Operational Research*, **53**, 337–47.

Dyczkowski T. (2015a) Mierniki dokonań organizacji pożytku publicznego. Możliwości i ograniczenia stosowania, *Prace Naukowe Uniwersytetu Ekonomicznego we Wrocławiu*, **398**, 146–58.

Dyczkowski T. (2015b) Financial and non-financial information in performance assessment of public benefit organizations, *Prace Naukowe Uniwersytetu Ekonomicznego we Wrocławiu*, **398**, 134–45.

Figueira J., Roy B. (2002) Determining the weights of criteria in the ELECTRE type method with a revised Simos' procedure, *European Journal of Operational Research*, **139**(2), 317–26.

Frumkin P., Kim M.T. (2001) Strategic positioning and the financing of nonprofit organizations: is efficiency rewarded in the contributions marketplace? *Public Administration Review*, **61**(3), 266–75.

Górecka D. (2010) Zastosowanie metod wielokryterialnych opartych na relacji przewyższania do oceny europejskich projektów inwestycyjnych. In: Nowak M. (ed.), *Metody i zastosowania badań operacyjnych*, 10, Wydawnictwo Uniwersytetu Ekonomicznego w Katowicach, Katowice, pp. 100–25.

Górecka D. (2011) On the choice of method in multi-criteria decision aiding process concerning European projects. In: Trzaskalik T., Wachowicz T. (eds), *Multiple Criteria Decision Making*, 10–11, University of Economics in Katowice, Katowice, pp. 81–103.

Górecka D. (2013) Applying Multi-Criteria Decision Aiding techniques in the process of project management within the wedding planning business, *Operations Research and Decisions*, **22**(4/2012), 41–67.

Górecka D. (2014) Metody PROMETHEE. In: Trzaskalik T. (ed.), *Wielokryterialne wspomaganie decyzji. Metody i zastosowania*, PWE, Warszawa, pp. 117–18, 121.

Górecka D. (2015) Zastosowanie metod wielokryterialnych w procesie ubiegania się o akredytację międzynarodową AACSB. In: Gajda J.B., Jadczak R. (eds), *Badania operacyjne. Przykłady zastosowań*, Wydawnictwo Uniwersytetu Łódzkiego, Łódź, pp. 69–88.

Górecka D., Muszyńska J. (2011) Analiza przestrzenna innowacyjności polskich regionów, *Acta Universitatis Lodziensis. Folia Oeconomica*, **253**, 60–2.

Górecka D., Pietrzak M.B. (2012) Zastosowanie metody PROMETHEE II w procesie rankingowania projektów europejskich w ramach Regionalnego Programu Operacyjnego Województwa Kujawsko-Pomorskiego na lata 2007–

2013, *Studia Ekonomiczne, Modelowanie Preferencji a Ryzyko*, 12, Zeszyty Naukowe Uniwersytetu Ekonomicznego w Katowicach, pp. 87–9, 97.

Górecka D., Szałucka M. (2013) Country market selection in international expansion using multicriteria decision aiding methods, *Multiple Criteria Decision Making*, **8**, 31–55.

Górecka D., Szałucka M. (2016) Foreign market entry mode decision – approach based on stochastic dominance rules versus multi-actor multi-criteria analysis, *Prace Naukowe Uniwersytetu Ekonomicznego we Wrocławiu*, **446**, 47–69.

Hinkle D. (1965) The change of personal constructs from the viewpoint of a theory of construct implications, PhD Dissertation, Ohio State University.

Liczba NGO na świecie, Zespół badawczy Stowarzyszenia Klon/Jawor. http://fakty. ngo.pl/wiadomosc/2069932.html (accessed 8 June 2017).

Macharis C. (2000) Strategic modeling for intermodal terminals: socio-economic evaluation of the location of barge/road terminals in Flanders, PhD Thesis, Vrije Universiteit Brussel.

Macharis C. (2004) The importance of stakeholder analysis in freight transport: the MAMCA methodology, *European Transport/Transporti Europei*, **25–26**, 114–26.

Macharis C. (2005) The importance of stakeholder analysis in freight transport, *Quarterly Journal of Transport Law, Economics and Engineering*, **8**(25–26), 114–26.

Macharis C., Brans J.P., Mareschal B. (1998) The GDSS Promethee procedure, *Journal of Decision Systems*, **7**, 283–307.

Macharis C., Turcksin L., Lebeau K. (2012) Multi actor multi criteria analysis (MAMCA) as a tool to support sustainable decisions: state of use, *Decision Support Systems*, **54**, 610–20.

National Institute in Public Information Bulletin, http://sprawozdaniaopp.mpips. gov.pl/Search.

Penley P. (2012) Nonprofit performance evaluation: financial management, *Alliance Magazine*, http://www.alliancemagazine.org/blog/nonprofit-performance-evaluati on-financial-management-part-2-of-6/ (accessed 10 January 2017).

Piechota G. (2015) Legislation on financing public benefit activities from tax designation in Poland, *International Journal of Not-for-Profit Law*, **17**(1), 86–91.

Rogers M., Bruen M. (1998) A new system for weighting environmental criteria for use within ELECTRE III, *European Journal of Operational Research*, **107**(3), 552–63.

Świderska G.K., Więcław W. (eds) (2009) Sprawozdanie finansowe według polskich i międzynarodowych standardów rachunkowości, Difin, Warszawa.

Trussel J.M., Parsons L.M. (2008) Financial reporting factors affecting donations to charitable organizations, *Advances in Accounting*, **23**, 263–85.

APPENDIX

Table 11A.1 Model of preferences and input data

f_k	Financial ratings											Information and reputation ratings					
	f_{F1}	f_{F2}	f_{F3}	f_{F4}	f_{F5}	f_{F6}	f_{F7}	f_{F8}	f_{F9}	f_{F10}	f_{F11}	f_{R1}	f_{R2}	f_{R3}	f_{R4}	f_{R5}	f_{R6}
EW-DM1																	
w_k	0.105	0.105	0.105	0.085	0.059	0.052	0.033	0.072	0.078	0.007	0.013	0.046	0.039	0.023	0.065	0.023	0.092
q_k	25%	25%	40%	50%	30%	40%	50%	15%	90	25%	1	30%	1 095	1	1	1	1
p_k	65%	65%	70%	100%	65%	70%	100%	50%	150	70%	2	70%	1 825	2	2	2	2
v_k	300%	300%	200%	500%	100%	100%	300%	95%	365	100%		100%		3	3	3	3
J-DM2																	
w_k	0.098	0.039	0.059	0.111	0.072	0.033	0.02	0.105	0.085	0.092	0.046	0.026	0.007	0.052	0.065	0.078	0.013
q_k	25%	10%	10%	10%	17%	15%	20%	10%	15%	15%	0	20%	20%	1	1	1	1
p_k	55%	45%	45%	60%	45%	35%	30%	60%	55%	55%	1	45%	30%	2	2	2	2
v_k	90%	85%	70%	95%	80%	80%	70%	90%	90%	90%	2	75%	70%	3	3	3	3
EM-DM3																	
w_k	0.085	0	0.046	0.026	0.052	0.059	0.033	0.092	0.072	0.065	0.013	0.039	0.02	0.105	0.105	0.105	0.007
q_k	30%	15%	10%	15%	10%	5%	25%	15%	7.50%	20%	0	30%	40%	1	1	1	1
p_k	60%	40%	35%	35%	40%	20%	45%	30%	15%	30%	1	50%	70%	2	2	2	2
v_k	85%	75%	80%	85%	85%	70%	98%	95%	90%	80%	2	90%	80%	3	3	3	3

Poland – Public Benefit Organizations

a_i $f_k(a_i)$ – evaluation of the alternative a_i (PBO) on the criterion f_k

a_i																										
A	27.7	27868.1	0.0	0.0	0.2	0.1	0.0	0.0	0.0	0.001	1	975.0	4475	1	3	3	2	3	3	3	3	2	2	3	3
B	253.9	89768.1	0.3	0.1	0.4	0.1	5052.1	0.0	8.0	0.000	0	308.9	4264	2	3	3	3	3	3	3	3	2	2	2	3
C	983.2	23660.4	−0.2	0.1	0.1	0.5	0.0	0.0	158.6	0.000	0	25.5	4373	2	3	3	3	3	2	3	3	0	0	0	0
D	303.9	13516.8	0.0	0.1	0.2	0.3	31217.2	0.0	70.5	0.000	1	43.7	2301	2	3	3	2	3	3	3	2	0	2	2	3
E	1.1	129.8	0.1	0.0	0.1	0.1	90830.2	0.7	23.1	0.000	0	29.9	2585	2	3	3	1	3	2	3	2	2	3	3	3
F	2615.2	16071.0	0.1	0.1	0.0	0.2	3042730.6	0.1	11.8	0.150	1	5.5	3101	3	3	3	3	3	3	3	2	2	2	2	3
G	43.7	11650.9	−0.1	−0.1	0.6	0.1	1593642.5	0.3	11.5	0.000	1	102.6	3676	2	3	3	3	3	3	3	3	3	3	3	3
H	1425.5	182195.4	0.0	0.1	0.5	0.2	1986.3	0.1	0.0	0.000	0	128.0	3338	0	3	0	2	2	2	2	3	2	0	3	2
I	6719.5	49527.5	0.1	0.2	0.0	0.7	0.0	0.2	14.6	0.000	−1	6.2	2836	1	3	3	3	2	3	1	2	0	3	0	0
J	1264.9	24429.5	−0.2	−0.1	0.0	0.6	2754.2	0.0	0.0	0.042	−1	20.7	2603	2	3	3	2	3	3	3	3	1	3	1	3

Source: Own elaboration.

Index